MW00610780

RED STAR WHITE NIGHTS

RED STAR WHITE NIGHTS

THE LIFE AND DEATH OF YURI SOLOVIEV

JOEL LOBENTHAL & LISA WHITAKER

Ballet Review Books

BR

Dance Research Foundation, Inc.

Red Star White Nights: The Life and Death of Yuri Soloviev
Copyright © 2019
Joel Lobenthal & Lisa Whitaker

The Cataloging-in-Publication data is on file with the Library of Congress
ISBN 978-1-6629-0539-1

Photo Credits: Any mistakes or omissions, please contact authors.
Jacket Cover and Title Page Photo: Courtesy Mariinsky Theater
Jacket Back Photo: Valentin Baranovsky

Website: yurisolovievballet.com

Ballet Review Books
Dance Research Foundation, Inc.
100 Hudson Street
New York, NY 10013

Book and Jacket Design: culturepilot.com

To Sons and Grandsons
—L.W.

In memory of Allyn and Anna Waterman
—J.L.

Возьми ж на радость дикий мой подарок…
превративши…в солнце.

Take then for joy my wild gift…
transformed into sunlight.

—Osip Mandelstam (1920)

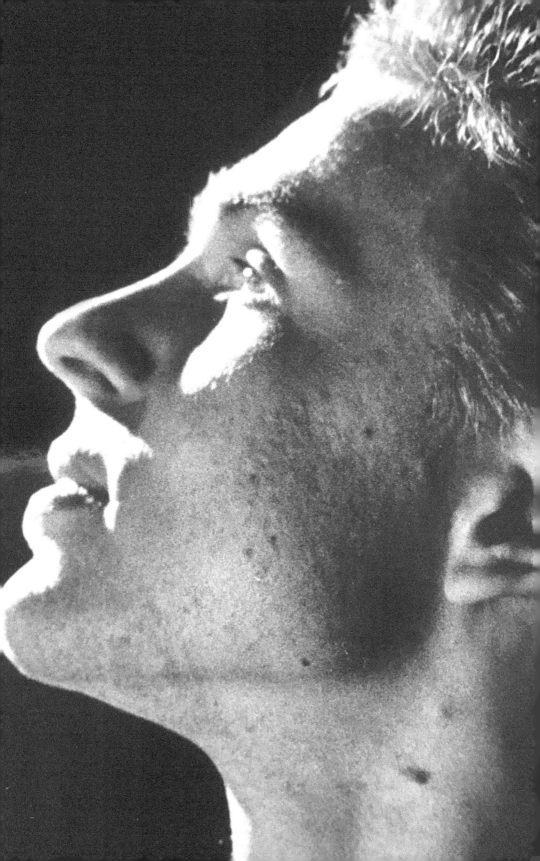

CONTENTS

Once again I struggle not to forget anyone while at the same time realizing that it is impossible to thank everyone who directly—or perhaps yet more difficult, indirectly—helped make this book happen.

I appreciate the way that Lisa Whitaker and the family of Yuri Soloviev went well beyond their comfort zone to ensure that his story and his achievements resonate in the record of history.

Nina Alovert, Patricia Barnes, Jennie Walton and Rosemary Winckley were incredibly generous with photographic materials.

Nina Baren, as always, has done so much to make my work with Russians possible. It was she who instant-translated my first interview with Tatiana Legat, now almost two decades ago! And I get to practice my Russian vocabulary with her on her downtime.

Marvin Hoshino has been a virtual collaborator from the very beginning of my Soloviev studies.

We had the luxury of taking time to try to get everything on the page as pristine and clear as possible. Olga Livshin, Kathleen Hall, John Morrone, and Sandra Grossman copy-edited and proof-read the book with alacrity.

Lisa and I were happy to accept Lynn Garafola's invitation to present on Yuri to the Columbia University Dance Seminar.

One more time, I took advantage of my now-elderly parents', Joseph and Shirley's, interest and willingness to read and/or listen to this book. As I told my parents and siblings on my last birthday, "I may be difficult, but it's your fault!" Just kidding. Thank you to brother Nicholas and sister Lydia for being very stringent critics.

The Jerome Robbins Dance Division at the Library for the Performing Arts is a haven.

And thank you, Merle Sue Gordon, for thinking of me.

Amid this time of darkness in America, Soka Gakkai International provides a beacon of light.

—J.L.

There are many kind and generous people, my guides on the path to this book, whom I wish to thank. Particularly the Soloviev family, Yuri's Russian friends, colleagues and contemporaries, many sadly no longer with us.

A special thanks to my friends, my guides to Russian ways, Natalya Pollack; Sergei Albert and his wife, Natalya Bespalova; to Sergei Kuznetsov; to Yuri Vasilkov and his wife, Irina, who were first to befriend and advise in those still-Soviet times. Among the Russians, those at the Vaganova Academy and its Rossi Street Museum and at the Mariinsky Theater who helped with the source material, time and advice. To Valentin Baranovsky. To Edgley International, Andrew Guild and his wife, Ai-Gul Kasina. My especial gratitude to Pierre Lacotte in France, for information and his singular insights. In the U.S., to Helen Atlas and Dina Makaroff, for a favorite picture. To Nina Alovert, Nina Baren, Kara Gray and to Sharon Williams, among many. To the late Fr. Desmond Reid, S.J., St. Ignatius Church, Singapore.

Among the unnamed, my thanks particularly to A.B., who, it appears, didn't rat.

And most of all, to Max and Alexander, far better sons than their mother deserves.

—L.W.

Великий могучий русский язык!
The great and mighty Russian language!

—Alexander Pushkin

The bane of any non-Russian speaker—as anyone who has read Russian novels will already know—is plowing through texts peppered with all sorts of variations of the names of characters encountered in the first chapters.

Russian, a melodic and highly nuanced, inflected Indo-European language, has approximately 150,000 words, not including variations of those words. Therein lies the rub, particularly in personal names.

Russians invariably have the following name sequence on their birth certificates: first name, patronymic (son or daughter of), last name. Period. For example, Yuri Soloviev was Yuri Vladimirovich (son of Vladimir) Soloviev. Had he had a sister named for Soloviev's mother, she would have been registered as Anna Vladimirovna (daughter of Vladimir) Solovieva (the feminine form of the noun). The mother's name is not indicated.

Russians, however, show a remarkable fondness for using all manner of diminutive nicknames derived from the first name. These show affection and intimacy. Even when addressing a colleague using "vy"—the polite personal pronoun which has disappeared in English ("vous"—"Sie"—"Usted" in French, German and Spanish, respectively), a speaker will use the diminutive to indicate friendliness or collegiality, even when none is actually present.

For example, as in English we have Bob, Bobby and Rob for Robert, the common name Aleksandr (male), Aleksandra (female) has many forms, the most common being Sasha, Sashenka, Sashok, Shura, Shurka, Shurochka, Shuronka, and Elizaveta becomes Lizochka, Lizonka, etc. The diminutives often end in "a," but they do not indicate a feminine ending, unlike English and other languages (Paul, Paula). Russian words present a further challenge. Pronunciation also changes depending on which syllable is stressed, e.g. CAT-a-log in English, where the first syllable is stressed. (In Russian the last syllable is stressed—каталог). In Soloviev, the stress is on the last syllable, whereas in Vasiliev, another common last name, the stress is in the middle. Hence the last syllable in Vasiliev remains unchanged, pronounced Va-SI-li-ev, but Soloviev is pronounced So-lo-VYOV and not So-lo-VI-ev, as he is known in the West. Both transliterations of the name "Соловьев" can be found in print and online, particularly in reference to the nineteenth-century philosopher, Vladimir Solovyov.

When Russians are quoted in this book, they will use several diminutives for Yuri Soloviev. The name "Yuri" is itself a variation of George.

The common diminutives are Yura, Yurka, Yurin, Yuronka, Yurochka, Yurasha. Reflecting their ancient animist religions reflective of the wilderness of their vast land, many Russian surnames are from nature, names such as Volkov (volk—wolf), Medvedev (medved'—bear) and so forth. Bird names are very common, from the lofty Orlov (orel—eagle), Sokolov (sokol—hawk) to the smaller ones, Kulikov (kulik—sandpiper), Vorobiev (vorobei—sparrow).

Soloviev, a common Russian surname, is one of these—solovei is the nightingale, a beloved, enchanted creature that appears often in folk tales and poetry. At Rossi Street, Solovei was the nickname of the subject of this biography. The nightingale, a solitary bird, that sings its entrancing melodies hidden deep in the forest, speaks deeply to the animist in the Russian soul:

И он поэт,—о, да!—и он поэт,
Мой чудный соловей, мой песенник унылый!
…Не терпит клетки он: в ней райского житья
Он, гордый, не возьмет за дикую свободу;
И только раз в году, весной, когда его
Любовь одушевит, поет он, сладкогласный;
И только чтоб развлечь грусть сердца своего,
В тоске восторженной, он гимн слагает страстный.
Жизнь сердца для него единственный предмет
Всех песен пламенных, всех томных вдохновений;
Жизнь сердца кончится,—в молчаньи и смиреньи
Он укрывается… о, да!—и он поэт!

He is a poet—oh, yes—he is a poet,
My wondrous nightingale, my lonely minstrel!
…He cannot bear the cage: for him the only paradise,
As he is proud, is the freedom of the wild;
And only once a year, in spring,
When flushed with ardor, he sings, sweet throated;
To try to entertain the sadness of his heart,
In rapturous anguish, he composes his passionate hymn.
Life of the beating heart exists alone for him,
All ardent songs, all languid inspirations;
Then, when the heart's life ceases, in silent mortification
He melts away… oh, yes!—oh, yes! He is a poet!

"And He Is a Poet"
—Evdokia Rostopchina (1840) *

* Unless otherwise indicated, all translations are Lisa Whitaker's.

PART 1: BEGINNINGS

Завтра в монастырь, а сегодня попляшем…
ну и что ж такое, Бог простит.

Tomorrow the convent, but today we will dance…
and what of it, God will forgive.

The Brothers Karamazov
—Fyodor Dostoevsky

1 INTRODUCTION

uri Soloviev emerged in the era of the *shestidesiatniki*, the iconoclastic and socially conscious Soviet cohort of the 1960s, many of them artists and writers. They came of age during the Soviet "thaw" that followed premier Joseph Stalin's death in March 1953. Soloviev was twelve when Stalin died, the future superstar already enrolled in Leningrad's fabled state-funded ballet academy on Rossi Street. Like so many in his generation, as Soloviev grew to adulthood, he believed that after the horrors of the 1917 Revolution, Stalin's multiple, perpetual purges, and the Second World War, an irrevocable turn in the road had occurred.

"When Stalin died, everybody rejoiced," Soloviev recalled in 1969. "We knew that now everything would start getting better. There were some, of course, who cried over him. But the people rejoiced."

Impulses toward liberalization began to stir immediately. But it wasn't until Nikita Khrushchev denounced Stalin at the Party congress in February 1956, that a message—as unequivocal as anything could be in the USSR—was transmitted, acknowledging that the state had committed atrocities on its population. "Excesses" had occurred. A new beginning was mandated.

Since the Bolshevik Revolution in 1917, Soviet ideology had for years promised society an ever-brightening existence. "Life is becoming more easy, life is getting more pleasant," Stalin proclaimed in 1935, two years before he launched what became known as The Great Terror with the murder of Leningrad Party Boss and presumptive rival Sergei Kirov. A further 1,000,000 Soviet citizens were to share his fate between 1937 and 1939.

But Soloviev and his generation could see with their own eyes an actual, quickening improvement. Indeed, by the time he was accepted into Leningrad's Kirov (now Mariinsky) Ballet in 1958, opportunities—for travel abroad, for cultural exchange with the West—were arising for him and his colleagues that would have been unthinkable before the thaw.

Soloviev incarnated the Soviet dream. His path to global cultural celebrity began in a single room in a communal apartment. "I always thought Yurka would be a metalworker," his father would say. "And as it turns out, he became a soloist in the ballet!"

Soloviev was a singular performer. He had a shapely and flexible body.

He had a very high jump exhibiting extraordinary ballon—a thrilling ability to remain paused in the air at the height of a jump. During the early 1970s, Ib Andersen, then a young principal dancer with the Royal Danish Ballet, took class with Soloviev when the RDB toured the Soviet Union. He recalled Soloviev "hanging in the air like I've never seen anyone do before or since."

"It gave the impression, even for us, as professionals," former Kirov ballerina Emma Minchonok recalled, "that God was pulling him up unto Himself. It would stop your breath; you would get goose bumps."

Soloviev's style was, more than anything, lyric, evincing a somewhat dreamy absorption. He had a reserved and often introverted stage personality that could also generate tremendous heat, strength, intensity.

In addition to glory, Soloviev certainly earned a measure of material comfort and privilege. Remuneration was nothing like it was for comparable celebrities in the West, but substantial by Soviet standards. Soloviev owned a car and a country house. Unlike the majority of Soviet citizens, he did not have to remain living at home into adulthood with three generations cohabiting in (at best) a cramped two-room flat. He was given a series of ever-larger apartments. From his frequent trips abroad, he brought back cameras and sports equipment unobtainable by the average Soviet citizen. The Soviet ruble had been withdrawn from foreign exchange markets. Its official value was artificially pinned to the dollar, but it remained worthless outside of the Soviet Union until the late 1980s.

Most important, liberalization during the thaw gave him the chance to expand himself, his intellect, his perspective. For Soloviev wanted to be a Russian, and Soviet, as well as a citizen of the world. He studied English. He read widely. He returned from his travels laden with reels of recordings he made on his movie camera. The sights and sounds of the great world entranced him. Former Kirov colleague Nikolai Ostaltsov recalled, "Before my eyes I can see his face when he was in Venice," where the Kirov performed in the summer of 1966. "He was so taken by the beauty—everybody was, but not as wonderfully as he."

Soloviev not only lived the dream, he believed in the dream. He turned down defection offers because of a host of personal ties, but also because he had been brought up to be sincerely patriotic, believing deeply that he belonged to the Russian people, Soviet collectivism. "All right, I know I'm an egoist," he would say when asserting his own opinion in conversation.

But before long, the dream soured, for Soloviev and for the Soviet Union as a whole. In truth, liberalization was continually buffeted all through the Khrushchev years by forces of reaction. The premier himself was buffeted as well. In short order, he was capable of wildly vacillatory cultural pronouncements. The tumultuous new cultural landscape was tentatively endorsed one moment, unequivocally denounced the next.

In December 1964, Khrushchev was ousted. And thus began the period of *Zastoi* (Stagnation) under the leadership of Leonid Brezhnev, who continued to rule until he died in 1982—a tenure twice as long as Khrushchev's.

Just how evanescent the Soviet thaw had been eventually became clear to Yuri Soloviev. Like so many *Shestidesyatniki*, however, he resisted acknowledging the truth. The inevitable result was despair, bitter teeth-gritting cynicism and soaring alcoholism, the latter becoming endemic in the previously largely immune intelligentsia. For Soloviev, indeed, his own eventual disillusion would lead to his death.

Ironically but not all that atypically, Soloviev's belief in the perpetuity of the Soviet state existed alongside a determination not to participate in what he knew remained of the abuses of the Communist Party. After surviving the horrors of the Great Terror, capture on the Eastern Front and years in German forced labor camps, his own grandfather had been imprisoned in the Gulag as a traitor, as all Soviet soldiers who had surrendered were classified by Stalin's Order No. 270 of August 1941.

A great-grandfather had been reduced from a prosperous estate steward to yeoman's duty at a lumberyard. Soloviev himself refused—repeatedly, adamantly and on principle—to join the Communist Party, which was insult to the state for someone as exemplary a public figure, the very embodiment of the *Homo Sovieticus*—the Soviet Superman—the state wished to idealize.

Despite his fame, his essential role in the life of the Kirov, without Party participation and thus devoid of patronage or protection, he was expendable. In his younger years, his talent made all political compromise unnecessary. Later his talent and dedication were no longer enough.

The last years of Soloviev's career were not a fall from grace, but were marked by a gradual, insistent and yet subtle disregard. As his friend and fellow Kirov dancer Evgenii Shcherbakov recalled, Soloviev was now "made to stand in line" behind dancers far less accomplished.

In January 1977, Soloviev was thirty-six. He not only faced the end of his performing career but was confronting a perfect storm of duress. On January 12th, the last night of the banned yet still observed Russian Orthodox calendar year, alone in his wooden cabin outside Leningrad, he put a sawed-off shotgun to his head and pulled the trigger.

2

"A MAN ALWAYS HAS TWO REASONS FOR WHAT HE DOES— A GOOD ONE AND THE REAL ONE."

"A man always has two reasons for what he does—a good one and the real one."

—John Pierpont Morgan (perhaps derived from Voltaire!)

In death, Soloviev's reputation was effaced. During his lifetime, three celebrated Kirov colleagues had made sensational defections to the West—Rudolf Nureyev in 1961, Natalia Makarova in 1970 and Mikhail Baryshnikov in 1974. Each was a great propaganda boon to Western powers: each a rejection of communism and the Soviet Union by an elite performer, presumed recipient of the best that the USSR had to offer. All three had already garnered tremendous success with the Kirov on tour in the West. Now they were lionized here.

Following them in 1974 were ex-Kirov émigrés, Valery Panov and his young wife Galina Ragozina, finally allowed to emigrate to Israel after years of obstruction and harassment by the state. Protests in the West eventually led to their release. Panov, however, was now thirty-six and had suffered two years of enforced inactivity in the USSR, including a prison stint. Nor had his career in Russia been built on the princely heroes; he thus conformed less readily to the West's most marketable archetype.

In 1975 came Soloviev's frequent partner Kaleria Fedicheva, who was also too close to forty to start again a new performing career. Aleksandr Godunov, defecting while on tour with the Bolshoi Ballet in 1979, had won fame in the West but was ultimately defeated by his own personal problems.

Yet well until the Perestroika years of the late 1980s, a veritable cult of defection permeated the Western ballet world, penetrating as well into the larger cultural macrocosm and geopolitical interface.

Defection was mythologized by the media as an existential quest for freedom, a heroic act of self-definition and self-assertion. But Soloviev had not defected, despite, as his widow Tatiana Legat recalls, "numerous offers, all the time." Thus in life he was rendered useless to the Western governments' diplomatic strategies in the Cold War against the Soviets. His death, however, was a black eye on the face of the alleged Soviet utopia. Suicide was akin to treason, a de facto political crime in the USSR. Russian theater critic

Iulia Iakovleva wrote in 2010 that Soloviev's death "became the most terrific accusation made not only against the stagnation of the Brezhnev era, but of the calamity in all Soviet art forms."

But by this point he was off the radar of any Western statecraft, eclipsed by the propaganda victories provided by the three superstar defectors. His death received surprisingly little notice, let alone exploitation by the West.

Soloviev had strong ties of collegiality and affection to the defectors. But their public reaction was silence. Part of the reason was undoubtedly residual fear of the long arm of the KGB—as well as its short arm within the USSR itself, for all had family remaining. Since defecting, each had assiduously said as little as possible about the politics of their home country. The Soviet Union remained officially at war with the capitalist world; Nureyev had been tried and sentenced for treason in absentia.

As news of Soloviev's death spread, "Leningrad shut down," Legat would recall. Each of the city's major theaters went dark for several days. All of the Kirov men refused to replace Soloviev in an upcoming performance for which he had originally been scheduled; the administration was forced to invite a guest artist from the Bolshoi Ballet in Moscow.

The official explanation given in the Soviet Union was that an accident had occurred while he was cleaning his gun. Officialdom, however, knew the truth, and interpreted his act as a highly embarrassing indictment. In the years immediately following his death, Soloviev was quickly reduced nearly to the status of non-person. Certainly his death, following multiple leave-takings of various sorts, did the Kirov itself no favors. Foreign tour opportunities for the troupe were further reduced. Still under the lash because of Baryshnikov's recent defection, the company was, as Clive Barnes wrote in *The New York Times,* "slowly dropping out of international consciousness."

For both Nureyev and Baryshnikov, Soloviev had represented an ideal of male ballet technique—a criterion to be equaled and, if possible, surpassed. Defection afforded them material reward and a multitude of life options beyond the imaginations of Soloviev and his colleagues who remained. Perhaps his suicide awakened some residual guilt as well as grief. From New York, Baryshnikov called Legat in Leningrad. "It would have been better if he had become a millionaire instead," he told her. He left unsaid the undoubtedly implied "in the West," which were taboo words in a phone call that was undoubtedly being monitored. Shortly after, Legat's telephone number was changed, cutting the family off from further contact. In addition, she was placed under a permanent foreign travel ban.

With the self-expiating collusion of his more fortunate colleagues, Soloviev became a Soviet incarnation of the Invisible (as well as Unmentionable) Man. His death gave the defectors an alibi, a justification, assuaging whatever guilt they may have felt. Their post-defection lives had been purchased at the price of their former colleagues, who were victims in Russia of increased retaliation and repression following each defection. Ironically, it now fell to the defectors to become, in a sense, operatives of the West, supporting a schematic narrative by their silence or even, in some cases, by their own statements.

Was Soloviev indeed, as Makarova insists in her 1979 memoir, *A Dance Autobiography*, simply "a Stradivarius which played beautifully, but never sang"?

3
RECLAMATION

LISA WHITAKER AND SERGEI VIKULOV IN THE MARIINSKY THEATER CANTEEN, NOVEMBER 2016. PHOTO: VALENTIN BARANOVSKY

ertainly Soloviev was a man of paradoxes. Described by so many who knew him as the gentlest of souls, he was also an avid hunter, and skilled angler and underwater spear fisherman. (His suicide weapon, in fact, was a gift from an admirer.) All extremes in the human psyche do perhaps meet as surely as in the ideological dogmatism of individual ends in a political spectrum. Not a bit of paradox or complexity remained, however, in the posthumous portraits of Soloviev, the man any more than the artist. Not only were his talent and achievements flattened out, but his personality as well. Thus emerged the legend of Soloviev the mute, phlegmatic balletic laborer of limited intelligence, devoid of anything beyond the most minimal artistic or cultural interests, insight or passion.

Perestroika brought a partial correction to the quite damning revisionist portrait of Soloviev. Indeed, Perestroika began to bring him what we might ironically term a "rehabilitation" of sorts, comparable, perhaps to the way that so many victims of Stalin were exonerated years after they were executed.

Perestroika meant that in the former Soviet Union, Soloviev was no longer a topic to be suppressed. In 1996, Galina Mshanskaia's documentary on Soloviev, *I Am Tired of Living in My Native Land* (a phrase from a poem by Sergei Esenin, to whom Soloviev had been compared), was released in Russia. It was shown in New York four years later, included in a program of Russian dance documentaries hosted by Elizabeth Kendall as part of the Film Society of Lincoln Center's annual Dance on Camera festival.

Joel Lobenthal was a teenager when Soloviev died. He had begun writing professionally about dance in 1983, but had seen little footage of Soloviev. He had, in fact, for years, tacitly acceded to the myth of Soloviev as somehow great but at the same time second-rate.

Yet much of the footage of Soloviev was astonishing. Anna Kisselgoff wrote in *The New York Times* that the "clips of Soloviev's dancing offer a rare chance to discover or rediscover the impact he produced on those of us who saw him in live performance. Soloviev, an indisputably great dancer, stuns even on film with the muscular grace of his artistry."

Certainly, critical and personal opinion about any performer will always remain above all subjective, but the video record put the lie to any estimation that did not acknowledge his phenomenal, indeed epochal gifts. "Looking at this film," Kisselgoff wrote, "one wonders if Mikhail Baryshnikov's purity of style would be the same had not Soloviev paved the way 10 years earlier."

After seeing the film, Joel wanted to write about Soloviev. He interviewed Tatiana Legat in Boston later that year. Early in the 1990s, Legat and her daughter Alyona moved to the United States. Both were teaching at the school of the Boston Ballet. He interviewed Soloviev's brother Igor in St. Petersburg in 2001, as well as a number of Soloviev's ex-colleagues, before writing a long profile of Soloviev the man and the dancer, published in *Ballet Review* in Fall 2003.

Six months later, he received a phone call from one Lisa Whitaker in Houston, Texas. Legat had mentioned her name to Joel. Lisa had known Soloviev in 1969, when he went on a pickup tour organized by Igor Moiseyev. Moiseyev frequently blended his own folk dance troupe with ballet soloists and ensembles to create touring units permitted to make extensive tours abroad. These tours generated much-needed hard currency for the Goskontsert organization's coffers, in partnership with foreign impresarios.

Lisa was the daughter of a French diplomat. Born in Manila, Philippines, she had lived with her family in Paris, in Calcutta and Madras, India, and in England, before her father was transferred to Washington, DC in January 1962, appointed First Secretary of the French Embassy. Studying at the Washington School of Ballet, Lisa had gone to each of three performances that the Kirov gave at the Washington Coliseum in December 1964.

"Nothing prepared me for the Kirov," she recalls today. "For those of us who hadn't heard of Russia's Imperial Theater traditions, it provoked the thought, Well, how could *anything* be wrong with the system that produced such perfection?" Makarova, Fedicheva and Soloviev in *Swan Lake* she found superb, but it was the corps de ballet in the dream scene of *La Bayadère* that obliterated every ambivalence she had about endorsing products of the Soviet system. As it was certainly intended.

A Soviet diplomat gave Lisa a book on Galina Ulanova, which fueled her enchantment with all things Russian. Her father, however, refused to allow her to study "the language of the archenemy of the country where we are guests." And so the fourteen-year-old started teaching herself. By 1969 she was a Russian studies major at the University of Melbourne in Australia, where her father was now French Consul-General. Australian impresario Michael Edgley presented Soloviev as a headliner of Moiseyev's "Forty Stars of the Russian Ballet."

Twenty years later, during Perestroika, Lisa went to Russia to learn of Soloviev's fate and to find his widow and their daughter. They were no longer in Leningrad, but "nobody could or would tell me where they were." Only after two more trips was she finally successful.

In 2003, Tatiana Legat, then living in Boston, told Lisa about Joel's article on Soloviev and that he might write his biography. She asked her to contact him for a copy of the article and to offer to help him, if needed, saying, "We are here in this country with nothing, you have languages, you knew Yura…" Reading the article, she felt a pang; Joel had captured the Yuri Soloviev she had known. And she found she liked Joel and respected his approach. In the summer of 2004, Lisa joined him for more interviews with Legat in Boston, some of which were eventually published in *Ballet Review* in 2011. Years passed. Lisa and Joel each made trips to Russia to interview more of his friends, family, and colleagues. But the book project languished. Lisa was abroad for two years. Finally, in 2016, as the fortieth anniversary of Soloviev's death approached, Joel felt it was now or never. He called Lisa and suggested they fully collaborate and make Lisa's own experiences integral to the final product. The time was right: Lisa was now retired, and she would summon the emotional fortitude. She felt liberated by Legat's remark to her: "You were dear to him. You were so young. It is a touching story. Tell it." This was her Nihil Obstat. Never having considered revealing, let alone translating, Soloviev's letters to her, she realized they were essential to the narrative and, steeling herself, crossed the emotional Rubicon. The manuscript took shape in the form of a true collaboration. We realized it was biography, personal memoir, and an autobiography all in one.

ANNA WITH HER SONS YURI AND IGOR AT THE DACHA
WHERE THEY RENTED A ROOM EACH SUMMER

4
HIS PARENTS

VLADIMIR WITH IGOR AND YURI AT HOME

oloviev inherited his dance talent from his mother, Anna Kondratieva, who studied dance in the evenings in studios set up around Leningrad especially for amateurs. Anna "was very talented," Legat said, recalling her mother-in-law's delicate wrists and ankles, as well as having "beautiful feet like Yura, long legs, great turn-out."

Anna's father was a cabinetmaker in a furniture factory. She grew up in typically post-Revolution poverty in what was then the rural outskirts of southern Leningrad, near the Moskovskie Vorota—the Moscow Gates. "They lived almost in a shed," Soloviev's paternal uncle Aleksandr said about Anna's parents. "I remember bringing them logs for the fire. They also kept a pig."

Anna met her husband, Vladimir Soloviev, when they were both working in the same factory. Before the Revolution, Vladimir's mother Olga Gamazina had grown up in Novaia Ladoga, on the lushly wooded southern shore of Lake Ladoga. Her father, Aleksandr Gamazin, was manager of a large estate belonging to a family by the name of Zhukov. Aleksandr Soloviev described his namesake grandfather's "two-story house, with a plot of land, a cow, an orchard—such things." By appointment to the Czar, Zhukov was a provisioner supplying seafood, fruits, berries and other northern delicacies to the Emperor and his court in St. Petersburg. Olga and her two sisters attended a gymnasium, a private high school for girls. A gifted student, Olga attended the first women's university opened in Russia, finishing the teacher training course, and she then taught school in St. Petersburg.

"Then some changes happened..." Aleksandr explained euphemistically. What indeed happened was the Bolshevik Revolution of 1917, which swept Lenin and the Communists into power. Post-Revolutionary persecutions and mass murder eviscerated the aristocracy, upper class, bourgeoisie, and intelligentsia. Also targeted were the pejoratively named *kulak* ("fist") class, enterprising peasants who had taken advantage of land reform and prospered. Eventually, fulfilling quotas meant expanding criminal criteria to indict any rural resident who owned anything, and eventually it meant rounding up on whim any rural resident in sight.

Gamazin suffered the indignity of not only losing his business but being reassigned to working at a lumberyard. "He worked delivering sand for cement, bringing lumber, building materials, et cetera. He suffered a lot," his grandson Aleksandr said. "He was distraught because he had lost his position in life, all of what he had, to end up as just a laborer at that site." It was there that he collapsed one day and died shortly afterward.

It was clear from the recollections of Olga's niece Mira Baklanova that the Gamazins considered Olga's marriage to Valentin Soloviev a *mésalliance*—Valentin not entirely worthy of the Gamazin pedigree and ambitions. Nevertheless, Valentin was "intelligent," Mira recalled. "Educated, well brought up. The way he presented himself, it was immediately apparent he was someone from the intelligentsia." Like so many St. Petersburg intellectuals, he had little affection for, and even less inclination to toil for the Communist cause, whereas other members of Mira's family believed passionately. Mira's mother Mariia was studying medicine in St. Petersburg when the Revolution intervened. "Mama followed the Revolution," moving to Moscow where she married a graduate of the Imperial Art Academy who had become a Red Commissar.

Valentin had a white-collar job, and together with Olga the family lived well enough to have a nanny for the two boys. Nevertheless, life in renamed Leningrad was not easy. "She went through a lot," Mira said. "The famines, the hard years…" The city had suffered famine during World War I and the revolutionary transition, while the horrors of forced collectivization of the peasantry in the early 1930s caused catastrophic shortages of fuel and food. "It affected her. Well, she was born with that kind of a personality…"

We may assume that Valentin was possessed of a charm that later aided him in surviving both German captivity and subsequent time in the Gulag. But his appeal to the fair sex ended his marriage to the very proper Olga. "I personally… don't know the story well… but I do know that Valentin was unfaithful to her," Mira recalled. Nevertheless, "they separated very quietly. In a cultured way. The boys remained with her, they were well brought up, like her. Very well mannered."

In the late 1930s, Olga fell ill. "She became paralyzed, from then on practically never left the house," her son Aleksandr told us. Her sister Mariia in Moscow was also in difficulties, having become the wife of an "enemy of the people." Her husband had become a well-known artist. But he was imprisoned, like so many revolutionary warriors, during the purges of the 1930s. Now branded as a "Relative of an Enemy of the People," Mariia didn't even dare telephone her ailing sister Olga in Leningrad for fear she might compromise her. Olga died in 1939.

Both Vladimir and Aleksandr completed their education in a *desiatiletka*, the ten-grade vocational high school. In the course of sowing wild oats, Aleksandr was arrested for some petty hooliganism and sentenced to a juvenile labor camp. Upon graduation, Vladimir joined an apprentice program at Elektrosila, the electrical power factory that made turbines, located near where Anna had grown up. He then was assigned to that same factory, where Anna was also employed as a typist. Vladimir was athletic and attractive, star of the factory volleyball team. He and Anna were each eighteen when they married in 1939. Soon after, she was pregnant with Yuri.

Reportedly, Anna's ballet training had been advanced enough that she was accepted into the corps de ballet at the Maly Theater, but her pregnancy terminated her theatrical dreams. Later in life, she would say that she enjoyed folk dancing more than ballet but sometimes speculated, "Imagine, I could have danced with the Maly!"

Yuri arrived on August 10, 1940, born with a small dark growth—technically, a "deformed lachrymal carbuncle" in the inside pocket of his right eye. In 1969, he told Lisa how much he had always hated it. "He must have been teased about it as a child," she muses today, and wonders how much it contributed to his shyness and reserve. It was, of course, invisible onstage.

At 4:00 a.m. on June 21, 1941, Nazi Germany broke the German-Soviet Non-Aggression Pact and invaded the USSR. Vladimir, Aleksandr and their father were all conscripted, Aleksandr inducted directly from the labor camp. Anna's father remained in soon-to-be besieged Leningrad, while she was evacuated with her mother and one-year-old Yuri to the Republic of Bashkiria, one of the seventeen republics of the Soviet Union. Their evacuation, however, was a far cry from the organized resettlement that the country's major cultural institutions enjoyed.

Survival was a matter of ending up somewhere and finding shelter. In Anna's case, it was finding a family to take them in, and making themselves sufficiently useful to share in whatever little food could be mustered.

Bashkiria (now Bashkortostan) is an ethnically Turkic republic situated 1000 miles south east of Leningrad, part of the southern Ural Mountain Range and the northern plains of Central Asia. Anna fought to stay alive in a corner of the *izba*—a peasant hovel in the barren steppes. Anna did whatever she could, from clerical work to hard physical labor that included splitting, hauling and stacking logs for others in the village. The *izba* would certainly have had neither plumbing nor heating other than a *pechka*—a hearth stove to heat and cook meals.

One morning her toddler son came to tell her, "Babushka won't get up." It is hinted by friends of Soloviev's that Anna's mother committed suicide. "Of course, it affected her mind," Legat said of her mother-in-law's wartime traumas. For the rest of her life, Anna would remain anxiety-ridden and suffer bouts of depression.

When late spring of 1942 arrived in blockaded Leningrad, which was still encircled by Wehrmacht and Finnish troops, every spot of grass was tilled during the region's short growing season by those still alive and capable of working. Nevertheless, starvation had claimed the lives of an estimated eight hundred thousand Leningrad residents over the first year of the siege. Growing season in faraway Bashkiria was similarly brief.

It was not blessed with the agricultural bounty of republics like Georgia yet further south. On the edge of the barren steppes of Central Asia, it had a climate comparable to that of Bismarck, North Dakota, or Saskatchewan, Canada. In all likelihood, Soloviev suffered the effects of malnutrition. Lisa once talked to a woman who also survived the war in the region: "We lived on spinach. People bloated and our skin turned green from it."

Vladimir originally served with his brother in the Seventieth Border Guards Detachment. A signals and radio operator, he was then sent to a unit being formed in the Urals, later to the European front. At the battle of Kursk in the summer of 1943, Vladimir's left knee was shattered by an exploding bullet. When he was stripped naked in the military field hospital, his athletic build led the doctors to mistake him for an officer, which meant that rather than amputating immediately, the surgeons fused his knee and saved his leg.

Vladimir and Aleksandr's father Valentin served in a Baltic unit that was surrounded. He was captured, remaining in a German forced labor camp until the end of the war. Since the Soviet Union had not signed the Geneva Convention, captured Red Army soldiers became slave laborers. Millions perished.

Liberated by the Americans, some Russian captives made their way to the US, but Valentin was repatriated to the Soviet Union. There he found himself not a war hero but a suspected criminal—the xenophobia of Stalin's USSR condemned all POWs as cowards, deserters and traitors. "Reform" for Valentin, who had been lucky enough to have avoided summary execution, was a matter of spending the next three years in a Gulag in the Urals.

His son Vladimir spent eighteen months recuperating in the hospital. However, he never could bend his left leg again, which, for one thing, made driving impossible. When Anna learned that her husband had been brought back to Leningrad, she applied and received permission to return from Bashkiria with Yuri. She took in typing work until Vladimir could finally return to factory work.

Wartime experiences changed everyone. Inevitably, Anna and Vladimir were now different people from the young couple they'd been in 1941. "They had problems when they came back together," Tatiana said. He left her for another woman, but divorce was out of the question, since a 1944 law now made the procedure labyrinthine and the cost prohibitive. Vladimir dutifully returned when he learned that Anna was pregnant. Anna, however, had not wanted a second child, but she had no other safe options, whether she had considered them or not. Abortion had been, and would again be, the primary form of contraception. But as of 1936 it had been outlawed. It was now, more than ever, a hindrance to the government's attempts to rebuild a population devastated by two World Wars, the Revolution and the Civil War. Anna gave birth to a second son, Igor, on June 25, 1946.

"You have to give him credit," Mira said of cousin Vladimir. "He came back from the front, with wounds... the time he spent in the military hospital... He remained always with the family and concerned himself with his children. He took care of his family. That's how he was."

5

CHILDHOOD

FIRST DAY OF SCHOOL, SEPTEMBER 1, 1946

oloviev grew up with his family in the communal apartment at 64 Fontanka Street, where Vladimir had originally lived with his parents and brother. They shared the apartment on the fifth floor with eight other families. They shared their own room with a beloved German shepherd named Amur, after the river that runs through Siberia. (Vladimir's brother Aleksandr was stationed there, and the dog was perhaps purchased with money or goods that he sent them.) The building had been financed in the late nineteenth century by the merchant Eliseev, whose magnificent Art Nouveau food emporium still remains in operation on Nevsky Prospect a few blocks away. Some feeling of spaciousness in the Solovievs' room was provided by two windows and a very high ceiling. It also had a beautiful old tile stove. In winter, Anna burned logs there to supplement the inadequate central heating.

Anna was "a wonderful cook, she baked beautifully," Legat recalled. "They were very poor, but she managed to feed them well." There was no water in their room, only in the kitchen and toilet. Anna would go to boil water on one of the three stoves in their communal kitchen. As almost everywhere in Leningrad, the prerevolutionary pipes were bad. The most reliable source of water, in fact, was the hand pump in the courtyard.

Anna was an avid reader, a trait she passed on to Yuri. Reading provided an escape from her life of drudgery and her lost dreams of a life in the theater. She would get up very early to send her husband off to work with lunch, then read in bed until the rest of the household needed her attention. Reading material was "whatever she could get," her granddaughter Alyona recalled, since it was no easy matter to hunt down worthwhile material. Quality books were usually printed in small quantities; the vast majority of published works were formulaic and propagandistic. When money became more plentiful, she and Vladimir subscribed to the literary, cultural and sports journals that began appearing with the Khrushchev thaw.

"There were no toys," Igor recalled, but they had an old wind-up gramophone and some records. Before the war, Vladimir had been an avid amateur athlete. His wartime injury obviously restricted what he could still do, but the family was keen on swimming, skiing and volleyball. In the summer they would rent a room in a dacha in Koloskovo, north of Leningrad on the Karelian Isthmus. It was a region of lovely lakes, forests, mushroom and berry patches, which were harvested as necessities for the next Leningrad winter, when no vegetables except potatoes were available.

Yuri "was very kind," recalled Vladimir's cousin Mira, who was "Auntie" to Soloviev. "Very captivating, a very appealing child, everybody thought so, not only I because I was his aunt. He was well-behaved: if told to do something he would go ahead and do it. He always paid close attention to what was going on; he was very perceptive."

When he was seven, "Yura told our mother that he wanted to dance," Igor recounted. Undoubtedly delighted, Anna enrolled him in after-school dance classes at one of the city's headquarters for Soviet children—dubbed "Young Pioneers." Parents had to pay a small stipend, so his father, a skilled metalworker, started an illegal home business of sharpening ice skates for professional athletes. Under Soviet law, any form of private enterprise, even on that scale, was a criminal offense. Had he been discovered or denounced by one of their neighbors, it would have meant arrest, gulag and catastrophe for the family. The fact that he got away with running this enterprise in a cramped communal apartment is based on the following essential factors for survival in Soviet times. First, the relationship between the families in the communal apartment was reasonably harmonious; there was no ardent *stukach*—snitch—among them. Second, Soloviev Sr. was a man who knew how to keep his mouth shut. And third, family well-being frequently depended on what one could do *nalevo*—on the left, that is, illegally, to survive, as it was often impossible to manage on individual salaries. It follows that every family in the apartment was, in all likelihood, up to something and everyone pretended to know nothing. *Ruka ruku moet*—one hand washes the other, as the saying goes.

The large, heavy family table in the center of their room would be cleared after dinner and Vladimir would go to work. He may have had no choice, for certainly Anna was not going to tolerate any obstruction to Yuri's tutelage. But his work must have been lucrative, because he kept at it long after Soloviev joined the Kirov.

For two years, Soloviev attended class three times a week at the *Dvorets Pionerov*—Palace of the Pioneer Communist Youth Group—in what had

been the Romanovs' Anichkov Palace. He was taught by Leonid Efimovich, who taught extracurricular dance classes at various schools in the city. Happy as Anna must have been at Yuri's initiative, how much more so would she have been to discover that he was gifted. "Even at home she made him practice," Aleksandr Soloviev recalled. "All that she had learned, she taught Yura." Long before the time he was old enough to audition, she would insist that if the Rossi Street ballet academy would accept him, it was there and only there that he was headed. "If they take him, he's going. I will only give him up for the *Choreograficheskoe!*"

Fortunately, Efimovich felt the same way. He had previously taught the Kirov's Alla Osipenko and brought her to audition on Rossi Street. Now he took Soloviev there in the spring of 1949. Years later, Efimovich was recognized with a modest title as a cultural worker by the Soviet government. "Yura and I wrote very supportive letters," Osipenko recalled.

6
UNCLE ALEKSANDR

FISHING TRIP WITH UNCLE ALEKSANDR

ow much fatherly affection and mentorship could battle-scarred Vladimir provide? Certainly he taught his two boys the outdoor pursuits of hunting and fishing. As adults, Yuri and Igor would cheer and clap as they watched televised sports matches together with their father. "If the women wanted to watch a movie," Legat recalled, "it was out of the question."

In Soloviev's lifelong pursuit of skiing, hunting and fishing, as well as competitive athletics, there may have been an effort to obtain his father's acceptance. Elena Tchernichova, who entered the Rossi Street school with Yuri in 1949, grew up in a neighboring building that shared an adjoining courtyard. She "visited us often," Igor remembered. "Yuri was always very quiet," she writes in her autobiography; Igor, "more streetwise and outgoing." Her impression was that Yuri was too sensitive to easily win his father's approval and understanding.

Vladimir's younger brother Aleksandr seems to have provided more of an engaged and sympathetic paternal presence. It was shortly after Yuri began to study on Rossi Street that the Soloviev household expanded with the addition of Uncle Aleksandr—"Dyadya Sasha," as he was known in the family. Aleksandr's ambition and his intellectual sophistication were greater than Vladimir's—or perhaps it would be more accurate to say, had more chance to be developed. "Because he married earlier" than Aleksandr, "there was no further studying for him," Mira said of cousin Vladimir.

Yuri and his uncle became close and remained so throughout Yuri's adulthood, so much so, indeed, that Aleksandr would blame himself for not being able to prevent Soloviev's suicide.

During the war, Aleksandr had served in the Soviet Far East, participating in operations to rid Manchuria of Japanese occupation. His unit, the Seventieth Border Guards, was stationed in the village of Kazakevichevo, some fifty kilometers from Khabarovsk. He remained there, serving at the confluence of the Amur and Ussuri Rivers until the Soviets returned Manchuria to China in 1949, upon its takeover by the Communists, led by Chairman Mao Zedong. "Of the 120 men in my unit, twelve of us survived the war," Aleksandr recalled with tears in his eyes.

Like many specialists, Aleksandr was considered valuable enough that he was required to stay in the Soviet army after the Allied victory. The work the men would have been performing as civilians was performed by women, children, Gulag slave laborers and millions of Axis prisoners of war, German, Hungarian, Italian, Romanian, Japanese, and others, including a handful of Americans. An estimated million POWs perished, others only permitted to return to their homeland years after Stalin's death in 1953.

"I was the company top sergeant," Aleksandr said, and in this capacity was able to send back to the Solovievs in Leningrad things that could be useful. "Whenever there was something I might happen upon, since I didn't need much, I would send it to them." Soviet soldiers were encouraged to take war booty, named *trofeinoe*—trophies—from occupied areas to send back to their devastated land. Presumably, these were the goods that Aleksandr "happened upon." (Soviet Marshal Georgii Zhukov is reported to have happened upon several trainloads of *trofeinoe* to send back to his family.)

In 1949, following demobilization, Aleksandr returned to Leningrad and moved in with the Solovievs in their 220-square-foot room. Anna and Vladimir slept on a large enamel and wrought iron bed, and their two boys shared a mattress. At night, Aleksandr would turn two chairs upside down, and put a board and mattress on them. "That was my 'territory,'" Aleksandr recalled in 2005, a lively and genial octogenarian when Joel and Lisa each interviewed him separately in St. Petersburg.

Aleksandr became the only member of the immediate family to earn an advanced degree, which meant first completing a college-prep high school diploma, then undergraduate and graduate engineering studies. Eventually he became a tenured professor of engineering at Leningrad's prestigious Bonch-Bruevich Institute of Communications.

He was attending school full-time during the years he lived with his brother's family. "After spending nine years on the border, I had to relearn everything: physics, mechanics, math… I had to study a lot." To do his homework, he would leave the Solovievs' room and repair to the communal washroom to study, lounging in the tub. (The toilet was housed separately.) The bathtub was nonoperational, recalled Legat, who moved in with them when she and Yuri married. "We used to go to the local bathhouse to bathe." There were also, of course, showers at the theater and school.

Although electricity cost only pennies a month for each family, apartment mates "would complain that I was using too much," Aleksandr said. As the light switch was in the hallway, "Sometimes someone would come by and switch it off on me!" But overall, "there wasn't much fighting" among neighbors in the communal apartment, crowded as it was. "Of course, if one of the families didn't clean the apartment when it was their turn, then people would argue."

Aleksandr recalled that "Yura was soulful. He was very quiet. He was kind, pleasant mannered always." He and Igor got along very well. Yuri "was the leader, he was older. He was very protective of his younger brother." Aleksandr recalled a time when Igor had the mumps. "He looked awful. Yura was greatly concerned about him, comforting him, sitting by him—he felt an obligation to help him."

Aleksandr found odd jobs at night in order to pay for living expenses and contribute to the family's upkeep. On Rossi Street, "Yura also had to study music, so he had to have a instrument. I helped pay for it." Together with Anna, Aleksandr helped the two boys with their homework. Yuri "always grasped ideas very quickly and managed well in all subjects," he recalled. Yuri also read a lot on his own, another trait inherited from his mother. Was he closer to Vladimir or Anna? "To his mother, of course," Aleksandr said. "Because she loved him very much… I believe it was mutual."

Aleksandr had joined the Party in 1945, motivated in part, he recounted, by the patriotic fervor that galvanized the USSR during the war years. But he was also ambitious. With the same forthrightness that characterized the entire family, Aleksandr allowed in 2005 that he remained committed "actually, right up to today, even though I can't really be considered a Party member anymore. I still stand for the same principles, with some corrections, of course." Vladimir, however, "didn't believe it," while Anna "never said anything about Party matters—she was busy with housekeeping, she was interested in the theater."

Fulfilling the role of Soviet citizen required disavowing so much that had been essential to the lives of prerevolutionary Russians. Religion was one of them. One of the major goals of communism, indeed, was the eradication of religion, which it correctly recognized as one of the greatest counterforces to its supremacy. In the empiricist, rationalist USSR, people were brought up convinced that believing in God was acutely embarrassing, shameful, akin to admitting one was illiterate or still wet the bed. But, like so much in prerevolutionary consciousness, belief lingered in the hearts of many. The Russian Orthodox Church continued to function in marginalized fashion. Perhaps it was a lingering strain of belief and observance that also explained Anna and Vladimir's indifference to the Party.

As an adult, Soloviev himself possessed what Lisa describes as a sense of reverence and a Wordsworthian spirituality. In Australia in 1969, Soloviev on one occasion fingered the cross she wore around her neck. "I was baptized," he said, almost to himself. "When Igor was still very small, Babushka took us to a church to be baptized." The grandmother he referred to was Vladimir's stepmother, Mariia, his father Valentin's second wife, a devout woman.

"Afterward, she made me swear never to tell anyone. I promised." Then he paused. "And now I have broken my promise." He paused again. "But I think it was all right to tell you, Babushka would not have minded." It would appear that he told no one else.

SEEING SOLOVIEV OFF AT PULKOVO AIRPORT FOR HIS FIRST U.S. TOUR, YURI, VLADIMIR AND UNCLE ALEKSANDR

ON ROSSI STREET

AS A PAGE IN THE KIROV'S RAYMONDA, 1950

A t his Rossi Street audition, Soloviev was chosen by a commission that included instructors Bazhenova, Gromova, Levin and Nadezhda Fedorova. Fedorova was his teacher for the first three years. She was followed by Boris Soloviev (no relation), who was reportedly very successful at developing strength in his young pupils.

Students at Rossi Street were on stage almost as soon as they began studying. There was much need for children's ensembles in both ballet and opera at the Kirov and at the Maly, Leningrad's number two venue for ballet and opera. Nikolai Ostaltsov, who was one year younger, danced alongside Soloviev on the Kirov stage in the Saracen children's dance in the second act of *Raymonda*. They took it very seriously and were nervous about it; the standard demanded of children was high and strict. "The discipline was unbelievable," Ostaltsov recalled.

FOLK DANCE ON ROSSI STREET, YURI SECOND FROM RIGHT

Each year more students were winnowed out. According to his class-mate Tchernichova, faculty were worried about Soloviev's height and even asked his parents to come in to see how tall they were. Soloviev was at one point in danger of being dismissed in favor of another boy, Igor Briantsev, "a pint-sized prince" who seemed more of a performer than the diffident Solo-viev. But it was Soloviev who remained, in part because Aleksandr Pushkin, one of the school's most influential teachers, argued for him.

Now, in his senior course, he started studying with Boris Shavrov. Shavrov had joined the then-Imperial Mariinsky in 1911, and remained a premier dancer there throughout the 1920s. As a teacher, he was precise, demanding, and rather dry. His son Aleksandr, a classmate of Soloviev's, boasted to Lisa years later… "We were all known as the *shav-rovchiki*—the Shavrov Gang—"always recognizable because of our clean techniques, especially jumps, entrechats. We could out-entrechat anyone in the yearly exams!" Soloviev himself credited Shavrov for making him the technician he became.

Marina Tcherednichenko, also a member of the class of 1958, recalled that Shavrov customarily addressed Soloviev by the pet name "Yurinka," and

DRAPED IN RED FLAG AND DOMINATING A VAGANOVA ACADEMY ASSEMBLY, THE GREAT HELMSMAN, GREATEST LEADER OF ALL TIMES AND ALL PEOPLES, GREAT FATHER OF THE PEOPLE, WISE AND GREAT FRIEND OF ALL THE OPPRESSED, GREAT LEADER AND TEACHER, TIRELESS FIGHTER FOR PEACE AND INDEPENDENCE OF PEOPLES, LOCOMOTIVE OF THE REVOLUTION, ARCHITECT OF COMMUNISM, ARCHITECT OF A NEW HUMAN SOCIETY, MOUNTAIN EAGLE, SON OF LENIN, HERO OF THE OCTOBER REVOLUTION, 3-TIMES ORDER OF THE RED BANNER, 3-TIMES ORDER OF LENIN, ORDER OF SUVOROV, MEDAL OF VICTORY, MEDAL OF VICTORY OVER GERMANY IN THE GREAT PATRIOTIC WAR, MEDAL OF VICTORY OVER JAPAN, MEDAL OF THE MONGOLIAN PEOPLES' REVOLUTION, TWICE ORDER OF THE WHITE LION OF CZECHOSLOVAKIA, GREAT GENERALISSIMO OF THE SOVIET UNION, GENERAL SECRETARY OF THE SOVIET UNION JOSEPH [IOSEB BESARIONIS DZE JUGHASHVILI] STALIN, CIRCA 1953.

FRONT ROW: YURI SECOND FROM LEFT, ALLA SIZOVA THIRD FROM RIGHT

"he would say it with such admiration." Shavrov taught him "not just how to dance," recalled Gabriela Komleva, Soloviev's classmate and future partner, "but how to hold his partner, how to treat her, the regard needed toward the partner, how to behave onstage." Excellent tutelage in partnering was also provided him in the pas de deux class of Nikolai Serebrennikov.

As he grew taller, Soloviev was given important solo roles in student recitals staged in the school's own tiny theater, which were attended

SCHOOL DEBUT
AS THE BLUEBIRD IN
THE SLEEPING BEAUTY

by administration and faculty, as well as fellow students. There he danced Nijinsky's solo from Fokine's *Le Pavillon d'Armide*, created in 1907 for the Mariinsky. It was after that, his friend Nikolai Gorbachev recalled, that Soloviev seemed headed for fame. Later Soloviev would assume the roles that Nijinsky had created in Fokine's *Chopiniana, Carnaval* and *Le Spectre de la Rose*. Shavrov also taught him an old variation that had once been interpolated into act 2 of *Swan Lake*. It included a manège of jetés in first arabesque that also excited his peers and instructors.

WITH CLASSMATES BUGANOVA AND VASILIEVA

The Solovievs lived just across the Fontanka River from Rossi Street. This was fortunate, for Yuri would return from school "completely exhausted," Uncle Aleksandr recalled, having clocked in a full day of dance as well as general academics. He was not as robust as he later became, and he strained

IN BORIS SHAVROV'S CLASS WITH LEFT TO RIGHT: KUMYSNIKOV, KORECHOV AND SHAVROV'S SON ALEXANDER. PHOTO: COURTESY VAGANOVA ACADEMY

his back in pas de deux class; the girls he was lifting weren't as thin as they became after turning professional.

At home, he was confronted by worsening tensions, certainly exacerbated by the proximity of the entire family in one room. Yuri's success at school could only have increased Anna's nearly obsessive attention; as Aleksandr said, "Anything and everything she did was for the sake of Yura alone." It eventually fell to Yuri to become her protector as well. When acrimony flared between her and Vladimir, Yuri came to his mother's defense.

Tchernichova recalled being assigned one of Cinderella's mime scenes from Konstantin Sergeyev's 1946 production for the Kirov as her graduation project in the acting class taught by Mikhail Mikhailov. She played the stepmother and Mikhailov picked Soloviev to play opposite her. She made up her face outrageously but, as her henpecked husband, "Yuri didn't wear a comic makeup; he didn't need to," she recalls in her autobiography. "Just be yourself," she told him, explaining, "he always seemed so very much inside himself. His own forlorn expression was perfect."

LAKE COUNTRY
OUTSIDE LENINGRAD

THE FONTANKA BRIDGE
CONNECTED HOME AND SCHOOL

Each of his contemporaries would have their own recollection of his expression, but all agreed that he lived within his own psychological perimeter. At school, Soloviev was "very polite," recalled Evgenii Shcherbakov, who was one year younger. "Very kind. Not aggressive, not sad," often wearing an enigmatic smile "like the *Gioconda*." He was "open-minded, very joyful, gracious," classmate Elena Shatrova recalled.

In school, as for the rest of his life, the face Soloviev wore in public was perhaps not a deliberate mask so much as it was part of his identity. "I understood later that he always had some kind of sadness inside, very, very deep inside," recalled classmate Oleg Vinogradov, who later directed the Kirov.

At a memorial service for Soloviev, Uncle Aleksandr would tell Shcherbakov that his nephew was extremely sensitive from childhood on, able to be deeply wounded by an unkind word. Aleksandr had tried to instill

PARTNERING NATALIA MAKAROVA IN THE BLUEBIRD PAS DE DEUX
AT HIS GRADUATION CONCERT ON THE KIROV STAGE, MAY 1958

GRADUATION REPORT
CARD, MOSTLY 5'S
I.E. A'S, INCLUDING
FENCING

GRADUATING CLASS, SOLOVIEV FAR LEFT

the psychological defenses that Yuri seemed to lack. Aleksandr was worried when, as a teenager, Soloviev began to bring up the subject of death.

Was this occasioned by threats made by Anna? One imagines that like her own mother, she too, may well have entertained thoughts of suicide during her wartime ordeal. But she had fought for her own survival in the knowledge that it was the only way her child would live. Rumination on the topic of suicide and death, however, seemed a constant theme for her. Soloviev's classmate Aleksandr Shavrov said that Anna had threatened suicide on more than one occasion. He didn't specify when. If during Soloviev's adolescence, however, it remained only an unspoken possibility, it was certainly something he was sensitive enough to absorb.

When Lisa interviewed Uncle Aleksandr, she sensed a palpable animosity on his part toward Anna. In surreptitious pantomime he indicated that her father drank, and that she was also not immune. He described her as "nervous." Lisa sensed that in the interests of civility he had stopped himself from using the more common epithet "hysterical." But a silent accusation was certainly there in the unblinking eyes staring at Lisa.

PART 2:
THE KIROV

MARIINSKY (ONCE KIROV) THEATER. PHOTO: VALENTIN BARANOVSKY

MARIINSKY INTERIOR. PHOTO: VALENTIN BARANOVSKY

LE CORSAIRE

8

NUREYEV, PISAREV, PUSHKIN

longside Soloviev's adolescent gentleness and intermittent melancholy went a potential for violence that perhaps foreshadowed his eventual fate. However, in his early adolescence it was a potential completely in key with the prevailing tone of Soviet mores. While there were certainly any number of gay and bisexual men in the Kirov and the Rossi Street academy, students were subject to the idealized hypermasculinity and ingrained homophobia of Russian and Soviet culture.

When weather was pleasant, the Rossi boys often used to hang out in "Katia's Garden." Named for Catherine the Great, the Ekaterinsky Garden abutted Rossi Street. It was notorious as an after dark gay pickup site, since there were public bathrooms there, which were a rarity in the city.

A favorite sport of Soloviev and his classmates was setting up the prettiest boy—often his good friend Marat Kumysnikov—alone on a bench as a decoy. Then the boys scattered and hid. When they saw a cruising man approach and begin to chat up their bait, the boys pounced on their prey and pummeled him.

"How could you do something like that?" Lisa asked, appalled when Soloviev told her the story in 1969. "They were repulsive, they pestered us, so we let them have it," he answered simply. She didn't think that he had considered how awful it was until then. But she could see he had registered her horrified reaction.

A more serious example of possible gay bashing during Soloviev's school years was the murder of a young Ossetian academic instructor at the school. He was tall, handsome and fair-haired, hailing from a historically Christian nation in the Caucasus. According to Tchernichova, he was found stabbed to death in the street. At the school, suspicion fell on the boys from Tajikistan; they had continued to carry concealed knives, according to tribal custom, despite attempts by the school administration to ban the weapons. But the entire matter was quickly hushed up.

As a senior student, Soloviev was invited to dance the *Swan Lake* act 1 pas de trois as part of the Kirov's performance calendar. This was a very rare honor. At his graduation concert on the Mariinsky stage in May 1958, seventeen-year-old Soloviev danced *The Sleeping Beauty*'s Bluebird pas de deux

partnering Natalia Makarova, who was one class behind him.

At school, Soloviev's gifts had attracted Rudolf Nureyev's notice as well as admiration. Nureyev envied not only Soloviev's natural talent but also the methodical schooling he had already received. Whereas Nureyev was seventeen when he entered the school, a native of Ufa in Bashkiria; he was basically just beginning serious training in the senior men's class taught by Aleksandr Pushkin.

Nureyev resented the excitement generated by Soloviev at the school. "Why everything for Yuri Soloviev and nothing for me?" Nureyev bemoaned to Menia Martinez, a Cuban student on Rossi Street who was his close friend. In fact, Nureyev never did entirely conquer his sense of inferiority. "You think I'm good?" he later rebutted adoring fans in London. "You should see Yuri Soloviev."

But Soloviev was too likeable and modest to become a nemesis. Instead, Nureyev perhaps in some way co-opted his rival by striking up a friendship. As it turned out, there would be more than enough glory for them both.

Nureyev was from the very first an electrifying and flamboyant stage presence. Kirov artistic director Boris Fenster decided that, contrary to

precedent, Nureyev would enter the company not as a member of the corps de ballet but as a soloist. Very soon, he was dancing leading roles way beyond what he could then manage technically, yet he made astonishing progress during his three years in the company. As was customary for Rossi Street graduates, Soloviev joined the corps de ballet, but he also was soon given solo roles.

Nureyev and Soloviev each had high extensions and beautiful feet, physical attributes that Nureyev exploited well beyond what was considered acceptable in male style in the company. Perhaps this was a way of compensating for the technique he was still struggling to attain; standing on higher relevé than the balance of the company's men also made his legs look longer. But then again, everything that Nureyev did on stage and off was more than

SOLOVIEV AS THE RIVER GOD IN
THE LITTLE HUMPBACKED HORSE

a little outlandish.

Moving into the dressing room they shared with a few other dancers, Soloviev was shocked by the way Nureyev took possession by throwing his things willy-nilly all over everyone else's personal space. His disdain for conventional etiquette, as well as Soviet regulation, indeed knew no bounds. Nureyev mocked Soloviev's modest dressing and undressing in a furtive corner. Nureyev himself was the consummate exhibitionist, intruding his charms into the sight lines of his dressing room mates as much as he encroached on their things. He mocked Soloviev's *pudeur*. "Oh, come on," Nureyev coaxed. "Give us a little look." This produced in Soloviev diffidence rather than anything like the brutality he and his classmates demonstrated in the Ekaterinsky Garden.

At times, Soloviev acted as a brake on Nureyev's heedless flouting of tradition. The Kirov usually took class and rehearsed in the school's Rossi Street premises. It was the duty of the newest company members to sprinkle studio floors with water to provide better traction against the old wood boards. But Nureyev refused to perform a task that he considered beneath him. The Kirov's Sergei Vikulov, who had joined in 1956, recalled that Soloviev threatened to punch Nureyev if he didn't comply. At least in that one instance, Nureyev did as he was told.

Certainly Soloviev and Nureyev were polar opposites when it came to imposing their will on the theater administration. "Why don't you go in there and just pound your fist on the table and tell them what you want?" Nureyev asked. That was something that Soloviev could not do then—or, for that matter, ever.

As soon as he joined the company, Soloviev began studying in the company class taught by Alexei Pisarev. Pisarev was coauthor with Vera Kostrovitskaia of a classic ballet textbook. An excellent coach, Pisarev worked with Soloviev on his first important successes on the Kirov stage, the pas de trois from *Swan Lake* and the Bluebird pas de deux, showcases for his phenomenal elevation and batterie.

Pisarev, however, was unfortunately caught in a tailspin of alcoholism, which led to his death in 1960. Soloviev then joined the parallel company class taught by Pushkin. He took Pushkin's class routinely until Pushkin's death in 1970, and was coached by him as well. Pushkin also continued to teach at the school, where he was a gentler personality than Alexander Shavrov. Pushkin's class was "freer and a little bit advanced," said Soloviev's colleague Ostaltsov. Both as teacher and coach, Pushkin "was a great gardener," said Shcherbakov: "When he touched a dancer, the dancer blossomed." Pushkin's guidance of Baryshnikov and Nureyev has been recognized, but not his influence on Soloviev, although it may have been equally profound.

"How could anybody be competitive with him in class?" asked Vikulov about Soloviev. "Who could do everything perfectly? Only he. Nobody compared to him technically." And yet, at least in Soloviev's own opinion, Shavrov's technical tutelage could not be surpassed. He told Lisa in 1969: "When I left Shavrov's class and went to Pushkin's, I started dancing worse."

GRADUATION BLUEBIRD PAS DE DEUX WITH MAKAROVA

TATIANA WITH GALINA KEKISHEVA AND YURI IN *SWAN LAKE*, PAS DE TROIS ACT I

9

TATIANA

Классический балет есть замок красоты...
и ангелы добра в невыразимой пачке.
И в силах пробудить от элизийской спячки
овация Чайковского и К°.
Классический балет! Искусство лучших дней!

—Иосиф Бродский

Classical ballet is a bastion of beauty...
And of virtuous angels in a silent bundle.
And able to awaken from the Elysian hibernation
The ovation of Tchaikovsky and Co.
Classical ballet! The art from the best of days!

—Joseph Brodsky

Choreographer Andrei Kuznetsov-Vecheslov once explained to Lisa why the Great Terror and other purges had not extended to ballet. Stalin liked ballet, replied Kutznetsov, son of Kirov stars Tatiana Vecheslova and Viacheslav Kutznetsov. The dictator liked its prestige and its imperial trappings that they conferred on him as the Communist "Tsar of all the Russias." And in addition, Kutznetsov quipped, Stalin might have believed that the nature of their work ensured that "dancers know how to keep their mouths shut." Dancers, indeed, were not considered intelligent, idealistic or intellectual enough to stoke the dictator's paranoia. Nevertheless, culture was in the same straitjacket as all important institutions. Just the way it did in every sector of Soviet society, Stalin's death opened up altogether new horizons for the Kirov Ballet. Soloviev joined the same year that it had hosted guest stars Yvette Chauviré and Liane Daydé of the Paris Opera Ballet, Cuban Alicia Alonso, star of Ballet Theatre in the U.S., and Beryl Grey, who had just left Britain's Royal Ballet. Cultural exchange meant that Kirov dancers were now also being sent to previously off-limits countries in the West.

In August 1959, the Kirov sent a stellar delegation to dance at the

International Youth Festival in Vienna. One of the numbers they performed was the pas de six from act 3 of Vakhtang Chabukiani's Spanish-accented *Laurencia*, created for the Kirov in 1939. A character-flavored classical divertissement amid a panoply of celebratory wedding dances, it was often excerpted for concert programs. In Vienna, the pas de six was led by Nureyev and Ninel Kurgapkina, while the four soloists were Galina Kekicheva and Tatiana Legat, partnered by Gennady Selutsky and Soloviev.

At twenty-five, Legat was an established soloist, sparkling and crisp onstage and off. In the Kirov, she and Soloviev were cast together not only in *Laurencia*, but in the *Swan Lake* pas de trois, *Giselle*'s Peasant pas de deux, and in a revival of Fokine's *Carnaval*. But during Soloviev's first months in the company, Legat hadn't paid much attention to him, "because Nureyev simply took all the attention. Yura was very shy," she said. "It came very slowly, very shyly. I started noticing him and he started noticing me."

Certainly Soloviev had not dated while he was studying on Rossi Street. Dating in the USSR was not the rite of passage it was for American teenagers. The school was a prized *zakrytoe zavedenie*—closed facility—on a par with military research institutes and it attempted to strictly supervise all the students' activities. Parents' incomes were minuscule by Western standards, and Vladimir Soloviev's worker salary didn't allow Yuri any pocket money to take a girl anywhere special. There were, of course, always the possibilities of movies and long walks.

In addition, the prospect of his developing any form of adult romantic relationship was, in all likelihood, not something that his mother relished. He had once brought to the apartment the very same Menia Martinez who was a close pal of Nureyev's. "Many men were courting her," Uncle Aleksandr recalled, but, he added, "I think he appealed to her." Anna was home, and the three sat and talked. Anna "had no reaction," Aleksandr said. "There were no emotions involved, so it was OK with her." Tatiana, however, would prove to be a very different story.

TATIANA WITH YURI IN *GISELLE*, ACT I PEASANT PAS DE DEUX

CINDERELLA STEPSISTER. PHOTO: TEJA-KNUT KREMKE

10

SURVIVOR

TATIANA, HER GRANDMOTHER ANTONINA LEGAT, AND HALF-BROTHER GERMAN OLSHLEGER

Certainly both Yuri and Tatiana's childhoods had been damaging in any number of ways, but they didn't discuss their wartime experiences. "We were just happy that we had survived." Legat's experience had been gruesome.

Tatiana came from a storied theatrical family impoverished, as most were, by the Revolution. Her grandfather Nikolai Legat had been a leading dancer, then director successively of the Imperial Mariinsky and the Rossi Street academy. Her grandmother Olga Chumakova had also danced with the Mariinsky. Nikolai married her after a long common-law marriage to her older sister. Nikolai left Russia in a rage in 1923. One of his treasured possessions had been the violin Enrico Cechetti had used to accompany his classes. During a tense meeting with a member of the young Soviet state's secret police, however, the officer broke Nikolai's violin in two. Legat then left his wife and child, and settled in Britain, where he became an important teacher. He eventually served Chumakova with divorce papers and remarried in Britain.

His abandonment of her grandmother haunted Tatiana in adulthood.

"How could he do that, just leave a wife and young child? I've asked people all my life, wanting to hear their answers, to explain. Looking at Alyona, I'd ask Yura, 'Look at our daughter, how could he do that, leave his family?'"

Tatiana's mother, Mariia, married a navy man, Nikolai Shilov, his rank unknown. Tatiana was born in Leningrad on April 8, 1934, moving to Murmansk, and then on to Novaya Zemlya, on the Arctic Sea, where her father served aboard ship. His mother disapproved of the marriage, and Tatiana was given her mother's last name at birth. Her father's last name is absent from her birth certificate. Her middle name—patronymic—Nikolaevna is, coincidentally, that of both of Shilov and her grandfather, Nikolai Legat.

Mariia and the baby lived in the settlement under appalling conditions. Tatiana ate coal from the fireplace where her mother cooked what little food was to be found in that arctic outpost. The marriage collapsed and Mariia returned to Leningrad before Tatiana was two years old. Mariia soon married German Olshleger (a Russian of German extraction), and bore him a son, also named German. As Tatiana was told by her grandmother, Mariia left Olshleger because she suspected he was an informer for the secret police (the then-NKVD, later KGB, now FSB).

"Mama was very bitter," Legat recalled to Lisa. "She had a childhood like a princess, like yours, Lizonka and then… That was why she had such a vicious temper. I was afraid of her, I'd close my eyes and pretend I was asleep when she got angry. I'd always tell Babushka, 'I want to stay with you, not Mama.'"

Tatiana, her brother, mother and grandmother all remained in Leningrad during the siege. After the Nazi invasion, many in Leningrad were unable to evacuate, or unwilling to leave their apartments and what little they had. Many parents also were reluctant to join the transports of dependents and noncombatants. Although there was a blackout of news from the front and being caught "rumor-mongering"—discussing the war—would guarantee a one-way trip to the basements of the Big House, people had heard horror stories of the evacuations. Children's transports had been abandoned by caregivers when their trains were overtaken by the approaching Wehrmacht troops. Small children too young to know their names had been lost forever, as horrified mothers learned from some of the older children who had managed to find their own way back to Leningrad. Tales of typhus epidemics spread by unsanitary conditions, and criminals robbing defenseless women and children on the railways were also a deterrent.

The winter of 1941–42 was one of the coldest in recorded history. Rations were reduced to an official 350 calories a day. However, bread rations amounted to far less, as grain was only one ingredient; sawdust and other fillers were added to create the required bulk. Buildings ceased to be heated, pipes broke; water, frequently contaminated by human waste, was collected with buckets or pans wherever it could be found, including the Neva River and canals.

Public transportation stopped early in Fall 1941. So long as she remained strong enough to walk to her office job, Tatiana's mother was able to bring home a staple of the office worker's diet: blocks of carpenter's glue. Made from animal bones—the proverbial glue factory that old horses were sent to—these were melted in the evening and set to gel overnight. A laurel leaf or any spice that remained was added to give it some flavor.

After Nazi shelling destroyed their building in the outskirts of town, Tatiana, German and their mother moved into Madame Legat's room in a communal apartment at 32 Marat Street. As countless Leningrad mothers chose to do, Mariia denied herself her ever-dwindling ration to feed her children. German was so weak that Tatiana would carry him on her back to the table to eat. As he became unable to hold utensils, Tatiana and her mother spoon-fed him.

Finally, Mariia herself became too weak to leave the apartment, further reducing the family's ration. In early 1942, hidden from her children in a cordoned-off corner of the room, she succumbed to starvation-induced hypertrophy and dysentery and was taken to a hospital. Legat's grandmother continued to work in the laboratory of another hospital. By putting on a white lab coat and impersonating a visiting doctor, she was able to sneak into the hospital ward where her daughter lay dying.

After the blockade was broken early in 1944, Tatiana was placed by her grandmother in an *internat,* a boarding school for orphans or children of indigent families. The Kirov company and school had by now returned from Perm, where they had been evacuated. Agrippina Vaganova had known Nikolai Legat and his wife very well before the Revolution. She had attended the christening of Tatiana's mother at the Vladimirovsky Cathedral.

After the war, Madame Legat took Tatiana to Rossi Street to seek out Vaganova. "I thought you were dead!" Vaganova cried. She gave Tatiana a fifty-ruble bill: "Your grandmother will buy you a present with this." Soon Tatiana was enrolled at Rossi Street. Vaganova arranged that her debilitated, destitute grandmother be given a bowl of soup daily in the school cafeteria. In 1953, Tatiana graduated and joined the Kirov.

Fate dealt more harshly with Tatiana's younger half-brother. Possessed of the inescapably Teutonic name German Germanovich Olshleger, nicknamed "Gitler"—Hitler—by his pals, was evacuated to Yaroslavl Oblast in a children's transport after his mother died in 1942.

Returning to Leningrad postwar, he was surrendered by his grandmother to a series of ever-rougher orphanages, ending up by a clerical oversight in a *desiatiletka* work-study apprenticeship in a Gulag sub-camp in Ukhta, in the Russian Far North. A tall, fine-featured adolescent with a

German name, he owes his survival largely to having been befriended by the German POWs still held there. Finally, Madame Legat petitioned the government that because she was failing, and claiming that he was her only relative, that she needed him. She was able to obtain a pass to bring him back to Leningrad for the summer. He then went AWOL. With irregular papers, he was unable to finish school. He found work as an apprentice in a factory that did choose not to scrutinize his documents as laborers were in short supply. He remained there until retirement.

11
NEWLYWEDS

GRANDMOTHER MARIIA, ANNA, VLADIMIR, TATIANA AND YURI ON
WEDDING DAY, OCTOBER 7, 1960, AT FONTANKA EMBANKMENT, 64

uring the 1959–60 season, Legat and Soloviev had many chances to spend time together amid exotic foreign locales. The Kirov was now beginning to tour internationally, and during that theatrical season it went on long tours to Egypt and Japan. Since the company numbered two hundred dancers, performances at home could continue seamlessly no matter how long part of the company was away.

By this time, Tatiana's grandmother was dead and she was living with a married couple, the Efremovs, childless members of the intelligentsia. He was an engineer; his father had been a well-known mathematician. A teacher at the school, Leonid Semionov, had once been a student of Nikolai Legat. Semionov knew the Efremovs, and it was he who made the introduction that led to them virtually adopting teenaged Tatiana.

At night, Legat and Soloviev, tired as they may have been, took the Efremovs' hunting dog on long walks through the city. Soloviev's feet were so high-arched that they were particularly prone to fatigue; nevertheless, love was a priority. It was the first time either had been seriously involved. "We only kissed and giggled about it," Legat recalled.

"Yura wanted to marry me," she said, but she was twenty-five and he was nineteen. She asked that they wait until he turned twenty, and if he changed his mind, "we won't even talk about it."

On August 10, 1960, Soloviev turned twenty, and they married on the next public holiday, October 7, Soviet Constitution Day. "We were so poor; we didn't even have wedding rings." She moved in with the Solovievs on Fontanka Street. The family had reluctantly sold their dog Amur to the border patrol because it shed so profusely. They grieved over the loss of the dog, but with that money his parents bought a convertible sofa for the newlyweds. His parents slept in one corner, while halfway down the room were the new convertible and a folding bed for Igor. Uncle Aleksandr had by now moved out. As a wedding present, Anna and Vladimir gave Tatiana a bolt of fabric that Yuri had brought Anna from abroad. Tatiana had a suit made from it.

"The cult of personality in the family was all about Yura," Legat recalled, appropriating the phrase with which Khrushchev had denounced Stalin in 1956. "Everything in the family was about him." High priestess of the cult was, of course, Anna, whose younger son took second place in her affections. Nor did she welcome her new daughter-in-law unreservedly. "How wonderful it is that you have no relatives," Yuri said to Tatiana. "That way Mama doesn't have anybody to fight with." Nevertheless, there still was Tatiana herself. Initially, Legat recalled, "his father liked me but his mother didn't very much. She objected to the fact that I was older. At first, she would go after me and push me around a bit. His father would say, 'Leave her alone, leave her alone,' and take me into the [communal] kitchen."

Relief came when Tatiana was named Honored Artist of the RSFSR (Russian Republic of the Soviet Union). The head of the local Komsomol, the Communist Youth League office, who had been a guest at their wedding party, arranged for Tatiana and Yuri to move to their own room in another communal apartment. It was on the Petrogradskaia Storona, on the other side of Trinity Bridge, a fashionable part of town developed at the turn of the century, with many attractive Art Nouveau buildings.

Eventually Tatiana and Anna developed a mutual fondness, so much so that Legat would describe them as "allies." Yet Anna's instability didn't lessen, nor did her emotional demands on Yuri. She routinely insisted that Yuri and Tatiana come to dinner after a performance, even though Fontanka Street is a considerable distance from the opera house.

From time to time, Legat recounted, something would "transpire" at the senior Soloviev household and Yuri would be called to deal with his mother. Tatiana wanted to come too, but invariably Soloviev would brush her off: "This has to do with my family. Stay out of it." It hurt her to be excluded. But Soloviev wouldn't hear of it. He always went alone and came back refusing to tell her anything.

THE STONE FLOWER BETROTHAL SCENE

12

ALLA SIZOVA

The remarkable resilience and instinct for survival Legat had already demonstrated found its lifelong channel in ballet. She was and remains infatuated. Ballet has been the anchor of her life. She continues to coach at St. Petersburg's Mikhailovsky, as the Maly is now called, reverting to its prerevolutionary name.

As a girl, she endlessly watched the Kirov when it used the school studios to rehearse. Her teacher Lidiia Tiuntina would pull her away from a studio keyhole: "You're going to get hit in the head when they come out. So show me, what did you watch?" And she would demonstrate what she had seen, precisely re-creating the personal mannerisms of the individual dancers. Tatiana developed a laser focus and an encyclopedic memory for ballet. Now, married to Soloviev, "We were trying to help each other to improve our performances," Legat recalled, "and we were always discussing everything." When she watched Soloviev dance from the wings of the Kirov, "he would say, 'When you're standing there you're so nervous, you make me nervous.' But after the performance he would ask, 'How did I do this, how did I do that?' I would say, 'If I didn't stay in the wings, I wouldn't be able to tell you.'" She tried, however, to lose herself in the crowd; that way, he wouldn't see her and would be more comfortable.

While individual Kirov stars had already made appearances in Europe, in May 1961, the Kirov was due to make its European debut as a full ensemble—an event that would prove momentous on all sides. Well before the tour, Soloviev experienced a watershed, creating his first major new role: the Youth in Igor Belsky's *Leningrad Symphony*, performed to a movement from Shostakovich's famed composition of the same name. Belsky was one of the company's leading character dancers. Two years earlier, he had created his first ballet for the Kirov.

In *Leningrad Symphony* Soloviev was paired with Alla Sizova, with whom he forged his first great partnership. Sizova had graduated with him in 1958. Like Soloviev, she was still a student when she danced the *Swan Lake* pas de trois on the Kirov stage. Sizova "was like Yura," Legat said. "She was easily wounded, very sensitive. They were together from adolescence, and he loved her and she loved him. They were happy dancing together."

Like Soloviev, Sizova had an extraordinary jump. She was small, with a high extension, perfect turn-out and a magical radiance. Not a "grand ballerina," she retained into her forties an air of girlish spontaneity, sincerity and impulsiveness. "Sizova would arrive and everybody would fall in love," Legat said.

She was academically trained, recognizably Kirov, and yet, like virtually all the Kirov ballerinas, completely herself. Doing things her own way did not always comport with the academic exactitude for which the company strove. "Her legs could go some strange way," Legat said, "or her head could stray on the turns, but she was so charming and delightful that the gates opened."

In the 1958 graduation concert, she and Nureyev had created a sensation dancing *Le Corsaire* pas de deux together. Nureyev was frequently her partner during his three years at the Kirov. But "Soloviev was always closer to me," Sizova recalled. "Nureyev gave me extra energy. Soloviev I always compared to the Volga River: big, slow, gracious."

The spontaneity she conveyed on stage was characteristic of her performance habits. Supporting her in pirouettes, Soloviev "was always afraid that she would fly off somewhere," Legat recalled. Sizova liked to impetuously try to fit in an extra turn: "You really had to watch it with Sizova. You had to keep your eye on her. Yura said, 'You cannot control her.'"

The great Kirov ballerina Alla Shelest was coaching Sizova during these early years of their partnership. "They were a wonderful pair on stage, youthful Sizova and Soloviev!" Shelest recalled in a posthumous tribute to him. "Both light, light in their jumps and in their natures, gifted with huge ballons, dancing in the expansive Russian manner—they both were aglow."

Shostakovich's Seventh "Leningrad" Symphony was completed in December 1941, during the hideous first winter of the siege. It was given its world premiere performance there the following spring. The Philharmonic had been evacuated, with almost all members eventually sent to the front, but the Leningrad Radio Orchestra was supplemented with military performers. The musicians were starving and exhausted and frequently collapsed during rehearsals; the fact that the concert took place at all was a triumph of will, broadcast by the Soviets to the German lines as a propagandistic salvo. Since

then, the music's place in national consciousness had become sacrosanct.

In the ballet, Soloviev's role was a frolicking youth who becomes a mar-tyred hero facing the marauding Nazis. Sizova danced his carefree beloved turned bereft survivor. "It was a youth performance," Sizova recalled. "Belsky was doing it with us in mind. It was quite new movements for us, based on classical movement but doing it a little bit in a contemporary way." Belsky "used combinations that I invented," recalled Gabriela Komleva, who alter-nated the role, "as I was rehearsing myself in front of the mirror." "It was very interesting for us," recalled Sizova.

Leningrad Symphony indeed figured prominently on a new page in Soviet choreography that allowed an inclination toward formalism after decades of *drambalet*—full-evening, plot-driven works that Stalin's cultural apparatchiks insisted be absolutely unambiguous to the presumed mass audience that would watch them.

Here in Belsky's ballet, the conflict between Nazis and Soviets emerged through choral-movement groupings. The ballet also reflected the heady pace of cultural exchange. Antony Tudor's *Lilac Garden* had been performed in Leningrad by American Ballet Theatre in 1960, and in his new ballet,

Belsky incorporated distinctive Tudor vocabulary.

. Shelest recalled a moment in the ballet when, "in the heat of battle, the two enemies clash in a plastic combat, not touching each other, and practically not dancing. But in the change of positions, clearly one reads the spir-

BATTLE SCENE, *LENINGRAD SYMPHONY*

itual victory of one of them—the Youth. Very rarely was anybody able to fill that static episode with strength of spirit—but Yuri did."

"Yura was a great artist," Belsky recalled in 1995. "He was a great helper in the beginnings of everything of in those days… I am grateful for everything that he did for me." In 1959, Belsky's first ballet, *The Coast of Hope*, had quickly vanished from the Kirov repertory due to the pernicious inclusion of some movement derived from rock 'n' roll. Indeed, very few new ballets survived long in the Kirov repertory, since officialdom considered all contemporary creations implicitly suspect. But *Leningrad Symphony* retains a place on the Kirov stage. For one thing, the music is beloved, identified with civic and national pride, forever a celebration of Soviet resilience and victory over the Nazis.

Seen today, Belsky's ballet is not quite the orgy of dogmatic nationalism that one might have expected. Socialist Realism, which had been decreed the USSR's official aesthetic in 1934, mandated optimism in a work of art's final resolution. Here that was missing. Neither the ballet nor the music suggested even the possibility of rebirth. In a final lamentation, Sizova stumbled across the stage, her arms dangling limply, a haunted figure of desolation.

Soloviev's performance, too, skirted the didactic clichés. He brought to the Youth a unique amalgam of vigor and sensitivity. Five months after the April 1961 Leningrad premiere, the Kirov brought Belsky's ballet to the Metropolitan Opera in New York during its American debut season. In *Dance Magazine*, Doris Hering saluted Soloviev's "honest and uniquely spiritual" impact in the role.

REHEARSING THE FATAL SHOT IN *LENINGRAD SYMPHONY*

FRONT, ALLA OSIPENKO, OLGA MOISEYEVA, INNA ZUBKOVSKAYA,
IRINA KOLPAKOVA, KONSTANTIN SERGEYEV, WITH NATALIA MAKAROVA
IN SUNGLASSES

13
PARIS

ELLES FONT PARTIE DES BALLETS DE LENINGRAD ET VIENNENT
DANSER A PARIS.

LES 120 DANSEURS DES "BALLETS DE LENINGRAD" SONT ARRIVÉS
CET APRÈS-MIDI À L'AÉROPORT DU BOURGET À BORD D'UN TUPOLEV
SPÉCIAL.
ILS OUVRIRONT LE 16 MAI LA "GRANDE SAISON DE PARIS" EN
PRÉSENTANT AU COURS D'UN GALA À L'OPÉRA, "LA BELLE AU BOIS DORMANT".
ILS DANSERONT ÉGALEMENT , PAR LA SUITE, DEUX AUTRES BALLETS:
"LA FLEUR DE PIERRE" ET "LE LAC DES CYGNES".

VOICI À LEUR DESCENTE D'AVION À L'AÉROPORT DU BOURGET, QUELOU..
JOLIES DANSEUSES DE LA TROUPE ENTOURANT LA DANSEUSE-ÉTOILE
ZUBOVSKAIA (EN NOIR).

11 MAI 1961.

PRESS RELEASE OF KIROV BALLET, LE BOURGET AIRPORT ARRIVAL

s scout for the Parisian Artistic and Literary Agency, Janine Ringuet went to Leningrad to watch the company in its home theater. Kirov director Boris Fenster had died of a heart attack in December 1960. The company was now directed by Konstantin Sergeyev. In Leningrad Ringuet faced down multiple ruses that Sergeyev employed to dissuade her from attending his wife Natalia Dudinskaya's performance with Nureyev in *Laurencia*. Sergeyev loathed the much younger Nureyev for his insubordinate insolence and would have loved to punish him by excluding him from the tour. But the Parisienne was electrified. She sent a telegram to Paris insisting that Nureyev be included.

Tour arrangements were dicey, subject to change up to the very last moment of departure. This was particularly true for an occasion as fraught with potential risk as the Kirov's European debut. Artistic distinction could easily prove irrelevant in the presence of any possible character flaw as defined by the Soviets. The primary determinant was the assessment by the KGB of the political reliability of the individual dancer. They decided who made the final cut, not the theater.

Four years earlier, Aleksandr Gribov had created the role of Danila in Yuri Grigorovich's *The Stone Flower*, which had been Prokofiev's final score. For Soviet audiences it represented a significant evolution from the *drambalet*. Much of the relationship exposition between the leads unfolded in long duets, with less reliance on realistic pantomime than the public was accustomed to. For Kirov dancers as well as the ballet-going public, the ballet became a watershed.

Alla Osipenko danced the Mistress of the Copper Mountain, who becomes infatuated with Danila, a stonecutter. Frustrated with his creations, he desires to see the Stone Flower that is the platonic essence of sculptural creation. The Mistress spirits him away to a magical kingdom she rules—there he will experience the Stone Flower and create to his heart's delight. Irina Kolpakova danced the role of his village sweetheart Katerina, to whom the Mistress eventually surrenders him.

The Stone Flower went to Paris and London, but Gribov did not. He was abruptly pulled off the tour roster shortly before the company left Leningrad. His crime, Osipenko later speculated, may have been his marriage to the Romanian ballerina Magdalena Popa. Gribov's absence would prove a boon to Soloviev.

Nureyev was allowed to travel—despite the fact that he was a living, breathing, pirouetting red flag (and anything but the communist kind). Already on Rossi Street Nureyev had demonstrated a contempt for rules and protocol that only increased after he entered the Kirov and instantly became a popular favorite.

Certainly the Kirov's General Director Georgii Korkin realized that Nureyev was as much a theatrical asset as he was a political nightmare. With byzantine skill, he and Sergeyev staged a Party meeting where Nure-

yev received a dressing-down and an oral but, shrewdly, not a written reprimand in a last-ditch attempt to control him and assuage the concerns of the KGB. A written one would have meant automatic exclusion. Thus finally they were able to secure his tour participation. His absence would have been a deal breaker for the French impresario.

KIROV THEATER GENERAL
DIRECTOR GEORGII KORKIN

Legat was not going to Paris, having been told she could travel either to Europe or to America, where the company would have not only a month in New York that fall but a two-month tour. She had already visited Europe; for her, even a Soviet bloc country like Yugoslavia was a chance to sample relatively capitalist territory. So she turned down Europe in favor of America, gaudiest and wealthiest capitalist citadel of them all. But first and foremost, she looked forward to spending three months away from home with Yuri. America would be the honeymoon they hadn't yet had.

According to her, Soloviev was the only member of the Kirov who would agree to be Nureyev's roommate in Europe; Nureyev was roundly disliked by the other male dancers. Most were sons of the ex-imperial city, and Nureyev's crudeness was all too reminiscent of his roots as the son of a Gulag camp officer in a far-off republic. Ethnicity played a role, too. They were Great Russians; he was a Tatar. They were also fearful: guilt by association would mean any infractions he was highly likely to commit would taint them as well. It was Soloviev's sense of fair play as well as his fondness for Nureyev that made him volunteer to live with him. The two young men laughed as they anticipated how each would be asked by officials to spy on the other. Given Nureyev's eventual defection as the company was en route to London, their living arrangements, however, would prove to be no laughing matter.

In Paris, the Kirov would first play two weeks at the hallowed Opéra, the balance of its monthlong season at the Palais des Sports in the suburbs. That was a far less prestigious and hospitable venue for ballet, but with a greater seating capacity (and the Opéra, too, had its own performance calendar to consider).

REHEARSING IN ROOFTOP STUDIO OF THE OPÉRA DE PARIS

The Kirov artists, escorted by the obligatory squad of KGB secret police operatives, were warned not to fraternize with their host population, but Nureyev wasted no time. After the opening night *Sleeping Beauty* on May 16, 1961, a meet-and-greet was held for the two companies in the Opéra's Foyer de la Danse, the lavish reception area behind the stage. The two national camps remained segregated. The Russians had been herded to one side of the long buffet table "looking uncomfortable in their ill-fitting, old-fashioned clothes," as choreographer Pierre Lacotte described. The French were relegated to peering at them from on the other side "as if we were observing a sight through binoculars." Nureyev, he noticed, deftly wove his way behind the dancers and around the table to go over to introduce himself in more-than-passable French to Paris Opéra Ballet étoiles Claude Bessy and Claire Motte, who were talking with Lacotte. Delighted at the opportunity to chat informally with a Kirov member, they eventually invited him to join them for dinner at Bessy's apartment. He explained that this was impossible without obtaining permission. Motte went over to ask Sergeyev himself, who relented on condition that Nureyev bring a colleague. Nureyev chose Soloviev, who just that same evening had enjoyed a great success with Sizova in the Bluebird pas de deux. The French were happy to meet him as well, and Soloviev "appeared delighted to go," Lacotte recently recalled.

At Bessy's apartment, Soloviev "barely said anything, as he didn't speak French and English like Nureyev," Lacotte recalled, "but he appeared very interested and frequently asked Nureyev to translate." Despite Soloviev's silence and, perhaps, some timidity about not speaking the language, Lacotte wouldn't have described him as reserved or even shy; rather, he was "quiet by nature… very gentle, like an angel."

Yet "he was confident, he was sure of himself, sure of his talents, you could see that, just not talkative like Nureyev. But he was smiling and enjoyed the company, enjoyed being *en famille* with us." Indeed, then and in years to come, Soloviev would appreciate all that France had to offer. "Yura was a Francophile," Lisa said. "He adored the French: French civilization and culture was the absolute cat's meow."

Gribov's absence meant that Soloviev would take his place in *The Stone Flower*, going on stage with very little rehearsal in the three-act ballet at the May 23 premiere. Making it easier for him, however, was the fact that Osipenko would reprise her role as Mistress, while his frequent partner Sizova would dance the role that Kolpakova had originated.

Eight years older than Soloviev, Osipenko had been the first of her generation of Kirov stars to delight Paris; she had been a guest star with Moscow's Stanislavsky and Nemirovich-Danchenko Ballet for a month-long season there in 1956. Around her there hovered an aura of chic, of sophistication, of flirtation—she was, indeed, something of a breath of Paris in Leningrad.

THE STONE FLOWER WITH ALLA OSIPENKO AS THE MISTRESS OF THE COPPER MOUNTAIN

"Osipenko was a senior master, but she wasn't a typically standard type of dancer," Legat said. "She was interesting, rather complex," and Soloviev "was beside himself with excitement that he was going to dance with her."

In Paris, when Soloviev's Danila bid farewell to Osipenko's Mistress in act 3, his response seemed to her suffused with his apparent guilt about usurping Gribov. It heightened the scene's emotional intensity; onstage Osipenko raised goose bumps.

Nureyev was a sensation in the Paris season, but there was, no question about it, more than enough glory to go around. On the ballerina side was an embarrassment of riches: Olga Moiseyeva, Inna Zubkovskaya, Xenia Ter-Stepanova, Gabriela Komleva, together with Makarova, Kolpakova, Sizova, and Osipenko. On the male roster, Oleg Sokolov, Vladilen Semyonov, and Igor Tchernichov were praised, while "for me it was Soloviev who was the Kirov's most impressive dancer," Claude Bessy would declare decades later. "*Comme un chat*—the leaps, the takeoffs, the landings. It was he who was the sensation in Paris, not Nureyev at all. They say that now, because of the furor caused by the defection, but it was Soloviev, not Nureyev, who stunned the public, the dancers, everybody."

For Lacotte as well, Soloviev "was the best dancer of them all. He had perception, plastique, technique, intelligence, everything. I'll never forget *Stone Flower* or *Taras Bulba*," from which an excerpted Cossack dance featured both Nureyev and Soloviev. "Oh, he was fantastic in that! He was so Russian, so good. Then again, there was Bluebird. Everything he did with ease and perfection. I cannot describe the effect it had on us in Paris."

BLUEBIRD PAS DE DEUX WITH ALLA SIZOVA

14

NUREYEV'S DEFECTION

n Australia, Lisa would tell Soloviev how passionately Nureyev had affected the girls at the Washington School of Ballet. "Ha, he was blue!" Soloviev scoffed. "Yes, quite a one." Lisa did not know that was Soviet slang for gay, and was dumbfounded. For her the Russian male dancers seemed so much more virile than most of their Western counterparts.

Living with Soloviev in Paris became a chance for Nureyev to enhance his friendship with a dancer he not only liked and admired but fancied. "Rudolf was always trying to get into my bed," Soloviev claimed years later to mutual friend Terence Benton, a wealthy British balletomane. "So I said, 'If you don't stop, I'll report you.'" The matter, however, was surely not as cut-and-dried as that.

In the West, Nureyev would become extremely promiscuous and almost something of a sexual predator. Throughout his life here he attempted, and sometimes succeeded, in seducing men who would presumably have been off-limits. Soloviev was twenty years old and his wife was at home in Russia. Nureyev undoubtedly saw his chance, and undoubtedly set things in motion with subtlety and élan.

The two young men got into the habit of massaging each other after performances. One night they were heard arguing and Nureyev was seen being tossed into the hallway. He had apparently gone too far. Soloviev hit him—a blow that Nureyev in all likelihood reciprocated, since he had a hair-trigger temper much more volatile than Soloviev's.

But it was Nureyev who appeared, in the recollections of some, with a black eye, which would have occasioned attention from the authorities. Major Vitalii Strizhevskii, commander of the KGB squad accompanying the Kirov and his deputy, Agent Smirnov, undoubtedly questioned Soloviev about the altercation, and about his relationship with Nureyev.

Regarding accounts that Soloviev went to the KGB officers himself to rat on his friend, we find that unlikely. Initiating contact with the secret police would have exposed him to charges of participating in illegal activity and could have led to his being blackmailed into becoming an informer. Also, people are true to their nature. It would have been uncharacteristic for Soloviev to go out of his way to inform on a friend or colleague.

But it may be assumed that the KGB made strategic use of tendentious inquiries: Had Nureyev really made a pass or had they been involved? If Soloviev had not reported the pass immediately, why hadn't he? If indeed Soloviev had reported the pass, hadn't he known before the tour that Nureyev was gay—why then would he have agreed to be his roommate?

It is quite likely that Soloviev was threatened under Article 121 of the Russian Criminal Code, which carried the sentence of a minimum of five years' imprisonment for male homosexual activity.

Over the previous four weeks there had been much that Soloviev could have reported to the authorities about his roommate's behavior, quite apart from whatever pass as did occur. Lacotte saw Soloviev "frequently, on and off stage," but with Nureyev he struck up a real friendship. Nureyev, too, was more assertive about exploring Paris beyond the company-imposed restrictions. When Lacotte would call their hotel room, it was almost always Soloviev who picked up the phone. "He would greet us nicely, then tell Nureyev, 'It's for you.'" Was Soloviev actually screening the calls? Lisa thinks no, comparing it to the way that Kirov ballerina Kaleria Fedicheva left it to Soloviev to fetch and carry for her in Australia.

Nureyev routinely returned to their hotel room very late at night, after socializing with his new French friends. It is unlikely, however, that Soloviev initiated any surreptitious surveillance. He was no collaborator, but he was also not the type to resist orders. "One day he came to me," Nureyev later recalled, "and said, 'Oh, Rudka, they made me open your bags. I looked for your plane ticket.'"

"The fact and fiction of Soloviev's actions in Paris will likely never be disentangled," Diane Solway writes in her 1998 biography of Nureyev. "But one thing is certain: Whatever happened was not significant enough to set Nureyev's recall to Moscow in motion."

Nureyev's behavior had indeed triggered alarms from the start. He repeatedly and intentionally insulted and provoked Major Strizhevskii. Midway through their month in Paris, acting upon reports from the enraged Strizhevskii, KGB headquarters in Moscow was already demanding Nureyev's return. Sergeyev and Korkin were desperate. At the Soviet Embassy in Paris, they pleaded for support from Ambassador Vinogradov, arguing that the company could not do without its superstar.

Soviet sources affirm that the reason Nureyev had not already been recalled had more to do with an internal power struggle between the ruling Politburo and Moscow KGB Chief Aleksandr Shelepin, rather than lack of concern about the actions of a ballet dancer.

Ambassador Vinogradov's apparently sympathetic response to Sergeyev and Korkin's plea to allow Nureyev to remain in Paris was dictated by the Politburo which was laying a trap for the ever more powerful Shelepin, regardless of collateral damage. And, as so often happened, the dancers were pawns.

In any case, matters culminated in Paris at Le Bourget airport on June 16, as the company prepared to board their flight to London. Once again, there are as many different recollections of Nureyev's behavior as there were eyewitnesses wanting to speak. Least reliable of all, probably, were Nureyev's own accounts: he later insisted that he negotiated the entire episode with unflappable sang-froid. In truth, he seems to have been reduced to a state of hysteria, as he realized that his career was now going to be virtually finished, the morning after he had closed the season with a triumphant *Swan Lake* partnering Osipenko. For Nureyev was now told that he would not go on to London but was being sent back to Moscow.

At Nureyev's request, Lacotte had come to the airport to see him off. Now he watched Nureyev's colleagues respond. "Some appeared very satisfied about the situation, gloating and happy because they were jealous of Nureyev." Now *they* could, artistically speaking, throw lots for his coat, divide his roles among themselves. Osipenko, Kolpakova, Sizova and Soloviev, however, went over to comfort Nureyev. "It was such a moving scene," Lacotte recalled. "Especially I noticed Yuri, quietly, gently comforting his friend. He had tears in his eyes, he was stroking Nureyev's face, stroking his hair, clearly trying to tell him something like 'It's going to be all right.' Then they were pushed away and I watched as Nureyev was encircled by the KGB goons."

Before morning had turned to afternoon, Nureyev had slipped his bonds and requested political asylum as his colleagues were flying across the English Channel. In his absence, Soloviev found himself promoted to the most prominent position on the Kirov tour roster.

15
LONDON

SIGHTSEEING IN LONDON. ALLA OSIPENKO FILMS WITH
SOLOVIEV'S NEWLY ACQUIRED 35MM CAMERA

BACKSTAGE MYSTERY
AFTER COVENT
GARDEN OPENING:
ANATOLII GRIDIN,
OSIPENKO, SERGEYEV,
SIZOVA AND SOLOVIEV'S
SMILING AT DELETED
NON-PERSON, LIKELY
POLITICAL FALL GUY
FOR NUREYEV'S
DEFECTION.
NOTE MARKS ON PHOTO

oloviev was received rapturously during the Kirov's four-week season at the Royal Opera House, Covent Garden. On opening night he again danced Danila opposite Osipenko and Sizova, winning "a huge ovation," reported *The Dancing Times'* A. H. Franks. A week later in *Giselle*, his act 1 pas de deux with Ter-Stepanova stopped the show "justifiably and inevitably," *The New York Times* reported.

Soloviev was "conquering London as Nureyev conquered Paris," Andrew Porter wrote in the *Financial Times*. "His leaps are astounding. Every limb of his body seems to fall, by natural enchantment, into its ideal position at each moment of a phrase. His motion is heart-catchingly beautiful. We have seen no one like him."

During the Kirov's stay in London, act 1 of *The Stone Flower* was filmed by the BBC, on stage but under studio-controlled conditions. Soloviev as Danila the stonecutter; Sizova as Katerina, his village betrothed; and Osipenko as the Mistress dance and characterize their roles as close to perfectly as could be imagined. Reviewing *Stone Flower's* Paris premiere a month earlier, Oliver Merlin had written in *Le Monde* that Danila was an "overwhelming role" in which Soloviev displayed "a heroism, a lyricism unaltered by any theatricalism." In light of the video record, this could be understood to mean a complete transparency. Soloviev embodies Danila's artistic idealism and frustrated quest, his joy with Katerina, his simultaneous resistance to and magnetized bewitchment by the Mistress.

Soviet cultural and political authorities preferred to limit the amount of cross-pollination possible between visiting foreign and native Russian performers. In all likelihood, this informed the Soviets' decision to host London's Royal Ballet in Leningrad exactly at the moment that the Kirov was on stage in London. Of course, this also freed up Covent Garden's stage for the Russians, and just as inevitably, much of the Kirov nevertheless remained in Leningrad.

"Dancing Through the Curtain" was the headline of the *Observer's* weekend section on June 25, 1961. Featured on the front page were parallel reviews of "Leningrad in London" and "London in Leningrad." Despite Nureyev's defection, it was easy to imagine that a true moment of cultural reciprocity had arrived. But behind the scenes, prudence was required. In Leningrad, the Kirov's Alla Shelest had been a regular visitor to Margot Fonteyn's dressing room during the Royal Ballet season. After the news of Nureyev reached Leningrad, Shelest no longer visited.

On June 19, the Kirov's opening *Sleeping Beauty* featured a Bluebird pas de deux by Sizova and Soloviev that was pronounced "breathtaking" by *New York Times* dance critic John Martin. In the monthly *Ballet Today*, Janet and Leo Kersley wrote that Soloviev had performed it in a manner entirely different from that to which London audiences were accustomed: he did not "treat it as a technical showcase in which to display batterie, elevation and pirouettes." The Russians' pursuit of dramatic authenticity à la Stanislavsky lent a different tone to easily excerpted exhibition pieces like this.

When the Kersleys managed to secure an interview with Soloviev, he explained his view of the Bluebird, consistent with the way that the pas de deux had originally been envisioned by Petipa in 1890. "But it is not a showcase," Soloviev told them. "The Blue Bird is a prince who has turned himself into a bird in order to see the Princess, and when he dances with her he is singing to her and she listens to his song."

The Kirov attempted to replicate the great success that Osipenko and Nureyev had enjoyed together in *Swan Lake* in Paris by now casting Soloviev in his place. It would be his debut as Prince Siegfried. The two dancers were permitted to take long walks together after rehearsal. Soloviev shared his anxieties, telling Osipenko repeatedly, "*Swan Lake* isn't for me… I'm too short for you." Whereas in *Stone Flower* she was meant to dominate, here they were supposed to be on more of a physical and dramatic par. Osipenko had been dancing *Swan Lake* since 1954. She tried to reassure him that Nijinsky had not been tall either, that he would dance wonderfully, and reminded him that in any case they had no way out and had to do the performance as best they could. They made their debut on July 12 and repeated the performance the following night—tour scheduling could be brutal, much more concentrated than the dancers' calendar in Leningrad. There, principal dancers usually performed only four times a month.

Reviewing their debut, Fernau Hall in *Ballet Today* opined that it was a triumph for each individually. "The whole season came into focus with

Osipenko's magnificent performance of Odette/Odile." Although Soloviev's partnering "was at times inept… one forgave Soloviev for everything as soon as he launched himself into Siegfried's variation, in which he brought pure male classical dancing to a higher point than anything seen in London for at least three decades, and probably since Nijinsky."

THE STONE FLOWER

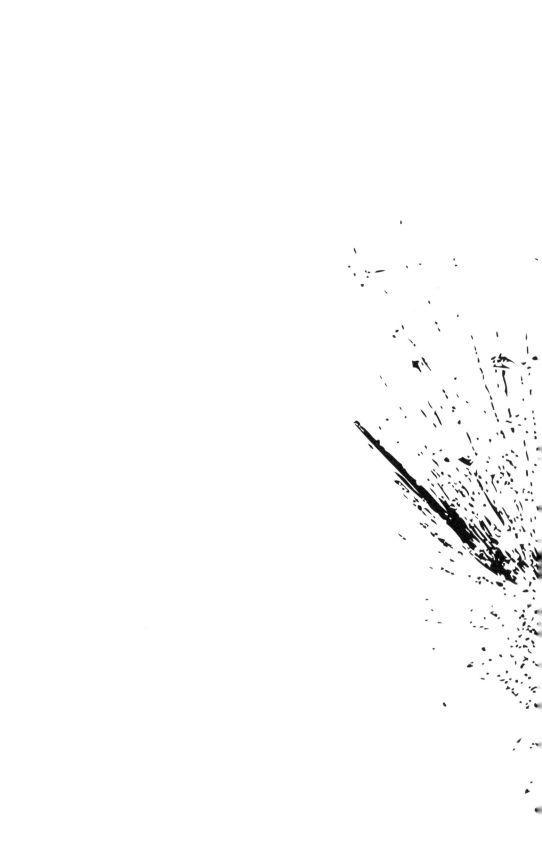

16
REPRISALS

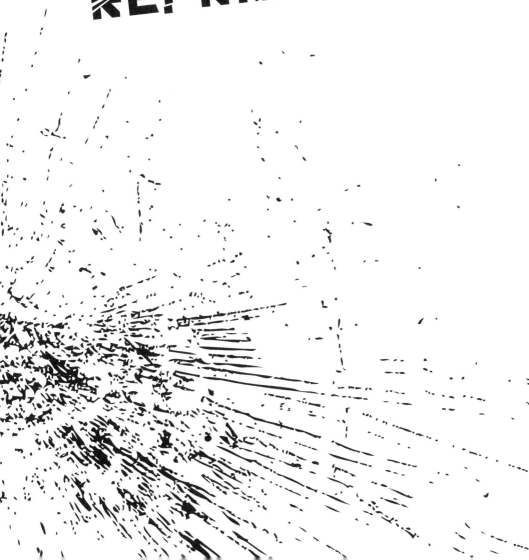

sipenko sat next to Soloviev on the flight home to Leningrad. She leaned her face close to his. He sensed an invitation and kissed her on the lips. "I have kissed Alla Osipenko!" he announced. Unfortunately for him, nearby company members had seen the innocuous buss. Soon after the plane landed in Leningrad, Tatiana was informed, and vented appropriately newlywed displeasure at her husband. But Osipenko and he would remain fond and friendly colleagues for the next decade. "He adored and admired her," Lisa said. "He told me that she was kind and generous to him, as an inexperienced partner."

Much more onerous than Legat's pique was the official censure awaiting Soloviev in Leningrad over Nureyev's virtually unprecedented act. Defection had not been a consideration under Stalin, since, apart from military forces, few people had been allowed to leave the country. Liberalization had made defection a possibility—and liberalization itself surely received its own body blows directly stemming from Nureyev's act. A similar situation was occurring simultaneously in East Germany, where the borders were now sealed, and the Berlin Wall erected to stop the further flow of citizens. One third of Germans in the Russian sector had already fled to the West.

In July 1961, the Central Committee of the Communist Party began an investigation into Nureyev's defection. The Kirov itself was gripped by fear. Nureyev was denounced at compulsory company meetings, and the very mention of his name in private conversation could bring unwelcome attention. Sizova was certainly a prime suspect since she had danced frequently with him beginning with their graduation three years earlier. "Nureyev won't fail in the West with *our* education," she happened to remark. This most patriotic of statements nevertheless elicited an immediate response from the authorities once it was reported. "Do you understand what you have said?" they asked Sizova. She thought fast and backtracked elegantly: what she had *really* meant was that it must be terrible to work abroad. She was out of the woods—somewhat.

Soloviev was just as potentially complicit, particularly as he and Nureyev had been rooming together all through the monthlong Paris season and, undoubtedly, because Soloviev had not come forward—at least until the alleged pass—with damning reports of Nureyev's many infractions. He found himself summoned more than once to Leningrad's Bolshoi Dom, KGB headquarters, the nerve center of internal security operations, for repeated interrogation. "He had to say how lucky he was that he hadn't been tainted by Nureyev," Legat recalled. Tainting, of course, could take many different forms.

Nureyev biographer Kavanagh reports that one ballet world rumor postulated that Soloviev "had been set up by the authorities to try to seduce Rudolf in order to prove his homosexuality." That would have vastly aided the state's case against Nureyev. Decriminalized by the Revolution, homosexuality had been recriminalized by Stalin in 1934, and redefined as treason, as participation in anti-Soviet conspiracy.

Unsubstantiated, but nonetheless persisting, are rumors that Soloviev was covertly gay. An American ballet critic once told Lobenthal that he thought Soloviev's suicide was due to KGB blackmailing him with homosexual exposure. Certainly, his subsequent close friendship with performer Makhmud Esambaev sparked rumors within the Kirov. Esambaev was a superstar in Soviet popular entertainment, performing dances often inspired by those of his native Chechnya. He had begun his training in ballet, however, and remained an avid admirer. Indeed, when the Kirov filmed *Swan Lake* in 1968, he would perform the role of evil wizard von Rothbart. Esambaev had provided himself with the obligatory wife, but there was a lot more to his sexuality than that.

Historically, Soviet society had been prudish, dogmatically asexual, although this would begin to change in the late 1960s. But there was no understanding or toleration of the gradations of human sexuality, certainly nothing like the groundbreaking Kinsey Scale. Published in 1948, it described six strata of sexual orientation from the exclusively heterosexual 1 to the exclusively homosexual 6, with an extra category for asexual.

As Legat recounted, "We had no idea even of what it was… We didn't think such a thing existed. Between men…? How could it be possible? We didn't know about Sergeyev and Dudinskaya, for example…" The two lived separately except when on tour or at their dacha. In Leningrad, Sergeyev lived with a man to whom he eventually bequeathed his estate. "Or what it meant that Pushkin's wife was such a masculine-looking person. Nobody

had heard of such a thing!" But despite the pronounced level of sexual ignorance in the USSR, Soloviev, of course, understood something of what the
"blue people" were, given his adolescent gay bashing.

What the security service operatives most wanted, however, was cor-
roboration that Nureyev had deliberately planned his escape during the four
weeks in Paris, rather than spontaneously bolting once he learned that he
was being recalled to Russia. This also would have aided the prosecution
subsequently launched against Nureyev in absentia.

Soloviev was hardly the character to resist the brutal onslaught of professional interrogation. Aleksandr recalled his nephew telling him briefly
about these sessions. To Legat, Soloviev said nothing, only that he had to go
to the Bolshoi Dom—the Big House, and "I knew what that meant."

Very few in the Kirov believed that Nureyev had been planning to
defect all along. The suitcase he'd checked in for the flight to Paris contained
new costumes he'd purchased on shopping trips with Kirov designer Simon
Virsaladze to find materials not yet available in Russia.

In Leningrad, Nureyev's friend Tamara Zakrzhevskaya was shocked
when she heard that Soloviev had indeed confirmed the KGB's accusations.
She confronted Soloviev, who didn't deny what he had said, citing as corrob-
oration the fact that Nureyev hadn't been buying as many consumer com-
modities as many of the other dancers. Nureyev biographer Solway found it
odd that no such statement survived in the files she inspected, but these files
were frequently purged.

Soloviev would certainly have known about an electric train set that
Nureyev's jet-set admirer Claire Saint had bought him. The two young men
had stayed up late one night playing with it.

If not part of a methodical plan, defection was an idea Nureyev had
entertained before essentially it became an act forced upon him by circumstance. In Leningrad he had learned English on his own. "What would you
think if I remained here in France?" he suddenly asked Janine Ringuet. She
did not try to hide her shock. With a laugh, he assured her that he loved
Leningrad and the Kirov too much to undertake such a rupture. He could
certainly have said something similar to Soloviev, who at the time would
probably have ignored it, considering it just another passing incident in his

friend's outlandish behavior.

Ten years later, when colleague Valery Panov requested permission to emigrate to Israel and was denounced at company meetings, Soloviev refused to participate. By that time, having doggedly resisted years of pressure from the Party to join, it further increased his disillusion with his country. Perhaps by the early '70s he knew or sensed that inevitably the chips were going to fall, making it easier to risk further retaliation. But as a young man, a *shestidesiatnik* believing in the future, perhaps he was more willing to conform, buoyed by a career that was taking off gloriously. He had after all, just had his first real taste of international fame and adoration.

A signed agreement not to divulge what had been discussed was KGB standard procedure. "I don't know what he did there," Legat said about his trips to the Bolshoi Dom, "what he was saying, but he was surviving in the company." Eventually, it was Kirov General Director Korkin who took the fall most directly; he was removed from his post and expelled from the Communist Party. But Osipenko's affair in Paris with Opéra étoile Attilio Labis and her own professional closeness to Nureyev proved very damaging. She was not taken to America that fall and would not be allowed to dance in Europe again for five years. Soloviev did go to America in September 1961. Indeed, he would star with the company on virtually all its international tours for the next decade and a half.

Nureyev's nemesis, Major Strizhevskii, was demoted but remained in the KGB. An apparently fit, middle-aged man, he was dead before the end of the 1960s. Strizhevskii's boss in Moscow, KGB Chairman Aleksandr Shelepin, the Politburo's target, was ousted at the end of 1961. For Soloviev, Nureyev's defection "was the beginning of the end for him, for his moods," the Kirov's Vikulov recalled. Beginning with Nureyev's defection, Uncle Aleksandr also recalled, his nephew became "more cryptic," particularly about what had happened between them and how Nureyev left. "After all, they were living together in the same hotel room. He did not like to discuss this topic."

"Obviously," said Aleksandr, "he was affected by—going over there," his euphemism reflecting the terror that the population retained about anything to do with KGB headquarters. "That played its role, I believe"—played its role in Soloviev's ultimate fate.

Yuri Soloviev
Nothing like him in recent memory.

Antor

By LOUIS BIANCOLLI

Louis Biancolli

If your taste is only the best Spanish dance, the place for you these nights is the City Center.

There the fabulous Antonio and his Ballets de Madrid opened their new engagement to resounding applause. Antonio is greater than ever, and so is his company — in size and quality.

A note of nostalgia was injected by the appearance as guest artist of Rosario, long the teammate of Antonio before they parted to form their own companies. Her artistry has mellowed to fine-spun innuendo.

The crowd greeted the Spanish charmer with the joyous acclaim reserved for a long-cherished friend. But it went completely wild over Antonio. Yuri Soloviev of the Kirov Ballet now has a rival matinee idol in New York.

In whatever he did, Antonio was breathtaking. The foot-tapping, finger-snapping, arm-work, and pantomime were inimitable. He is the ultimate in male grace—a poem in motion. And a poem of passion.

But it wasn't only flamenco fire that was in his dancing. There was the consummate poise of classic Spanish

Women Leap For Red Star

By JOHN FERRIS

The woman, standing in line at the Metropolitan Opera House for tickets to the Leningrad Kirov Ballet, leaned closer to the box-office grill.

"Is Sol—S o l o v—oh, you know whom I mean—Soloviev. Is he dancing tonight?"

The ticket seller smiled and nodded. It was the question women have been asking since the Russians opened their stand at the Met. New York suddenly found a new matinee idol —blond, Russian, handsome and only 24.

* * *

His full name is Yuri Soloviev and he was born in Leningrad, went to ballet school there and joined the Kirov in 1958. In no time at all, thanks to the power of his brilliant dancing he was the company's youngest principal soloist, performing such roles as The Bluebird and Prince in "The Sleeping Beauty," Albrecht in "Giselle," Prince Siegfried in "Swan Lake," the Prince in "Cinderella" and the leading role of Man in the new ballet, "A Distant Planet."

"There's been nothing like it in my memory," a company spokesman said."

Soloviev is thrilled by it all. "It's wonderful," he said. "Yes, it happens in Russia, too, but it is different. Here, people scream and gasp. At home, they just applaud."

In Russia, he said, it is customary to send a male dancing star flowers or throw bouquets on the stage. "That hasn't happened here so far," he added, with a grin.

* * *

The applause in Soloviev's case is something rarely heard at an American ballet performance. It bursts forth spontaneously—a gasp, a cry, a shout of "Bravo," and then the handclapping—as he makes one of his great effortless leaps and seems for an instant to be sustained in the air.

He lands only to rebound and is off again, soaring through space with unbelievable ease. His power and his good looks have made him an idol—but Soloviev doesn't care. He's happily married to one of the girls in the company—Tatiana Legat.

"I'm not jealous," his wife said, "I enjoy his success."

Century Houses Show 'Invasion'

"The Secret Invasion" is the current feature at Century's Freeport, Shore, Floral (L. I.) and Marine (Bklyn.). "The New Interns" is at the Sheepshead, Brook (Bklyn.), Bliss and Queens (L. I.), while "A Shot in the Dark" is on view at the Elm (Bklyn.).

"The Best Man" and "Seven Days in May" are co-featured at Century's College (Bklyn.), and Baldwin (L. I.), "What A Way to Go" is at the Kingsway, Rialto (Bklyn.), Fantasy, Prospect and Roosevelt Field (L. I.). "Becket" is the feature at the Green Acres, Meadows, Grove, Plainview L. I.) and Avalon (Bklyn).

17
AND NOW AMERICA

WITH SIZOVA OUTSIDE MADISON SQUARE GARDEN

fter the acclaim as well as the trauma of the previous months, we may presume that the Soloviev who flew to America with the Kirov in September 1961 was not the same young man who had blithely left for Paris four months earlier. At least professionally, however, he was continuing to benefit from Nureyev's defection, even dancing in New York the *Corsaire* pas de deux. Nureyev had made it his own since performing it with Sizova at their graduation concert three years earlier. The man is meant to be a slave from Moorish regions, and in this pas de deux Nureyev's exotic flamboyance was shown to perfection. Without the same degree of feral personal projection, Soloviev nevertheless danced it unsurpassably.

Presented by Sol Hurok, the Russians enjoyed good performance conditions in New York. They arrived sufficiently early to acclimate to the time change, to the unfamiliar stage of the Metropolitan Opera House. At the September 11 opening, Zubkovskaya and Semyonov led *Swan Lake*, while the act 1 pas de trois was danced by Makarova, Sizova, and Soloviev. "A unique pas de trois," Legat recalled of the luxury casting of these three young stars. "It was a sensation."

Skittish about the possibility of another defection, the Kirov would rarely take husbands and wives together on tour. One or the other usually remained in the USSR as a guarantee against defection. Although determined to preempt the possibility of coordinated action, the administration permitted the recently wed Solovievs to room together in the U.S. Tatiana and Gabriela Komleva did, however, room together in certain cities. Nevertheless, Legat said their three months in the U.S. were "almost like our honeymoon."

Offstage, the Russians' movements were almost as strictly deployed as they were in balletic choreography. They were told never to travel in anything less than a small group. But "we wanted to walk around a bit, to be free," Legat recalled. They decided to chance an independent excursion on Manhattan's subway. Much to their surprise, they wound up in Harlem, "and we were terrified." Soviet newsreels depicted urban U.S. ghettos via the most alarming optics. They dove into a taxi, for them a forbidden means of conveyance, and returned downtown. "Thank God nobody had caught us!"

Frequently in attendance at the Met were elderly émigré Russians, dancers and spectators of the company in its prerevolutionary incarnation. They had originally approached with "grave misgivings," Martin reported, about how well the Soviets had maintained the aristocratic lineage of the ballet. But they kept coming back, and with "an increasing mellowness" that Martin found "both touching and profoundly reassuring"—reassuring, one takes it, that Communist Leningrad ballet had retained the old St. Petersburg virtues. Martin observed tears in the eyes of some old imperial veterans—"there has never been more nostalgic warmth in a ballet audience hereabouts."

George Balanchine was certainly present. He was at this point the most internationally influential alumnus of St. Petersburg ballet. In 1948, Balanchine had co-founded New York City Ballet and made the one-act ballet without explicit storyline the American template. NYCB was in season at the New York City Center on West 55th Street, Kirov dancers attended several performances. Kolpakova had seen no fewer than four. Soloviev told critic Anatole Chujoy of *Dance News* that NYCB's Diana Adams and Yvette Chauviré of the Paris Opéra Ballet were the two foreign dancers who most impressed him.

Curiosity worked two ways: Mimi Paul, then a rising ballerina in NYCB, recalled senior colleague Violette Verdy taking her to the Met to watch the Kirov rehearse or take class in the opera house's upstairs studio. Allegra Kent, Balanchine's favorite ballerina at that moment, was in the opening night Met audience—"what a fantastic dancer!" she recalled, thinking back to seeing Soloviev in New York.

Having left the USSR for good in 1924, Balanchine himself remained stigmatized by official Soviet culture. He watched the Kirov warm up on the Met stage before performances, but stayed on the periphery, presumably to prevent trouble for the dancers should any interchange occur. But a year later, some rapprochement would occur when his company agreed to the U.S. state department's request that it accept the Kremlin's invitation to perform for two months in five Russian cities, including Balanchine's native St. Petersburg (then Leningrad).

In London in 1961, Sizova had danced her first-ever performance of

Aurora in *The Sleeping Beauty* on the closing night of the Covent Garden season. On September 22, in the New York premiere of the Kirov's *Beauty,* she was partnered as Aurora on her twenty-second birthday by Soloviev as Prince Désiré. It was the very first time they had danced these roles together, which they committed to film two years later. Louis Biancolli of the *New York World-Telegram & Sun* wrote that "in less than two weeks that little enchantress has become the toast of New York," while "it would be hard to name another man as graceful on his feet as Mr. Soloviev."

America at its peak of post–World War II economic expansion was "stupefying," Legat said. Luxury goods in department store windows dazzled, but almost more tantalizing was the relatively easy availability of high-quality household appliances. A novelty for the Russians was chewing gum, and it quickly became a fad in the company. Before they went on stage dancers might spit it out in the wings, and a couple of people tripped over gum stuck on the floor. Sergeyev was furious. "He got all of us together and he banned chewing gum."

Material abundance did not extend to the nonprofit sectors of ballet and opera. Russian ballet and opera had been recognized by the communists as cultural institutions that engendered national pride and cultivated the proletariat. Since the end of World War II, ballet had also become valuable as heavy artillery in cultural exchange and propaganda. And so it was quite lavishly funded by the state. Equivalent culture in the U.S. was entirely privately funded and was chronically in need. The 1883 Met was itself in a state of disrepair. Slated for eventual destruction as Lincoln Center was being constructed, the physical plant perhaps received even less attention than it once had. On stage the Russians were startled to see rain descend— sluicing through holes in the Met's old roof.

Due to popular demand, two days after the Kirov's Manhattan debut, Hurok announced that after its three weeks at the Met, it would move for an additional ten days to Madison Square Garden, then located on Eighth Avenue. Opera at the Met had to take its pride of place, but a makeshift stage at the Garden didn't allow for scenery, although the dancers stayed in costume.

After its final performance there October 11, the Kirov began an arduous two-month tour of the country. Few of the many stages on which Soloviev danced were as hospitable as the yielding old wood boards of the Met. Few had been built with dance in mind. The stage of the Chicago theater was very hard, but Sergeyev insisted national pride would not permit any shirking, his message an insistence that "our Russians *will* dance."

WITH TATIANA IN MANHATTAN

During a performance there of *Leningrad Symphony*, Soloviev tore his Achilles tendon, which is one of the most severe injuries a dancer can sustain. In fact, his plié on the right leg was never entirely the same after that. Legat was watching from the wings—"it was horrible to see." Soloviev crawled offstage. Vasily Ivanov, dancing in the ensemble, stepped into his role. Soloviev was taken to a hospital emergency room, where the torn tendon was surgically repaired. He hobbled on crutches for the rest of the tour.

Many Kirov colleagues visited him in the hospital. Nikolai Kalabash-kin from the administration brought him five apples—fresh fruit, of course, always being appreciated by the residents of frigid Leningrad.

In Russia, removing a plaster cast meant tearing the hair on the injured limb. The American method was far more pleasant. Soloviev's leg was sheathed in a cloth stocking, the plaster applied on top and a rubber heel added to facilitate walking. The padded American crutches, too, were more ergonomically sensitive than the bare wood ones available in the USSR.

After the company's return to Leningrad in December, Soloviev's cast removal became a performance witnessed by curious medical staff unfamiliar with American methods. Soloviev got on the table. "I steeled myself to be ready," he told Legat. But the stocking covering his skin meant that there was no pain when the plaster was pulled off. Kirov colleague Galina Ponomareva was so intrigued by his novel crutches that she asked if she could take them now that he was healed. By all means, he told her—he never wanted to see them again.

Venturing into the belly of the hyper-capitalistic beast brought the inevitable realization that the "enemy" was as much familiar as alien. In theory, tours made to both sides of the Iron Curtain were designed to promote mutual understanding. But in practice, certainly for the Soviets, as Nureyev had discovered, too much enthusiasm about Western society and culture was very dangerous. Three years later, the Kirov's Evgenii Shcherbakov came with the company on its repeat visit to the U.S. When he returned, he told his father, a disillusioned sixty-year-old former true believer, that America was something altogether different than what he'd been led to believe. The elder man cautioned his son never to repeat anything like that to anyone else.

WITH TATIANA AND COLLEAGUES AT A GARDEN PARTY FOR THE KIROV
PHOTO: LYUDMILA MELNIKOVA

IN LOS ANGELES

Between Ballets

There's no rest for the weary ballet performer. In the midst of a strenuous week of seven performances at the Capitol Theater, members of the Leningrad Kirov Ballet company were called yesterday for a rehearsal at the Washington School of the Ballet, 3515 Wisconsin ave. nw. In the photo above, the troupe strikes an arabesque pose while facing a wall mirror. In the foreground—and also reflected at far left—is Inna Zubkovskaya, who has been a "people's artist" in the Soviet Union since 1951. She dances as Odette-Odile in Swan Lake. Facing the mirror, at right, is Konstantin Sergeyev, artistic director of the ballet.

Konstantin Sergeyev executing a leap he

THE KIROV TAKING CLASS IN THE STUDIOS OF THE WASHINGTON SCHOOL OF BALLET. ZUBKOVSKAYA AND SERGEYEV IN FRONT.

Mis Sizova, youngest soloist of the Kirov group, dances

of the rehearsal by
ers to duplicate.

SERGEYEV REHEARSES SOLOVIEV AND MAKAROVA IN LONDON, 1970
PHOTO: ROSEMARY WINKLEY

18
DUDINSKAYA AND SERGEYEV

REHEARSING WITH SERGEYEV (PARTIALLY OBSCURED) AND DUDINSKAYA

fter Soloviev's injury, he and Legat expected a visit to their hotel room from Artistic Director Sergeyev and his wife, the former Kirov prima ballerina Natalia Dudinskaya. But no visit was forthcoming, nor did Sergeyev and Dudinskaya make any mention of the incident at all, as if this would dispel any onus of possible responsibility or blame. Ignoring or deflecting any situation that might cast a compromising light could have been one of the survival strategies that helped ensure Sergeyev's longevity as director. There were periods when he was forced to share power with Fyodor Lopukhov and Boris Fenster. Nevertheless, Sergeyev functioned in a directorial capacity from 1951 to 1970. It was all the more extraordinary a run since neither he nor Dudinskaya was a member of the Communist Party. Sergeyev was religious, a devout member of a Russian Orthodox sect founded by his mother, and "deep down hated Soviets so much," Baryshnikov recalled to Julie Kavanagh.

During his first ten years directing, Sergeyev was also onstage. Both he and Dudinskaya, who had established a common-law marriage at the end of World War II, danced past age fifty. They were still prominent in classical leads during the first years of Soloviev's Kirov career. In fact, both Dudinskaya and Sergeyev had originally intended to dance during the Kirov's European debut. The pair had hoped to perform what they viewed as their swan song as a balletic pairing, or, to put more it correctly in French, their *dernier tour de piste*—their last lap, in the City of Light. But their decision was vetoed by the European impresarios as well as by Korkin. As late as 1967, however, fifty-five-year-old Dudinskaya was performing special numbers at Kirov galas in Leningrad.

Like all younger dancers in the company, Soloviev had to contend with the ruling couple's ambivalence about their respective successors. Each was generally more supportive of younger dancers of the opposite sex. Lacotte observed during the Paris season that Sergeyev "was nasty to Yuri, although I noticed how fond Dudinskaya was of him; she mothered him."

Following the Kirov's closing performance in Washington, DC, in December 1964, Lisa's teacher, Igor Schwezoff, was planning to go to dinner with Dudinskaya and Sergeyev, his former classmate in prerevolutionary St.

Petersburg. Schwezoff didn't drive, and he asked her father to take them to a restaurant in Georgetown. Schwezoff sat in the front seat, with Lisa sitting between Sergeyev and Dudinskaya in the back. Dudinskaya asked her in Russian which Kirov dancer she had liked best. "Makarova." "And of the men?" "Soloviev." Sergeyev turned away and scoffed.

Kirov ballerina Alla Shelest was six years younger than Dudinskaya. She, too, was reaching the end of her career on stage there—to a large degree, as a result of Sergeyev fiat. For Dudinskaya had always perceived Shelest as a particularly menacing rival. Both ballerinas commanded enormous followings within and beyond the company. Shelest, however, was singularly expressive and intellectual in the way she approached dance.

Dudinskaya had been teaching a women's company class since 1951. Shelest, too, in accord with company tradition, was already teaching before she stopped dancing. She was Alla Sizova's principal coach, and in that capacity now worked with Soloviev on *The Stone Flower*, after his injured leg had healed. Shelest was at that time the common-law wife of Grigorovich. She had worked closely with him during the long months it took the ballet to progress from initial idea through administration approval and finally public exposure. After Soloviev's hastily prepared Paris debut in the ballet and his subsequent performances in London earlier in 1961, Shelest now rehearsed him in Leningrad in the part for two months. "He gave all of his creative and physical strength," Shelest recalled. "Although he had already gained great love and recognition, Yura possessed a developing intellect and therefore did not fear searching and learning."

Together with *Leningrad Symphony*, *The Stone Flower* initiated Soloviev into the archetype of Russian and Soviet hero, a genre he next assumed in Sergeyev's *The Distant Planet*, first performed in April 1964. Sergeyev's choreography to date was concerned with revising nineteenth-century ballets or creating a new one, such as his 1946 *Cinderella* to Prokofiev's score, which perpetuated the classic formulas. In *The Distant Planet*, however, Sergeyev addressed a topical and patriotic theme, as the cultural commissars kept insisting that the company must do. Yuri Gagarin, the first man catapulted into outer space in 1961, was a hero throughout the Soviet Union and a worldwide celebrity. Soloviev, who had an equally blond, blue-eyed Slavic face, was himself termed a balletic counterpart to Gagarin—"Cosmic Yuri."

Now one space conqueror would evoke another: Soloviev was cast in Sergeyev's ballet as a cosmonaut who danced duets with two ballerinas, personifications of Earth and of the Distant Planet. Soloviev's friend, economist Nikolai Gorbachev writes that "in his whirlwind rotations on the ground and in the air he had demonstrated an active aggressive strength and will of the Youth—Spaceman with an endless quest for deeds and discovery." The ballet didn't last long in the repertory, but a brief, silent excerpt filmed by a New York balletomane, Dr. Michael Truppin, exists at the Library for the Performing Arts, filmed during the company's 1964 return to New York. In it, we see Soloviev assume stances of ardor and aspiration, launching jumps that deconstruct into flanges and rotors.

WITH GABRIELA KOMLEVA
IN *THE DISTANT PLANET*

Inevitably, choreographers will take a dancer's virtuosity and push it to its limit and beyond. Certainly Sergeyev reveled in giving Soloviev as much as he could possibly handle: after every *Distant Planet* solo, he'd collapse in the wings. His nose bled from the exertion.

The more classical steps in a ballet, the more truly it *was* classical ballet—this was the precept observed by choreographers who incubated in the immediate post-Revolution years. Internationally, it was Balanchine who most influentially distilled the art form by eliminating plot. That was impossible in the Soviet Union, but it was nevertheless in this spirit that Sergeyev staged his revivals of nineteenth-century ballets. It was in the same spirit, augmented by the desire to introduce more dance into these ballets, that Sergeyev had choreographed a new solo for himself as Albrecht in act 1 of *Giselle*. "Yura was the only other person who was allowed to dance it," Legat claimed.

It seemed to her that Sergeyev continuously gave to Soloviev with one hand but slighted him with the other. When Soloviev received Paris's Nijinsky prize in 1963, all those who received awards were then invited to perform in a gala in Paris. "But the authorities, Sergeyev probably, said no, he is busy, he is working, and they sent Maya Plisetskaya instead."

A rare and rarefied gift was a little piece entitled *Zéphyre and Flora* that Soloviev, Makarova and a small ensemble performed on Soviet television

ON TOUR IN ITALY, 1966:
STANDING: SOLOVIEV, RACHINSKY, SERGEYEV, VIKULOV
SEATED: MAKAROVA, KOLPAKOVA, KURGAPKINA, FEDICHEVA,
OSIPENKO, DUDINSKAYA

during the mid-1960s. It was created by Sergeyev as homage to the "Anacre-ontic" ballet of mythological subject popular in the late eighteenth and early nineteenth century. Charles Didelot had created a famous *Flore et Zéphyre* that made it to St. Petersburg in 1808. Since then, it had remained in ballet's collective consciousness; Leonide Massine had created a Jazz Age iteration for Diaghilev in 1924.

As wind god Zephyr, Soloviev turns and jumps but relaxes the pointed attack of balletic articulation in his own way. The historicist premise was well suited to Soloviev's naturally plush and less incised attack. Here it is less percussive—he is the wind after all, and drifts with a kind of invisibly propelled momentum.

Flore et Zéphyre survives as testament to grace, somehow apart from technique, a dialogue across the eras, an ability to grasp authentic period style. Bare-legged in archaic tunic, Soloviev evokes the pastoral tradition behind the Anacreontic ballet. Soloviev would himself contribute to the evolution of men's style, repertory and technique. Here we seem to be watch-ing him situate himself retrospectively into a formative line of descent.

WITH KOMLEVA IN *THE SLEEPING BEAUTY*, ACT 3

19
DANSEUR NOBLE

DRESS REHEARSAL, ALBRECHT IN GISELLE
PHOTO: JENNIE WALTON

"ura was always very attentive when he understood that somebody could teach him something," Legat said. Certainly he realized that Sergeyev had a lot to teach, and no more so than when it came to the danseur noble repertory. Sergeyev's aristocratic manner and assurance in the Prince roles of nineteenth-century ballet was much admired.

And these were the roles, the repertory of the danseur noble, which constituted the most storied and prestigious genre within the company. The Soviets had chosen to preserve the old masterpieces of Petipa as the heart of the repertory despite the Party's constant exhortation that more works with contemporary relevance were needed. In fact, these hallowed works were closest to the Kirov company's heart. For while Communist recruitment in the Kirov became more aggressive after Nureyev's defection, the ballet company still belonged as much to old St. Petersburg as to the city now named for the leader of the Revolution. Even more than technique, the relevant criterion at the Kirov was a convincingly aristocratic style.

Sergeyev could help Soloviev with his acting. The company's acting standard was exceptionally high, every member of the corps de ballet submerged into the drama, eloquently a part of what was going on. Indeed, on stage at the Kirov, the Soviet ideal of collectivism seemed to achieve its realization. Everyone on stage appeared to be working together to achieve a peak experience.

Students at the school were taught the Stanislavsky method, and Sergeyev certainly presided over its implementation in the company. Osipenko said that when he rehearsed her for Lilac Fairy in his new *Sleeping Beauty* in 1952, he encouraged her to construct a matrix of subtextual relationships between the fairies and the King and Queen.

Although Soloviev had received high marks in Mikhailov's acting class, he was noticeably self-conscious in this repertory when he first took on these roles. His personal reticence and awareness of his singularly proletarian background, compared to most others in the school and company, must have inhibited his entrance into this rarefied world; he had after all, told Osipenko that "*Swan Lake* isn't right for me."

But Albrecht in *Giselle* was the role Soloviev wanted most to dance, he told Anatole Chujoy of *Dance News* during the Kirov's visit to New York in 1961. In act 1 of *Giselle*, antihero Albrecht is a nobleman disguised as a peasant so that he can woo villager Giselle. Ideally, the audience will recognize both his disguised identity and the underlying pedigree. But Soloviev's younger colleague Boris Blankov writes that Soloviev in his early performances of Albrecht "lacked the noble manners required when he made his entrance on stage at the beginning of the ballet. One could sense he was ill at ease."

Soloviev's classmates Nureyev and Nikita Dolgushin, each of whom soon after graduation made debuts as Albrecht, were able to imprint their character immediately. Soloviev could not. Irina Kolpakova, who would later dance *Giselle* with him many times, watched him from the audience dance Albrecht early in his career. She found his performance very studied—"I thought, my God…"

Inhibition may have arisen also from his finely gauged understanding of the society in which he lived. Offstage, he was very aware of what could be betrayed in a look. Could anyone in Soviet society afford not to be? The face crime existed far outside the pages of Orwell's *1984*. Evgenii Shcherbakov, twelve when Stalin died in 1953, recalled laughing hysterically when he heard the news, then recoiling in terror that he would be arrested for reacting in a way deemed inappropriate by the state.

In the Kirov aesthetic, what the face looked like was just as important as the eloquence of emotion expressed. Governing ideas about casting were built on the typecasting dictates of *emploi*: dancers were slotted into categories and distinct repertories. *Emploi*'s yardsticks encompassed the face as much as the dance personality and physique. The preferred look was Eurocentric. To that end; Peter the Great had built St. Petersburg from the ground up; patterned after European capitals, it was to be Russia's window on the West. But Soloviev's high cheekbones, full lips and broad features were quintessentially Slavic. "What embarrassed Yura a little bit was that his face was very Russian, not cosmopolitan," Ostaltsov recalled.

Critic Arkady Sokolov-Kaminsky claimed that when Soloviev made his initial entrance in Petipa's *Raymonda*, an apparition in a dream of the heroine, "the audience gasped—so little did he resemble a romantic hero."

SIEGFRIED IN *SWAN LAKE* WITH MAKAROVA AND NIKOLAI OSTALTSOV AS VON ROTHBART

For some, the earthiness in his face was contradicted by the makeup department's pasting what Elena Tchernichova describes as "a finicky painting on his face, which was much more attractive without this maquillage."

Oliver Merlin in *Le Monde* would complain when the Kirov revisited Paris in 1965 that Soloviev was "always so beautiful despite atrocious makeup." When Soloviev danced a Prince role his blond curls were sewn with thread into a mat, then lacquered. London's Fernau Hall would complain that although he looked "magnificently heroic and virile" in *Leningrad Symphony*, his face had "a round, slightly girlish cast which is ill-suited to the traditional classical roles."

As was Kirov custom at the time, he also frequently wore a wig in the classical roles, particularly to enhance realism if he was playing a Latin or

Eastern character. The Stanislavsky influence was intended to provide maximum aid to suspension of disbelief, but for Soloviev himself the attempt was sometimes inadequate. In Konstantin Boyarsky's *The Pearl,* based on the Steinbeck novel, he donned the requisite wig and dark makeup to dance an African fisherman, accentuating his full lips. "He laughed about himself in this role," Ostaltsov recalled. "He was very ironic about himself." For Ostaltsov as well, Soloviev's face could limit suspension of disbelief. As Eurasian prince Ferkhad in Grigorovich's *The Legend of Love*, Soloviev "danced brilliantly, but his image was not Oriental."

Considerations of *emploi* naturally extended to the body. Height was preferable in maintaining the illusion of noble authority. Soloviev was medium-tall, around five foot nine. He was well-proportioned; his legs were not exceptionally long but were long enough. Today it is a bit puzzling why his thighs have been so frequently mentioned as a bar to perfect satisfaction in the Prince roles. Men's training in Russia built bigger thighs than ballet features today. Male dancers' thighs were employed in the service of aerial elevation and became ballast for a certain type of strength and control. That said, women's legs, too, were often less lithe than their contemporary counterparts. But even in Russia today, when men are more streamlined, they emerge with a distinctive thigh. And Soloviev's were certainly noticed outside of Russia as well: in London, A. H. Franks commented in 1961 that they were "more like a weight lifter, than a ballet dancer."

Soloviev's cushioned physique gave him and his thighs a plushness that was not the striated greyhound mold of the prototypical danseur noble. Plushness connotes health and vigor rather than elite aristocratic indolence.

But while most dancers—Western as well as Russian—had considerably more meat on their bones than they do today, weight is always an issue in ballet. Soloviev liked to eat and drink and, like many dancers, his weight fluctuated. When Clive Barnes visited Leningrad for the June 1967 White Nights Festival, he complained in *Dance and Dancers* that Soloviev had "put on a great deal of weight since I last saw him." Reviewing the Kirov's 1970 season in London, John Percival in *Dance and Dancers* described him as a little heavy in his *Corsaire* pas de deux on opening night, but much thinner when he danced it again later in the season. "His

build is big anyway, so that he will never look slight."

At the Kirov during the 1960s, however, minute attention was paid to things that were less important in the West and are hardly thought about today anywhere. Today, in fact, there is hardly any *emploi* at all either in the West or in Russia. *Emploi* gave the Kirov a coherence and tended to preclude the miscasting we see too much of on the contemporary ballet stage. Equally, it harnessed rigid confinement of performer and trained attention on considerations that should be secondary when discussing an exceptional artist, who to some extent makes his own criteria. The objectified ballet body as well as face can become fetishized in admiration or disparagement—such seems to have taken place with Soloviev.

STAGE REHEARSAL, *SWAN LAKE* WITH FEDICHEVA IN LONDON, 1966
PHOTO: ZOË DOMINIC

HERE AND PAGE 143: *THE SLEEPING BEAUTY*
FILMED AT LENFILM STUDIOS IN LENINGRAD

20

THE SLEEPING BEAUTY, 1963

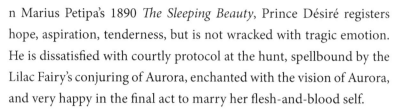

n Marius Petipa's 1890 *The Sleeping Beauty*, Prince Désiré registers hope, aspiration, tenderness, but is not wracked with tragic emotion. He is dissatisfied with courtly protocol at the hunt, spellbound by the Lilac Fairy's conjuring of Aurora, enchanted with the vision of Aurora, and very happy in the final act to marry her flesh-and-blood self.

Perhaps the role's dramatic demands were made to order for the fledgling Soloviev. Of all his princely repertory, Soloviev's Désiré seems to have pleased more people earlier in his career than any of the other roles. Shelest recalled his Désiré as "taut, inspired, in perfect technique: he understood what the style demanded and was faithful to it." It is his only classical role for which full-length recordings exist: the 1963 film and a 1976 performance filmed live for transmission over Japanese television.

In 1963, the Kirov considered Sizova and Soloviev together as good as it got in *Beauty*. They were the leads when a cinematic adaptation of the ballet was filmed at the Lenfilm studios in Leningrad. The film was to be released internationally and that may also have been why Sizova and Soloviev, after their success together in Europe and the U.S., were chosen.

The Kirov performed Sergeyev's 1952 production, the most sweeping in a series of revised versions at the Mariinsky that began in 1914. In the cause of modernization, Sergeyev's production eliminated as much pantomime as possible. Nevertheless, translated to film the dancers had lots of opportunities to be framed in cinematic close-up, and here they reflect not only the demands of the camera but the new style of acting at the Kirov. Rehearsing *The Stone Flower* for its 1957 premiere, Grigorovich discouraged the dancers from using too much facial expression. Instead, he wanted to let the body alone speak as eloquently as possible. It signaled a shift in Russian ballet expression.

For *Beauty*, in which Sergeyev and Apollinari Dudko shared directing credit, elaborate sets were tinged with the *bizarrerie* of a Cocteau art film, and some new sequences designed specially to maximize cinematic possibilities. Soloviev is first seen astride a horse, mustering his retinue with a hunting horn. He later recalled to Lisa, an avid horsewoman, that it had been a particularly intelligent horse. Although he hunted for sport, Soloviev's love for animals was keenly felt.

Rather than the curtain falling on the awakening scene with Sizova and him posed in a tableau of betrothal, as on the Kirov stage, on screen the scene ends with a wonderful pan of Soloviev pursuing her ardently into the palace.

When the film reached London in the fall of 1965, Alexander Bland in *The Dancing Times* wrote that Soloviev had "acquired much more style and attack than when one saw him last in London, without losing his amazing softness," but that he was lacking "the virile dash of the ideal film hero." Film heroes, of course, have registered strongly even without "virile dash"—Soloviev's adolescence saw the heyday of James Dean and Montgomery Clift. And yet this was nothing else but a ballet film. We are left to wonder: Did Soloviev—like his contemporaries Nureyev and Dolgushin—actually work an original twist on the danseur noble? Were his lack of conventional princely entitlement and the vulnerability he brought to the stage the ingredients of a new synthesis?

21
IGOR

TATIANA AND ALYONA GREET RECENTLY DEMOBILIZED IGOR

nna had not wanted Soloviev's brother, Igor—hadn't wanted a second child. Her affection was not increased by the fact that Igor was less shapely, shorter and stockier than Yuri. His face and shape more closely resembled his father's, and he had inherited grandfather Valentin's slightly hooked nose that had indeed endangered his grandfather while in German captivity.

Igor too, had been given a recommendation that he audition on Rossi Street. As he recounted to Lisa with some bitterness, he had a cold on the day he was to audition. Anna declared he was too sick to walk the two blocks to school and refused to take him.

It was Yuri who was to be the artist. Igor would be a factory worker like his father. Yet, "I could jump as high as Yura," he said ruefully, and indeed truthfully. For Igor later played with Yuri on the Kirov volleyball team, where his own phenomenal elevation was noticed by Yuri's varsity colleagues. In Anna's defense, she may have felt overwhelmed at the thought of putting two children through the grueling demands of Rossi Street and further strain on their poverty. But Uncle Aleksandr recalled that instead Vladimir "used to take him to the Pioneers' Palace where Igor sang in the children's chorus."

IGOR WITH TATIANA AND HIS PARENTS ON THE FONTANKA

In St. Petersburg in 2001, Joel was startled to meet Igor: he looked almost exactly as Soloviev might have if he were still alive. Igor had a wry sense of humor and a very attractive smile, but he was quiet, reflective, sad-eyed, obviously burdened by memories of his brother and his family. "I regret that I didn't continue to sing," Igor told Joel. Had he ever regretted not having a chance at ballet? "Sometimes a little bit."

Anna's pronounced disposition toward Yuri did not make her any more eager to countenance Igor's independence. "Once Igor was interested in a girl, it even went as far as introducing her to his parents," Aleksandr recounted. "But Anna put her foot down. She was against it, wouldn't have her. Igor never forgave her for that."

After trade school, Igor worked as a welder in a rocket parts factory, until he retired on disability. The military factories were notorious for exposing workers to chemical and radiological toxicity. Post-Perestroika, he began a new career restoring historic wrought-iron works, among them the famed stallions and Atlantes on Anichkov Bridge linking two stretches of Nevsky Prospect crossing the Fontanka.

In 1972, Igor married Anna Kakabadze, a beautiful dark-haired woman, the sister of his factory foreman. Her Russian mother had married Leonid Kakabadze, a scion of a wealthy wine-growing dynasty and a gifted and passionately communist Georgian, studying engineering in Leningrad. She bore him two sons. Although mobilized in 1941, Kakabadze managed to pull strings to evacuate the family to his homeland. Anna was born there after the war. Fleeing a disastrous early marriage, Anna escaped to Leningrad where her mother and siblings had returned. She was forced by her former in-laws, however, to leave her daughter Nonna behind.

Anna wanted to study medicine, but neither Igor's nor her own worker's salary permitted it. But Nonna is now head nurse in the neonatal department of the St. Petersburg 1st Children's Hospital. Igor and Anna's daughter Ekaterina was born in 1974.

At first, Igor and Anna shared the communal apartment on Fontanka, but finally received an apartment of their own after Igor joined the Communist Party. Anna was very fond of both of her in-laws, whom she called "Mama" and "Papa."

LANDOWNING GEORGIAN GRANDPARENTS OF
IGOR'S WIFE ANNA KAKABADZE

Anna was praised by Legat as deeply devoted to Igor, her household, and family. Igor's dreams of a closer involvement with art or theater seemed to have eventually been mollified by the success of his daughter, Ekaterina, a Mariinsky soprano who also sang Mimi in Baz Luhrmann's *La Bohème* on Broadway in the late 1990s.

The two brothers shared artistic and athletic pursuits, but what Aleksandr called "their ideology," as in their view of the world, "was different," he said. When Igor was drafted, his father arranged for him to get on an army sports team through the connections he'd made in his work sharpening skates. "While there, he figured out how life works," Aleksandr said. "It had an effect on him, his time in the army. The athletes always sought out opportunities for themselves, and he learned these things. But even when

Igor was small, he already knew how to count, how to count money." His mother used to refer to him by the unfortunate moniker "the sly Jew."

"I rarely got to go to theater," Aleksandr said, "because Anna Vasilievna was so in love." (Talking to us, Aleksandr always used Anna's formal patronymic, which is highly uncharacteristic for a Russian speaking of close family members.) "She always kept all the available free tickets, very rarely she would give up one to me. She mostly went herself."

Where Yuri's art was concerned, Vladimir "showed some interest because of his son, but he wasn't interested in ballet, in theater, in culture." Vladimir "was a limited person," his younger brother said.

But Igor followed his brother's career closely, enraptured by the magical alter ego of his brother on stage. "Deeply in my soul I understood that this was my brother," Igor recalled. "But it was another type of acceptance. When I looked at him onstage, he was not a brother, but an artist, the image of a hero.

"I became like a professional critic," Igor said, "because when Yura danced one role, Vikulov danced another. When Panov danced one, Yura danced another. I compared them. Sometimes Yura was the best, sometimes the other. It was very interesting for me." The two brothers and their wives become "our artistic council. We discussed everything: mistakes, about what to do better. Now I do the same with my daughter."

IGOR ALOFT RESTORING IMPERIAL MONUMENTS

22

ALYONA

During the summer of 1963, Tatiana was pregnant and not wanting to travel. She had been diagnosed with preeclampsia, a common complication in pregnancies of child survivors of the Siege. Soloviev took a three-week vacation with his uncle Aleksandr instead, driving to Sudak on the Black Sea in the Crimean Peninsula in his new Moskvich car. He was subsequently allowed to purchase a used Volga, a great privilege as this was the Mercedes of Soviet automobiles. He then gave the Moskvich to his uncle; his father's knee injury made it impossible for him to drive.

Yuri and Aleksandr toured the rugged coastline, filled with secluded beaches reached though winding paths in the rocks. Wherever they wanted, they stopped to swim, fish and sunbathe. Soloviev brought mask and flippers he had purchased abroad. He would take long swims so very far out from the shore that Aleksandr would worry, although he knew how strong a swimmer Yuri was. Soloviev indeed won competitive swim meets represent-

ON CRIMEA TRIP, 1963

ing first the ballet academy and then the Kirov. At one rocky spot, Aleksandr climbed up a cliff to watch him swim. "I saw him out there, swimming with the dolphins. It was amazing to watch him with them. Because he was swimming like one of the dolphins himself."

Back in Leningrad Tatiana's father made an entirely unexpected reappearance in their lives. She retained no childhood memories of him. He now had a second wife and additional children. First, he paid a surprise visit to Yuri at home. They talked through the evening. Then he came to see Tatiana in the hospital, promising that they would resume or, more truly, begin their relationship after the baby was born. But neither Yuri nor Tatiana ever heard from him again. In retrospect, she thinks he was merely indulging a fleeting curiosity about how she had turned out.

Alyona was born in Leningrad on October 31, 1963. She was registered as Elena on her birth certificate, since the authorities would not let them use the historic variant they preferred. "They told us we could call her whatever we liked at home but we could only register her as Elena," Soloviev told Lisa.

During Tatiana's pregnancy, her mother-in-law had told her flatly, "If you give birth to a boy, I am not sitting with him. I am done with boys. I have had it up to here with boys." But she was delighted to have a granddaughter, and as a child, Alyona would become very close to her grandmother.

Soloviev also wanted a daughter. Due to her preeclampsia, Tatiana had been admitted prior to labor. In Soviet maternity hospitals, no provisions were made for families: no visiting hours, no attendance at birth, and no anesthesia during normal labor. Anesthesia was provided only when the birth required surgery. There was no waiting room. Expectant fathers stayed where they were and awaited telephone notification. "And so they called Yura in a rehearsal," Legat recalled, "and told him Alyona was born, and he cried for joy."

23
INTERESTS AND HOBBIES

"Yura soaked everything up like a sponge," Legat said. "He wanted to know and understand things about the world, about many things." He sought out books wherever he went, in the Soviet Union and in Russian bookstores abroad. Classics were often in short supply in Leningrad bookstores, snatched up by the city's educated population. Soloviev searched local kiosks around the republics, hunting for editions of classics and good literature that was of less interest to regional publics. Large print runs were reserved for new, officially sponsored, usually didactic literature, despite the fact that they might remain largely unread. Even with a willingness to pay scalper's prices for, say, a slim volume of good poetry on the black market, the pickings were very slim indeed.

Soloviev carted the bundles of books back home and they "didn't go on the shelf until he'd read them," Legat said. His three favorite authors were Jack London, Erich Maria Remarque and Aleksandr Belyaev. Belyaev, who had trained as a lawyer before the Revolution, was a founding father of Soviet science fiction. He died during the Blockade. His sensitive, nuanced books, influenced by H. G. Wells, depicted dystopias created by human scientific efforts gone awry. They were thought-provoking and as enlightening as they were entertaining. Yuri "read and reread them constantly," Tatiana recalled. Why? she asked him. He didn't answer. But he loved to read about trips, travelers, nature. At home they subscribed to the literary journals, as well as to *Around the World*, something of a counterpart to the *National Geographic Magazine.*

He held the books close to his face while he rested his legs. "I was always saying, 'You will destroy your eyesight,'" Legat recalled, "and he didn't pay attention." It was his prodigious reading, Legat believed, that led to one of his eyes becoming nearsighted; the other one was not. On tour in Japan an optometrist crafted a tailor-made set of glasses for him.

Overseas travel also made it possible for him to amass an extensive collection of LPs, from jazz to classical to popular, augmented by barter or sale with other collectors at home. Soloviev's economist friend Nikolai Gorbachev was also always eager to hear his opinion of foreign films he'd seen abroad, describing Soloviev "a connoisseur of theatrical scripts, movie production and directing." In Leningrad the two often went to the movies together "and discussed the work of great actors; we tried to study their works analytically."

Stigmatized by the government, Western jazz nevertheless was the rage among the new generation. In 1964 two Kirov colleagues, Aleksandr Pavlovsky and Vasili Ivanov, decided that they would start a jazz band. Ivanov was known throughout the company for his extensive knowledge of jazz and was also a skilled pianist. Pavlovsky played saxophone. They recommended the trumpet for Soloviev, "since you have big lips… You could be like Armstrong." He learned how and they started jamming together.

Yuri and Tatiana had now traded up to an apartment on Lenskaia Street on the eastern edge of the city limits, but the apartment was private and had a small balcony. Legat now ordered the budding jazz combo to practice on the balcony so as not to disturb infant Alyona. But the noise nevertheless brought threats from neighbors. They worked for a few months and then disbanded. However, his love of jazz remained; he particularly liked Satchmo and Dixieland.

LENINGRAD INTER-THEATER SWIMMING CHAMPIONS. ONE PARTICIPANT WAS BELIEVED TO BE A STUKACH, A SNITCH

Sports were equally a passion: swimming, volleyball, cross-country skiing. In 1961 Soloviev began scuba diving lessons at an institute on Dekabristov Street. "Yura dragged me there," Ostaltsov recalled. "'Let's go! You can swim, right?'" Scuba diving was "something completely new in the 60s." They were taught how to deal with the equipment, then they practiced in the pool. "Yura really loved it."

Returning from overseas with new fishing lures and reels, Yuri and his brother and father would pore over them as though "nothing else existed in the world," Legat recalled, "sitting on the floor almost like little kids." Koloskovo, where Soloviev bought a wooden vacation cottage, a classic Russian dacha, was certainly a prime place to fish since the area is dotted with many lakes. Soon after joining the Kirov, Soloviev and Aleksandr Shavrov rented a dacha there. It was one train stop away from Kolokoltsevo, where Yuri had vacationed with his family as a child. Then, in 1965, Soloviev and Legat borrowed money from friends and family to purchase their home.

Soloviev owned a laika, a Russian hunting dog similar to huskies, which he used to flush out rabbits and small game. Legat hated the brutality, hated cleaning game and stinky, scaly fish. To her he defended his pursuit by saying he did it mainly because the dog had to have part of the kill as motivator to wander the woods with him.

Yuri Vasilkov, a principal dancer at Leningrad's Maly Theater, recalled, "Yura was always very kind, very generous." Then he added, "But he was so happy in the country, there he was even kinder and more generous as a host."

Soloviev and his family spent Augusts together in the country. His birthday was August 10, and Igor's wife's Anna's was the next day. At night they'd play lotto, sitting on the veranda. Their property included a small apple orchard. One night the family was gathered when Legat's brother German happened to venture into the orchard to relieve himself. The house itself had no indoor sanitation. Taciturn as he was, Soloviev's father nonetheless had a prankish side, as did the entire family. He now sounded a sham alarm. "Oh, look, look... there are some guys coming to steal the fruit," he said knowing full well who it really was. And he roused all hands to conduct a search that ended, as it was meant to, in hilarity.

Mariia Aleksandrovna, Grandfather Valentin's second wife, was devout

FRONT: ANNA, DEVOUT STEP-GRANDMOTHER MARIIA,
GULAG-SURVIVOR GRANDFATHER VALENTIN.
BACK: VLADIMIR, YURI, ALYONA, IGOR AND UNCLE ALEXSANDR.

and observant. She would always invite Yuri and Tatiana over to their tiny room in a communal apartment to celebrate Easter, the most important religious feast day on the Russian Orthodox calendar. "She would paint eggs and we would follow all traditions in celebrating, saying the prayers," Legat recalled. Sometimes Mariia and Valentin lived all summer at Koloskovo.

Neighbors would say, "If the Solovievs have already passed through, there'll be no mushrooms left in the woods." It was Soloviev's mother who led the family in the venerable Russian pastime. Anna had long experience, having scouted and harvested the area during their earlier summer vacations. If it so happened that Soloviev was going to be touring on his birthday, she gave him a little jar of preserved mushrooms to open up on the day. She was astute as well at harvesting blackberries, black currants and other berries that grew in profusion during the short summer season.

Yuri had an inflatable boat with motor—"I remember working on the engine with him," Uncle Aleksandr recalled. Always handy, Soloviev also became an able mechanic.

Not long before his death, talking with several colleagues, he was asked why he had never defected. "If I could take Koloskovo with me," he said, "then I could think about it."

SIZOVA AS CINDERELLA. PHOTO: TEJA-KNUT KREMKE

24

"WHEN YOU DANCE WITH YOUR BALLERINA, YOU FALL IN LOVE WITH HER"

REHEARSING ALEXIDZE'S ORESTEIA WITH FEDICHEVA
PHOTO: COURTESY MARIINSKY THEATER

nna had helped them move to Lenskaia Street, and from that point on was a fixture in Yuri and Tatiana's apartment; Vladimir remained with Igor and later with Igor's wife as well. Before leaving for a return visit to America in the fall of 1964, Legat and Soloviev selected a new apartment on Novocherkasskii Prospect in one of the five-story apartment blocks on the outskirts of town put up by Khrushchev in the 1950s. He had extended the city limits with a building boom designed to address the severe housing shortage ignored by his predecessors. They featured modern conveniences. Apartments were individual, not communal; each had its own private kitchen, bathroom and balcony. They were named *khrushchevki* in Khrushchev's honor by a mostly grateful, but also somewhat cynical population that had endured decades of overcrowding in slum-like living conditions.

Returning from the long U.S. tour, Yuri and Tatiana discovered that their apartment had been given away. They were left with another, less desirable one in the same building. The layout was like one of New York's "railroad flats," the rooms offering no privacy since one led directly into the other. But they were nevertheless happy to get the extra few meters and a second bedroom.

At the Metropolitan Opera and across America, the Kirov again featured Soloviev's partnership with Alla Sizova, which had been so acclaimed during their U.S. debut three years earlier. Michael Truppin's silent footage of them dancing Sergeyev's production of *Cinderella* is housed in New York City's Library for the Performing Arts. No more poignantly ideal incarnation of Cinderella than Sizova could be imagined and Soloviev portrays a most captivating young nobleman. In the opening scene of act 2, he swaggers playfully with his retinue. The final pas de deux is filmed in its entirety: it is slightly melancholy, achingly tender, as befits Prokofiev's music. Their performance together lifts the ballet to a peak of resolution and closure that gives ample promise of future bliss.

But Sizova was not Soloviev's exclusive partner during the 1964 New York season and subsequent tour. For one thing, their repertories did not entirely overlap. He was also frequently paired with Kaleria Fedicheva, who wielded singular power over the company all through the 1960s. Pyotr

CHICAGO'S AMERICAN, M

ANN BARZEL

'Cinderella' All Soloviev's

THE KIROV BALLET SHOWED two Cinderellas in the Arie Crown theater on Saturday and a gala program of dazzling dances yesterday afternoon.

"Cinderella," a story everyone knows, requires only the sketchiest dramatic line. This version by Konstantin Sergeyev, planned in collaboration with Composer Prokofiev, is a frame for dancing. This is in the style of the Leningrad company, which devotes itself to the art of classical dancing and lets drama and theatrical devices take second place. The interpreters do not delve into motivations. They give their all to the pirouettes and arabesques.

Frederick Ashton's British "Cinderella" borrows its boisterous stepsisters from pantomime—men in travesty. Leningrad's stepsisters are ballerinas, whose ugliness is in their manners—vainglory and bad temper. And it takes top ballerinas to do these demanding roles.

THE RUSSIAN "Cinderella" is flavored with a bit of mockery. It is in Prokofiev's score and the choreographer translated it to a Prince Charming who doesn't take the prince business too seriously, and an attendant who is a parody of effete court manners.

The afternoon "Cinderella" belonged to Natalia Makarova, dancing the role for the first time. She danced with exquisite precision and wistful lightness. Her prince was Sergei Vikulov, a paragon of technique who tossed off triple air turns, among other fireworks.

The matinee lagged, but the faults were not of the visiting company. There was obvious backstage fumbling of the intricate production and some tangled formations by the charming local children involved.

to see them do the whole ballet.

Kolpakova and Oleg Sokolov, in excerpts from Vainonen's "Nutcracker," used the newer vocabulary of flights and lifts and sent the audience into ecstasies. Kolpakova is truly irresistible and Sokolov is a worthy addition to the list of virile male dancers who make classical ballet a healthy art.

Leningrad Kirov

Russians Bring Ballet of Magic

By Robert Commanday

The magical illusions of great classical ballet, the traditional Russian gift, returned to the Opera House with the Leningrad Kirov Ballet's opening performance of "The Sleeping Beauty" Friday night.

The array of blithe spirits dancing with effortless grace and ensemble precision is enough to justify bringing the whole troupe of 165 from Leningrad to California. But when the climaxes of the featured solo performance are reached, then one is not merely impressed, but spellbound by a special romantic enchantment.

In order to achieve this effect, the dancers must overcome an elaborate and lengthy pageantry of miming and play acting which sets the background for the story and frames the dancing. It is soon worth waiting out, for Aurora, in the flying electric person of Alla Sizova, and Prince Desire, a bold and smooth Vladilen Semenov, create the exquisite motion in space that marks their distinguished art.

VIRTUOSO

sion of the ballet seems wholly self-contradicting, but the pleasure of the dance portion is happy reward for adjusting to this anachronism.

The Leningrad Kirov Ballet presented "Cinderella" on Saturday afternoon and evening and will give a Sunday matinee gala at 2:30, with Bayaderka, the Polovetzian Dances and solo excerpts from well-known ballets.

YURI SOLOVIEV
A virtuoso performance

Rachinsky, who had succeeded Korkin as general director of the Kirov opera house, had adopted Fedicheva as his principal mistress in the company. Rachinsky had no compunction about promoting her. In fact, Sergeyev, doubtless buckling to pressure from Rachinsky, locked horns with impresario Sol Hurok in New York about the opening night *Swan Lake*. Sergeyev wanted Fedicheva; Hurok was equally insistent that Makarova dance. Sergeyev, too, would probably have preferred Makarova were aesthetic considerations alone at play. Eventually a compromise was reached whereby Makarova danced White Swan Odette and Fedicheva was Black Swan Odile. The opening night could thus go ahead as scheduled, and each ballerina was seen to her best advantage. Dividing the part like this was an arrangement that the Kirov sometimes worked at home as well.

The same arrangement prevailed throughout the tour following the Met season. In Washington, D.C., Lisa saw him dance Prince Siegfried opposite his two Swans. Makarova was the Kirov ballerina who most exactly mirrored Soloviev's lyric dance temperament, while Fedicheva interjected a certain sexual aggression, something rarely seen on stage at the Kirov. The contrast between them was stunning.

As Soloviev later explained to Lisa, the ballerinas swept him into the plot requirements of the ballet. Emotion flowed freely: "When you dance with your ballerina, you fall in love with her."

"Since his last appearance here Soloviev has grown as an actor," Doris Hering wrote in her *Dance Magazine* review of the Met season. Legat notes that Soloviev's acting skills "were very much developed by his relationship with his partners." Each enhanced and expanded his interpretative response. Fedicheva elicited "dynamism, strength, courage." She was muscular, never quite as streamlined as her ballerina colleagues. If Soloviev was, as *Dance and Dancers*' Arthur Todd wrote from New York, now "considerably huskier than he was three years ago," it was certainly due in part to lifting her, although she would sometimes tell him during rehearsals just to mark the lifts. She was also tall for him, so much so that he wore shoes with special heels to partner her. Nicholas Dromgoole of the London *Daily Telegraph* found this a bit incongruous when the Kirov returned to Covent Garden in September 1966. On opening night of the season, they performed *Swan*

Lake—Fedicheva now dancing both White and Black incarnations. She was "too large" for him, Dromgoole reported, noting his "high-heeled shoes to keep level," while he dashed into the wings to replace with ballet slippers before his Black Swan solo. Changing shoes this way however, was a tradition dating back to the czars, perpetuated today in Act 3 of *Beauty.* Again it was a matter of verisimilitude, preserving court attire except when the performance ventured into the most technical of balletic languages.

Partnering challenges weren't the only inconvenience Fedicheva presented; Rachinsky's protective intervention could rankle. Sometimes Fedicheva and Soloviev danced concert appearances around Leningrad. On the day of one scheduled concert, he came down with an infection and soaring temperature. Legat called the theater and told them he was indisposed. "Well, is he really sick?" The opera house dispatched one of its own doctors by ambulance to assure themselves he was not malingering. "Oh, yes, Yuri Vladimirovich, yes you do have a temperature. Take it easy, lie down." Soloviev was enraged. "They wouldn't believe my word… Rachinsky had to send somebody to check if I was faking?"

Fedicheva herself also expected deference. In Australia in 1969, Lisa was eating out with them. "Gimme a cigarette," the ballerina commanded and Soloviev did so without batting an eye. Lisa's surprise was written on her face. Soloviev responded with a look and a rueful tilt of the head that seemed to say, "Oh well, that's how she is."

As onerous as Fedicheva could be, she certainly used her power in the company to boost Soloviev's career. Together they enjoyed a joint "Creative Evening" at the Kirov in 1964. This was the ultimate honor accorded a principal dancer, the chance to select his or her own program, an opportunity to commission new works and star in them.

Both dancers were able to show a wide creative range. Soloviev danced opposite Natalia Bolshakova in a springtime love duet to Rubinstein's *Waltz* that had been choreographed by Gulbat Davitashvili at the Maly in 1960. He danced opposite Fedicheva in the pas de six from the Spanish-inflected *Laurencia.* He also partnered her in the *Corsaire* pas de deux. Fedicheva stepped entirely out of her customary repertory by including in the program the "Panaderos" Spanish character dance from *Raymonda*, accompanied by lead character dancer Konstantin Rassadin.

What developed into what Legat calls "an extremely delicate and complicated situation" arose with Irina Kolpakova's equally intent determination that Soloviev would begin to partner her. "Women were always a great support to him," Legat said, "and there was a time he was sort of pulled back and forth between Fedicheva and Kolpakova. Fedicheva needed him, and Kolpakova needed him. In actuality, he was so beautifully paired with Sizova." Sizova, however, did not dance all the ballets in his repertory and she had no taste for political intrigue. She was also sidelined with a back injury for two years in the mid-1960s.

Fedicheva was very sure of her position, capable of talking back to a coach or choreographer, which was something formerly only Nureyev would have dreamed of doing. She certainly had no hesitation about facing down Kolpakova, who was a Leningrad Party Deputy in the Supreme Soviet (parliament of the USSR), who also had the support of Leningrad Party boss Grigory Romanov. Soloviev, of course, had no stomach for political intrigue and conflict, and partnered selflessly whomever he was assigned.

Kolpakova and Soloviev's partnership was predicated on the intriguing contrast between attracting opposites. She also had a high jump, but less projectile-like than Sizova's, and lighter, less catlike in its spring than Soloviev's. She was the same height as Sizova but, unlike Sizova or Soloviev himself, Kolpakova was very long-limbed, with famously elegant arms and a small head.

When the Kirov returned to London in 1966, it was not Sizova but instead Kolpakova whom Soloviev partnered in *Cinderella*. During the early 1970s, Kolpakova would be revitalized by her partnership with the young Baryshnikov—they were dancing together in Canada when he defected in 1974. Something similar seemed to have happened with Soloviev during the 1960s. Kolpakova customarily projected a more glittering illumination than the mellow tenderness of Sizova, but in *The Dancing Times*, Mary Clarke wrote that in her *Cinderella* with Soloviev, Kolpakova displayed "a new warmth and confidence and she sailed and spun round the stage like a sparkle of sunshine, a shower of stars."

"Certainly he inspired her," Legat said. At twenty-six, Soloviev had by

now progressed considerably from the hesitant Albrecht Kolpakova had been bemused by early in his career. In *Giselle*, "he completely changed" from the inhibited novitiate, she recalled. "Rather than being like somebody had taught him, he began to do what he felt.

"He was an absolutely natural actor on the stage and deep," she insisted. "I remember his eyes," which were blue-gray and ever-mobile on stage, she recalled, whipped by volatile storms of emotion. Perhaps in this particular pairing it was Soloviev who supplied the native fire. Kolpakova was "like an encyclopedia," Legat said, "she was very smart, very musical. "But she wasn't a natural actress." Kolpakova herself understood that. "Therefore she would work so hard."

Kolpakova's clout in the company helped Soloviev. Their rehearsals were scheduled immediately after class. They had the best studio, the best piano player. "It was an optimal situation for him to work and therefore it brought out a perfection in his work," Legat said. Highly stressed before each performance, Soloviev was prone to entertain every worst-case scenario about how it might unfold. Kolpakova, however, "was such a master of her craft that although, yes, she was nervous, she never showed it. So it was reassuring for him to dance with her."

A ballerina like Sizova could spontaneously expend extra energy on a particular movement and wind up temporarily deflated in Soloviev's arms. Kolpakova, however, "knew how to pace herself," Legat observed, "she knew you use this much here and this much there." Adagio was not the easiest muscular expression for her, but Soloviev was able to impart additional stretch and sensuality to her movement. Aurora in *Sleeping Beauty* was Kolpakova's most acclaimed role, but she was taxed by the act 2 Vision duet. Watching frequently from the wings, Legat discerned a certain amount of tension on Kolpakova's part as she surmounted and, with Soloviev's strength and adept partnering, conquered the duet's demands—as can be seen in the 1976 filmed record.

Kolpakova showed her gratitude. After Igor and Anna moved out of the family's room on Fontanka, Anna and Vladimir were given an apartment in a not-very-desirable area. The process of changing apartments could take years, but Kolpakova arranged for them to move to a one-bedroom apartment of their own in a newly constructed residential area near the city's dry docks. Vladimir's status as wounded war veteran also helped their eligibility. He and Anna still preferred, however, to spend most of their time with their individual children.

Yet another rival ballerina or her fans—the Solovievs were never quite sure—would deposit letters in their mailbox: "Yuri Vladimirovich, you fall so flat when you are dancing with others. But when you dance with X, you are on another plane." Indeed, Soloviev's ballerinas seem to have been unanimously appreciative of his support.

Emma Minchonok danced the Bluebird pas de deux with him many times. In the coda, Bluebird supports Princess Florine in a repeated sequence of pas de chats followed by a pose in attitude back. By the time this arrived, Minchonok was often tired and finding it difficult to lift her leg high in attitude each time. "And I, brazenly, shamelessly, pressed down hard on his hand in order to lift my leg higher. Not once did he complain to me, for which I was and remain very grateful to him!"

"However much work was involved, he did it uncomplainingly," said Gabriela Komleva, with whom he also danced many ballets. "He never made any demands or conditions about the work. You understand, it is very important in work, when you are free. Working with him, I always felt that freedom."

BLUEBIRD PAS DE DEUX WITH EMMA MINCHONOK
PHOTO: NINA ALOVERT

REHEARSALS WITH MAKAROVA IN LONDON, 1966
PHOTOS: JENNIE WALTON

HERE AND NEXT PAGE: *GISELLE, ACT 1*

25

PERSONAL STYLE

REHEARSING ALBRECHT
PHOTO: COURTESY MARIINSKY THEATER

oloviev enhanced the impact of his jump by never seeming to be going into overdrive. Never suggesting that he was dancing on his capital didn't suggest strain or expose a threshold or limitations. "His elevation is prodigious yet always at the height of the jump he has power in reserve," Mary Clarke wrote in her *Dancing Times* review of his London appearances with the Kirov in 1966. "He could have jumped even higher," said Tchernichova. Clowning around before pas de deux class began, she recalled, Soloviev would sometimes unleash his full elevation, which was almost frightening. Later, in Kirov company class, he would astound his colleagues with a trick only he could perform: jumping straight up in the air and landing on top of the piano.

Nureyev could make theatrical content out of his effort to do the steps, a genuine struggle in his early years occasioned by his technical rawness; he maintained this as performance trait after he became much more adept. Baryshnikov too, particularly in the West, made creative histrionics by seeming to register the air's resistance to his body's passage into space. For Soloviev, legato flow and the concealment of effort were nearly always paramount. Regarding Soloviev's opening night Siegfried in London in 1966, "He had just one fault, so far as the first-night audience was concerned," John Percival wrote in *Dance and Dancers*. "He made everything look easy, and many of the typical 'gala night' audience… responded as if they thought it really was easy."

"There was a harmony in him that you could feel," recalled Jean-Pierre Bonnefoux, a star of the Paris Opéra Ballet, and then New York City Ballet. Bonnefoux saw Soloviev at close range when he joined Pushkin's class on visits to Leningrad. From Soloviev's turns on the ground to movement way above the ground, "the balance of the body was perfect," Bonnefoux recalled. It enabled Soloviev to rapidly and seamlessly change positions, speeds, directions.

The Spanish style in ballet was diametrically opposite to Soloviev's characteristic expression, and that made it perhaps all the more something that he wanted to master. His experience with Chabukiani's *Laurencia* went back to his first season in the company when he had danced the pas de six.

LAURENCIA

At his 1964 Creative Evening, he performed another excerpt, this time as the lead, Frandoso.

Filmed for Soviet TV, his incendiary Spanish brio is restrained but understood. Two years later he danced the entire ballet opposite Natalia Bolshakova, demonstrating an impressive swagger in the amateur footage in Legat's collection.

"I think it suited him very well," Vinogradov said. The hyperventilating display may have been impossible for Soloviev, but "the inner temperament, inner emotions, he always had." By contrast, Vinogradov added, most dancers, "when they try to show the Spanish character, they look to me like epileptics."

Dancing the full-length *Don Quixote* however, was not something Soloviev could seem to make happen, which aggrieved him and aroused his competitive instincts. Once during the 1960s Vladimir Vasiliev was visiting from Moscow and came to watch Pushkin's class. Before his eyes, Soloviev impetuously whipped off a manège of barrel turns—quotation from the coda of *Don Quixote*'s act 3 grand pas de deux—this Vasiliev's most famous role. Vasiliev asked Soloviev how long he had been rehearsing the manège.

Soloviev replied that he hadn't been rehearsing it at all.

Rehearsing for a planned debut as Basil, he twice injured his back in the one-handed lift of act 1. Finally, he thought about seeking help in Moscow from Alexei Yermolayev, who had coached Vasiliev in it. A Bolshoi star of the 1930s and '40s, Yermolayev was now estranged from his former company. Neither Yuri nor Tatiana knew him personally; they didn't have his phone number. What was needed was a personal trip to the Bolshoi, a face-to-face conversation with Vasiliev, and a request that Vasiliev speak to the senior dancer. Soloviev did in fact go to Moscow to appeal to Vasiliev, taking class with the Bolshoi for ten days. But Yermolayev was on an alcoholic bender and died not long after that.

After Soloviev cancelled a planned debut, Shcherbakov gave him a suggestion about how to improve his grande pirouette, an important step in the coda of the act 3 pas de deux. Some Kirov danseurs substituted chaîné turns, but Soloviev intended to do it according to precedent, But Soloviev did not want to listen to Shcherbakov. Rather, he seemed to have closed a door on this particular turn, and did not want it reopened.

WITH ELENA EVTEEVA IN *LE SPECTRE DE LA ROSE*
PHOTO: COURTESY VAGANOVA ACADEMY

26
NIJINSKY
REPERTORY

oloviev admired the way that sixty years earlier Nijinsky had held his hands: he found them as relaxed and unself-conscious as a baby's. Soloviev's own career was entwined with that of his Mariinsky forbearer's from his student days, when he danced Nijinsky's solo in Fokine's *Le Pavilion d'Armide*. Like Nijinsky, Soloviev epitomized a central paradox of ballet: the way robust muscularity creates the illusion of gravity-defying weightlessness. Nijinsky was huskier still than Soloviev; watching Soloviev, "I understood it was sort of the way Nijinsky was built," Baryshnikov recalled, "but much more beautiful." Both Nijinsky and Soloviev became legendary for their jumps and beats; both had the ability to seemingly pause in the air at the height of their jumps. Yet they had a different manner of getting into the air. According to Nijinsky's contemporary Fyodor Lopukhov, Soloviev's deep soft plié seemed quintessentially Russian, while Nijinsky with a quicker take-off conveyed the flavor of his native Poland's Mazurka.

It was inevitable that Soloviev would inherit some of Nijinsky's repertory, making him the unlikely inhabitant of most un-Soviet imaginative places. For Nijinsky had wrought a revolution in men's repertory, particularly in the roles he created for Diaghilev's Ballets Russes. As Tamara Karsavina, Nijinsky's partner both at the Mariinsky and for Diaghilev, wrote in old age, "The new dimension of male dancing was revealed by Nijinsky in *Les Sylphides*. 'Graceful' when applied to a man may carry a hint of effeminacy. This epithet could be safely given to Nijinsky. The unfolding of his arms in arabesque spelled poetic dreams, the response of his whole body to the music."

Any hint of effeminacy, even channeled into poetic ambiguity, would not have been overly welcome in gender-specific Soviet culture. But Fokine's 1908 ballet remained in the Kirov's repertory, performed under its original name *Chopiniana*. Nijinsky's role was rapt poet conjuring fantastic forest creatures evocative of the nineteenth-century Romantic ballet, frolicking with them in flights of his own imagining. Nijinsky's ability to transmit this sense via his very muscular physique speaks of his power of chameleon-like transformation, a gift one doesn't associate with Soloviev. But Soloviev too, was able to suggest time and space limits were being transcended. "I'm sure that Yura must have rehearsed *Chopiniana* with Pushkin," Legat said. "Because of the result. Because he got so much out of *Chopiniana*."

Snippets of film of his Mazurka solo are riveting: his softly prolonged landings into arabesque fondu are crucial to the pervading musicality of Fokine's movement. Here frequencies are meant to suspend and prolong all but indefinitely. Irina Baronova, who rehearsed the ballet with Fokine during the 1930s, recalled, "Nothing stands like a rock in *Sylphides*, because that music, although you can't hear it, the animals can still hear it, and the Japanese can hear it even after the animals. It's still in the air, that one note that goes on."

During the 1966 London season, Soloviev's *Giselle* with Makarova was described by James Monahan in *The Dancing Times* to have sur-

HERE AND OVERLEAF: *GISELLE* DRESS REHEARSAL WITH MAKAROVA, LONDON 1970. PHOTOS: ROSEMARY WINKLEY

passed "any other in my experience." Sadly, we have not come across footage of their *Giselle*, a taproot of Romantic style informing Fokine's later homage. But in their filmed performance of the waltz from *Chopiniana* their jump, ballon, and melodious sensuality complement each other perfectly. Soloviev's sonority balances her occasional flights into exquisitely art nouveau ornateness.

Living in New York were any number of retired Russian dancers, most of them now teaching, whose careers dated back to the Mariinsky and to Diaghilev as well as successive Ballets Russ incarnations. (Had Nijinsky lived, he would have been just about seventy when the Kirov first visited New York.) Meeting them "was incredible for us" Legat said.

Andre Eglevsky was a former star of both Ballets Russ and then New York City Ballet. Anatole Gridin, one of the Kirov's leading character dancers, recalled that in 1964 Eglevsky tried to persuade him to defect. He toured him around his school on Long Island, which also was headquarters for his own small ballet company, and invited him to his large home nearby. There Gridin noticed a small oil portrait of Alla Sizova and a larger one of Soloviev, whom Eglevsky considered the apogee of male ballet dancing.

Eglevsky suggested to Soloviev that he dance Nijinsky's role in Fokine's *Le Spectre de la Rose*, the two-character ballet Karsavina and Nijinsky had created in 1911. Eglevsky himself had danced the role in the 1930s. A *Spectre* costume of Nijinsky's was on view in the Rossi Street Academy's museum. Soloviev rehearsed the ballet in New York with Eglevsky, who wrote him two warm, admiring letters before the Russians left America. "It was a great pleasure to work with you." He enclosed sixteen pages of notes on the choreography. He requested signed photographs from Soloviev and Makarova and posters from the Kirov for his school.

Soon after, Soloviev performed *Spectre* at his second Creative Evening. Eglevsky had envisioned Makarova as Soloviev's perfect partner in the ballet, but it was instead Legat herself who first danced it with him. They looked for old pictures of Nijinsky and Karsavina to check their poses as they prepared to inherit their roles. He was the spirit of the rose she has just worn at her first ball.

The role is many different things: one big jump after another, stylization in the arms suggesting the bewitchment of rose perfume, short sequences of partnering in which he arouses the girl's slumbering recollection. "I didn't see anything," Legat recalled about their performance in the ballet. "You don't dance in the real world. You're somewhere else. On the one hand, certainly you're just in your body, because you're using your technique, but at the same time it is totally, completely unreal. You remember the ball and it is so beautiful. "

Soloviev later filmed the ballet with Elena Evteyeva, who entered the Kirov in 1967, another superb ballerina in this great age of the Kirov.

Needless to say, Soloviev's time, place and temperament prevented him from falling into excesses of swooning "rosiness." His flawless execution evokes something of the feral quality for which Nijinsky was famous. His final exit, a jump across the window jamb, clues us again to the sensation Nijinsky created as he seemed to pause in the air before disappearing from view.

Nijinsky's widow Romola and his sister Bronislava were sometimes to be seen in the audience when the Kirov appeared in Europe. Romola also made trips to Leningrad, where she saw the company perform on the stage that had reared her husband. During the mid-1960s, rumors circulated about a British biopic about the legendary dancer. Soloviev was considered for the lead role, but it wasn't until after Soloviev's death that Herbert Ross directed *Nijinsky*, which starred American Ballet Theatre's George de la Peña.

SPECTRE. PHOTO: COURTESY VAGANOVA ACADEMY

27

WORLD TRAVELER

YVETTE CHAUVIRÉ

SIGNED BY YVETTE CHAUVIRÉ
"TO YURI SOLOVIEV, THE DANCER WHO FLIES"

"**N**othing but Russians, Russians, Russians and ballet, ballet, ballet," Soloviev once complained to Lisa about his life in Leningrad. He found too much of the conversation and thought patterns around him limited and conventional. His daughter reflects on how his life might have been enriched had he been able to spend more time with artists from different theaters, the same ones he competed in inter-theatrical sports meets. Or more time with the worldly and intelligent set surrounding his friend Makhmud Esambaev. But the foreign travel Soloviev enjoyed opened up vistas of experience, exposure and the intellectual stimulation that he craved.

Most of the big Kirov tours were undertaken in the summer, cutting into the dancers' vacation time. But "they could do whatever they wanted with us," Legat said. Vacation time they were prepared to forgo; what they feared was the ever-present possibility that they would be scheduled, then subsequently eliminated from a tour. Better to be superstitious: "Let us not say that we're going on this trip, because we'll ruin it." Only as they were sitting in a plane headed abroad would they acknowledge out loud that they were indeed headed abroad.

GARLANDED IN INDIA

He decided that he would begin to study English—that both he and Tatiana would. "It was the right thing to do," Legat agreed. "Of course you needed to speak English." But lessons could prove risky. Like all students on Rossi Street, Soloviev had studied French. For a time during the mid-1950s, English had been taught in some elite Leningrad schools. But now Soloviev couldn't enroll in a foreign language course at the university or elsewhere—it would have immediately marked him as suspect for defection. Instead, he arranged for a linguist, who taught freelance and illegally, to come to their apartment to work with them.

"I was no good at it," Legat said. "I still have my little notebook where I would write. Alyona always says, 'You've been working on English, working on this notebook for thirty years, and it still hasn't gotten anywhere.'" They soon dropped the lessons altogether.

As it was, the KGB did not consider him a particular security risk. He traveled not only with the Kirov, but also with tours organized by Igor Moiseyev. He could also travel independently with a partner. Once he and Kolpakova went to dance *Giselle* at a festival in Berlin. Another year they also performed together at the Venice Biennale. Without any minders, they found themselves stranded in an Italian airport, unaware that they had to move to the domestic terminal for a connecting flight to Venice. But even-

FRIENDS IN JAPAN

GUEST STAR IN JAPAN WITH SIZOVA

tually they made it to their engagement. On another occasion, Soloviev and Sizova went together to Japan as guest artists with a ballet company there.

Traveling the world, he received confirmation that his gifts were equal or perhaps superior to any other dancer on the international stage. "If Soloviev is the greatest male dancer in the world, where does Nureyev—who is the most publicized dancer in the world—come in?" Richard Buckle asked in London's *Times* in September 1966, midway through the Kirov's four-week return to Covent Garden.

> Soloviev has not got Nureyev's photographic and fascinating face, nor has he his interpretive power. From the beginning I said Nureyev was more amazing for his expressive qualities than for his dancing: he excels in certain steps, but Soloviev excels in all. Nureyev has not Soloviev's supreme flow and lightness, nor has he been subjected to so steady a course of discipline. Soloviev, slightly the younger of the two, is now better than in 1961: purely as a dancer he is incomparable and unsurpassed.

ソ連の男性ソリストの中で最も著名なソロヴィヨフは、気品と優雅さをそなえた典型的なダンスール・ノーブル（王子役舞踊手）で跳躍の名手としても知られ、最近ますます円熟の度を加えている。1967年以来、毎回日本公演に参加し、「跳躍と安定度、たくましさはむしろバレエの英雄といえよう」「品があり、その巧みなリードはベテランの味」、「優雅な気品あるプリンスを演じ、すばらしい跳躍の美をみせ、至難なテクニックのかずかずを披露」と毎回激讃されている。ソロヴィヨフはレニングラード・バレエ学校を卒業後、1958年キーロフ劇場に入り、「ジゼル」のアルブレヒト、「白鳥の湖」「くるみ割り人形」「眠りの森の美女」「シンデレラ」の王子、「白の花」のダニーラ、「愛の伝説」のフェルハード、「レニングラード物語」の青年、「イカルス」のイカルスその他多くの主役を演じ、あるいは世界各国で公演して完全な技巧、驚くべき柔軟さ、すばらしく高い跳躍、正確で詩的で深く抒情的な入魂の表現力によって大成功をおさめてきた。1963年および65年のパリ国際バレエ・フェスティバルでニジンスキー賞、最優秀舞踊手賞を受賞している。

ユーリー・ソロヴィヨフ
ソリスト／ソ連邦人民芸術家
YURY SOLOVIYOV
Soloist, People's Artist of the U.S.S.R.

The most typical "danseur noble", a dancer who is most suitable for prince, with nobility and grace, Yury Soloviyov is the most popular male soloist in the Leningrad Ballet. He is also known as the most skillful performer of high jumps.

His many repertoires include the Prince in "The Swan Lake", "The Sleeping Beauty", "The Nutcracker", and "Cinderella", Danila in "The Stone Flower", a Youth in "Leningrad Symphony", Ferkhad in "Legend of Love", Albrecht in "Giselle", and the title role of "Ikaros". He was awarded the Nijinsky Prize and the Most Distinguished Dancer Prize respectively at the International Ballet Festivals in 1963 and 1965 in Paris.

SOUVENIR PROGRAM, JAPAN 1976

DER INTENDANT DES HESSISCHEN STAATSTHEATERS WIESBADEN

62 Wiesbaden, den 24. Juni 1968

Herrn
Juri Soloviow
Kirow-Theater Leningrad

Leningrad
UdSSR

Sehr geehrter Herr Soloviow,

eine Umfrage bei den Theaterkritikern, die an den Internationalen Mai-Festspielen 1968 in Wiesbaden teilgenommen haben, hat ergeben, dass

Herr György Melis   — Ungarische Staatsoper, Budapest
Herr Juri Soloviow   — Kirow-Theater, Leningrad
Herr Rudolf Nurejew   — Royal Ballet Covent Garden, London
Frau Margot Fonteyn   — Royal Ballet Covent Garden, London
Frau Irina Kolpakowa   — Kirow-Ballett, Leningrad
Herr Georges Descrieres — Comédie-Française, Paris

die besondere Anerkennung der Kritik gefunden haben.

Im Auftrage der Jury, bestehend aus den Herren Walter Brad (Hessischer Rundfunk), Dr. Walter G. Russe ("Wiesbadener Tagblatt") und Dr. Hans Klaus ("Wiesbadener Kurier"), habe ich die Freude, Ihnen zu Ihrem persönlichen Erfolg sehr herzlich zu gratulieren und Ihnen die "FEDER DER KRITIK" zu übersenden.

Mit den besten Grüssen bleibe ich

Ihr ergebener

(Dr. Drews)

FESTIVAL INTERNATIONAL DE LA DANSE
DE PARIS

Paris, le 9 février 1968

Le Directeur Général
Jean Robin

Monsieur Youri SOLOVIEW
C/o Théâtre Kirov
LENINGRAD

Nouvelle Adresse
Théâtre de la Musique
Gaîté Lyrique
76, Rue Réaumur
PARIS - 3e
Tél. 508 19-75

VIIème FESTIVAL INTERNATIONAL DE LA DANSE — NOVEMBRE 1969

Cher Monsieur,

J'ai l'intention, pour clore le Festival International de la Danse de 1969, d'inviter tous les danseurs et danseuses ayant obtenu l'Étoile d'Or du Festival ou le Grand Prix de la Ville de Paris.

Je vous serais donc reconnaissant de bien vouloir réserver la dernière semaine de novembre 1969. Je vous demanderai dans cette semaine vraisemblablement quatre représentations, étant bien entendu que vous serez libre de choisir votre partenaire pour ces soirées. Le programme sera exclusivement composé de Pas de Deux, en principe je vous en demanderai deux.

Inutile de vous dire combien je serais heureux que vous puissiez accepter et je vous prie de me faire part, dès maintenant, de vos conditions, incluant votre partenaire.

Dans l'attente du plaisir de vous lire, je vous prie de croire, cher Monsieur, à l'assurance de mes sentiments les meilleurs.

- Jean ROBIN

Théâtre des Champs-Elysées.   15, Avenue Montaigne - Paris. 8e   Tél. Balzac 1968

TELEFON 39331

UNIVERSITE de la DANSE

26, Villa Mageux, (8e)   Institut Chorégraphique
Centre Culturel Chorégraphique
International   Paris, le 1er Juin 1963

PRIX 1963

1.- PRIX DE L'UNIVERSITE (10ème Année)
À Igor MOISSEIEV et son ensemble Russe .... (U.R.S.S.)
À ANTONIO et son ensemble Espagnol .... (Espagne)

2.- PRIX Serge de DIAGHILEV (10ème Année)
À Tatjana GSOVSKY
pour l'ensemble de son oeuvre Académique en Allemagne .... (Allemagne)

3.- PRIX Anna PAVLOVA (8ème Année)
À Carla FRACCI, Étoile du Teatro Alla Scala
pour son interprétation poétique et lyrique de Chloé dans
"Daphnis et Chloé" Ballet de Fokine sur la Scène du Théâtre SCALA ... (Italie)

4.- PRIX Vaslav NIJINSKY (7ème Année)
À SOLOVIEV, Danseur Étoile du Théâtre KYROV de Leningrad
pour son interprétation de "l'Oiseau Bleu" de Petipa
à l'Opéra de Paris en 1958. .... (U.R.S.S.)
À Erik BRUHN, Danseur Étoile du Th. Royal de Copenhague. ... (Danemark)

5.- PRIX Maurois de CUEVAS (5ème Année)
À Nina VYROUBOVA
À POLJAJENKO
Les Danseurs Étoiles du Ballet du Marquis de Cuevas ...... (France)

6.- PRIX Docteur HONORIS CAUSA (6ème Année)
À Olivier MERLIN
À Elvio ANTHIRAL
Les critiques et les Écrivains de la Danse. .... (France) (Japon)

7.- MEDAILLE de l'UNIVERSITE de la Danse (6ème Année)
À Konstanze VERNON
Première Danseuse du Deutsche Oper de Berlin. .... (Allemagne)
À Nanon THIBON, Première Danseuse de l'Opéra de Paris. ... (France)

Léone RAIL
(Vice-Directeur de l'U.D.)

Serge LIFAR
(Directeur de l'U.D.)
Maître de Ballet du Théâtre National
de l'Opéra de Paris.

M.F. CHRISTOUT
(Secrétaire Général de l'U.D.)

Michel GEORGES-MICHEL
Président de l'Association des
Écrivains et Critiques de Danse

à Soloviev

Pour le 30e anniversaire de l'Ecole de l'Air
UN GALA EXCEPTIONNEL

plus discutés, ceux qui n'étaient pas forcément dans la ligne

A-t-elle changé ? Pas le moins du monde. Elle avait trente ans lors qu'elle décida de quitter la tournée du Kirov et de rester à Londres. Rien de prémédité. Le coup de tête d'une danseuse dans sa maturité et la pleine possession de ses moyens. Il serait vain de donner la liste complète des chorégraphes avec lesquels elle a travaillé. Disons qu'en plus des ballets classiques elle a voulu tout connaître, tout expérimenter : Martha Graham, Roland Petit Balanchine, Jerry Robbins, Mac Millan, Tudor, Cranko. Puisque c'était cela la raison pour laquelle

elle quittait le Kirov, comment s'étonner ? Elle était partie pour échapper à la routine, la routine du répertoire, la routine des pas. « Exécuter un pas » ou « danser un pas », pour elle toute la différence est là. Ce pur produit du Kirov qui n'a jamais renié ce qu'elle doit à son pays natal, qui parle volontiers de la dette éternelle qu'elle lie à sa patrie et à son si précieux passé, Natalia Makarova danse comme elle parle et comme elle pense. Elle est la liberté même.

Aucune danseuse ne donne autant qu'elle l'impression de toujours être sur le point d'inventer.

EDMONDE CHARLES-ROUX

Natalia Makarova : Odette dans Le Lac des cygnes avec Youri Soloviev : Siegfried, et Nicolas Ostaltsov : Rothbard.

Ci-contre :
Youri Soloviev : La Légende de l'amour.

Youti Soloviov en répétition avec Natalia Pavlova dans Giselle.

66

Photo X

DANSE MAGAZINE LE KIROV

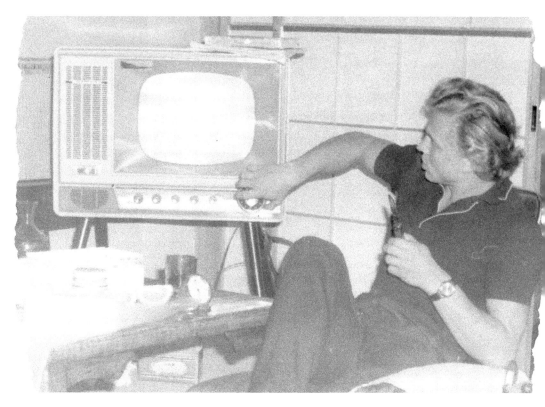

TOURING APPURTENANCES IN JAPAN HOTEL ROOM

PHOTO: COURTESY VAGANOVA ACADEMY

28

A GISELLE DEBUT

oloviev's travels undoubtedly provided artistic dividends as well. Boris Blankov writes that Soloviev's frequent touring cost him coaching preparation in the role of Albrecht, and yet travel itself broadened and deepened his approach. "He began to perform the role phenomenally well" after the Kirov's summer 1966 tour. "The trip had somehow had an effect in broadening his views of the world, of his craft."

So much so perhaps, that when Emma Minchonok made her Kirov debut as Giselle, it was her "good fortune" to be partnered by Soloviev as Albrecht. "I trusted him, trusted him completely," she recalled. "We found a common language right away, mutual understanding."

Sergeyev and Vecheslova—"two superb coaches"—worked on the role with her, and the rehearsal process became all-consuming. "I stopped sleeping; I lost my appetite, stopped thinking about anything but *Giselle*. I could hear only its music. I could only think about the rehearsals." She felt that Giselle's madness when finding herself betrayed had infected her as well: "I was like a *nenormalnaia*."

WITH MINCHONOK IN *THE LEGEND OF LOVE*
PHOTO: NINA ALOVERT

In rehearsal, Soloviev's response to her matched her own belief in the role. "Yura really helped me a lot… Because it was great tragedy that we were recreating in the rehearsal hall.

"In the fullest sense of the word, in the theatrical, I fell completely in love with him." Partner and role merged, so that at the end of act 1, when Giselle's peasant lover is unmasked as a philandering nobleman, "I simply couldn't believe it! I simply couldn't, in no way. I was sure it just couldn't be happening. I continued to love him, to justify him, and that went on into the second act."

In act 2, Albrecht visits Giselle's grave and her ghost fights to save him from the undead, man-hating Wilis. "There I also continued to love him and protect him somehow. Tried to help him and buffer him away from those Wilis. Evil creatures. He was someone near, someone beloved, dear little soul."

Central to the ballet are the themes of forgiveness and repentance— Giselle's forgiveness, Albrecht's repentance. As Albrecht, Soloviev was "so truly distraught, so real, that I believed him completely."

29
DEFECTION?

ureyev's love of the Kirov had not abated in the years since his defection. He frequently attended their performances on tour, making persistent attempts to renew contact with ex-colleagues. More often than not, his approaches were rebuffed by the anxious dancers. "I wasn't supposed to meet him," Sizova recalled about one occasion. "But I had enough courage to pull myself together and meet him. But I did it quietly."

In Milan in 1966, Soloviev, Legat and Kirov colleague Arkady Ivanenko were walking out of La Scala's stage entrance when Nureyev beckoned from an adjacent outdoor café. "Hello, Yura!" Nureyev called out loudly, and waved. Soloviev nodded quietly. Ivanenko recalled that Tatiana too may have also nodded slightly, but nevertheless she and Ivanenko himself froze. Another day the three were walking into the theater when they once again encountered Nureyev, now standing by the stage door. He executed a bow and extended his hand with a flourish, saying, "Welcome to my theater!" They had no reaction. "We couldn't," Ivanenko claimed. "We couldn't do anything."

Nureyev's influence on Western ballet had been cataclysmic. The West was ready to welcome eagerly the next sensation, and potentially there was a great deal of money to be made all around. Ostalstov recalled a later Kirov appearance in Barcelona, where Baryshnikov invited him and his wife to dinner in his hotel room. It was filled with silverware, diving equipment, oxygen tanks, water skis, winter skis—all hard to find in the USSR, all supplied by solicitous impresarios. Ostaltsov believed that Soloviev received equivalent bounty.

But it was not riches but rather autonomy that would have been most alluring. Soloviev "wanted to live independently," Ostalstov said. "His talent required it. But at the time it was impossible to live independently in our country."

Yuri told Igor that he had received several invitations to defect. "If he wanted to, he could have," Igor told Lobenthal in 2001. "He didn't want it. He liked Russia, nature and fishing. Of course," as Igor added with a wry laugh, "he could have gone fishing in Australia too." (Words spoken years before Lobenthal met his coauthor.)

Lisa agrees: "Yura no more wanted to leave his country than he wanted to go to the moon. He was a decent man and he wanted to behave decently. He didn't want to be cut off from his country, branded as a traitor or harm his family. What he wanted to do was to live in his country as he chose to live. His mistake, which he shared with his fellow *shestidesiatniki*, was the illusion that this was at the very least in the realm of possibility. It was not. It was an either/or proposition."

Well before his death he must have realized that. Tchernichova recalled a Rossi Street class of 1958 ten-year reunion. Tongue loosened by alcohol, yet his voice kept down, Soloviev told her about a defection offer that he'd turned down. "I think I made a mistake... I was so stupid."

Aleksandr Shavrov believed that Soloviev could not defect because a certain result would have been his mother making good on her suicide threats. And of course, as of October 1963, there was also that most compelling of hostages remaining back home: his daughter.

A bold leap into the unknown would not have been a characteristic move. "On the one hand, everybody knew that to go off was to become free," Ostaltsov said, "but what kind of freedom? Nobody knew..." And yet, "I *know* he had remorse that he hadn't defected," Pierre Lacotte says today. "Yuri sacrificed himself and his great talent to his duty, to his obligations. In the West, he would have been liberated from the mask he wore."

30

GEORGI ALEXIDZE

FEDICHEVA AND SOLOVIEV: AEGISTHUS AND CLYTEMNESTRA
PHOTO: COURTESY MARIINSKY THEATER

oung choreographer Georgi Alexidze gave Soloviev the chance to be a heavy, an antihero, to radically expand his range of characterization. Alexidze was a graduate of the Bolshoi Ballet school in Moscow and of a choreography course taught by Lopukhov at the Leningrad Conservatory. Lopukhov was a hero to the younger generation, having graduated into the Imperial Mariinsky, won and lost the position as director post-Revolution, and choreographed many ballets that were considered daring and new. His work was eventually banned, too modern for the reactionary aesthetic turn of the 1930s. But he had survived to enjoy an Indian summer of reappreciation.

In 1965, Leningrad French-horn player Vitaly Buyanovsky and his wife Tatiana Bazilevskaya organized an Ensemble of Chamber Music and Ballet. Still in his twenties, Alexidze over the next five years would have opportunities to choreograph for them in concerts held at the Leningrad Philharmonic. Kirov principal dancers frequently participated.

Alexidze was "very musical," Legat recalled, "and emotional like a true Georgian. Very charming." His work, however, freely investigated the dark side of existence. He decided to cast Fedicheva in a new duet portraying the amoral couple in nineteenth-century novelist Nikolai Leskov's classic short story "Lady Macbeth of the Mtsensk District." It chronicles the illicit love affair of a bored young provincial wife, and its ruthless path to homicide. In 1935, Shostakovich had turned it into an opera that was quickly banned, but since the thaw had become part of Soviet repertory.

Probably at Fedicheva's insistence, Soloviev danced opposite her as the loutish estate steward Sergei. She was perfectly cast, but Alexidze was apprehensive about him, wondering if Soloviev could break out of the classical emploi. Here there would not be the flowing lines and movements that was echt-Soloviev, but angularity, the balletic genre of "grotesque." But as Alexidze later wrote, "Paradoxically! The master of classical style had discovered himself in the capacity of a grotesque dancer with a great potential to self-expression."

What Alexidze describes as Soloviev's "extraordinary musicality and his phenomenal muscle memory" were conducive to the creation of new work. They stood him in good stead when Alexidze asked him to film a piece opposite Sizova that he had created to an orchestration of a Shostakovich piano fugue. The production schedule was tight and Soloviev managed to learn his part in a single rehearsal. Alexidze was astonished.

For her second Creative Evening in 1968, Fedicheva commissioned *Oresteia* from Alexidze, a kinetic transposition of Aeschylus. Alexidze wanted Soloviev to portray Aegisthus, again in the movement language of grotesquerie. Despite the success of the *Lady Macbeth* duet, Alexidze was once more worried that Soloviev would be unwilling to step away from his characteristic lyricism. Alexidze shared his doubts with Lopukhov. The grand old man offered to discuss it with Soloviev. He explained Alexidze's concept for the ballet, the literary references, the culture and philosophy of ancient Greece. To drive his point home, Lopukhov quipped to Soloviev that *Swan Lake*'s Prince Siegfried was "a rather limited young fellow. His burning problem is that he cannot choose a bride out of many zealous princesses who want him. And I doubt if that image can be interpreted on the scene in the newly experimental way."

AS AEGISTHUS WITH V. LOPUKHOV AS ORESTES
PHOTO: BOYAROV. COURTESY MARIINSKY THEATER

At the first rehearsal, Alexidze himself talked to the dancers, describing the atmosphere of Agamemnon's palace. His fears were immediately allayed. "Yura breathed together with my ideas; he didn't need to be convinced about anything. His open mind could accept any abstract idea."

Leningrad composer Yuri Falik wrote music in which leitmotifs substituted for melody; his composition was scored with trombones, trumpets and percussion. In a riveting monologue of harshly pressured steps, Soloviev conveyed these instrumental timbres with exactitude. Alexidze "opened up something very tragic and dramatic in him," Legat said, a dramatic contrast to his customary temperamental benevolence.

Watching from the audience, Kolpakova was impressed by the way Soloviev sometimes suggested a tragic mask from ancient Greece. She felt that he used his eyes and face with the nuance of a film actor. "Plus his wonderful body."

"My husband, as a choreographer, could see and bring out the inner qualities of a dancer, even ones that they didn't know they had," Alexidze's widow Marina Alexidze reflects today.

SOLOVIEV AND ALEXIDZE
PHOTO: COURTESY MARINA ALEXIDZE

AEGISTHUS IN ORESTEIA. PHOTO: BOYAROV. COURTESY MARIINSKY THEATER

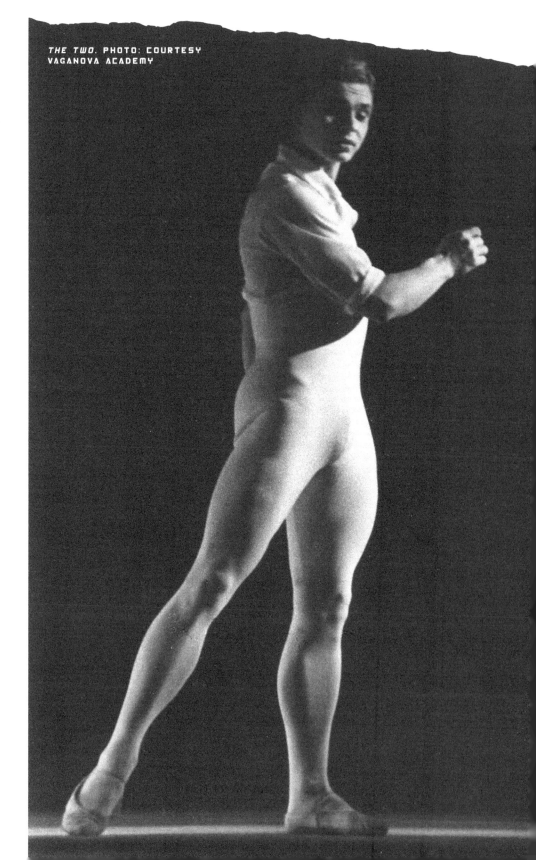

31
CREATIVE EVENINGS

WITH KOLPAKOVA
IN THE TWO

REHEARSING *LAND OF MIRACLES* ON STAGE AT THE MARIINSKY, 1967 PHOTO: COURTESY VAGANOVA ACADEMY

ndeed, it becomes apparent that a new interpretative handle on Solo-viev is needed that does not consider his primary arena the classic nineteenth-century repertory. Should Soloviev instead be looked at the way we do a Balanchine star, a Suzanne Farrell or Edward Villella? Balanchine created new repertories for his stars, exploring their unique attributes, and it was in their own repertory that they were judged supreme.

An ambitious Kirov dancer who sought the highest position and acclaim, Soloviev needed to commit himself to the classic repertory, and there were parts of them that he profoundly enjoyed. But as a *Shestidesiatnik*, he was keen to embody the creative vitality of his own time, the relevance of the new. Soloviev's major dissatisfaction with his Kirov career, his brother Igor recalled, was the dearth of new ballets. He certainly wasn't alone: the dancers all craved the opportunity to create new, especially made statements. But although they almost never lasted long in the Kirov repertory, Soloviev did eventually create at least fifteen major new ballets over the course of his career—an impressive tally even when stacked against a Western contempo-rary like Villella. He was sought out by many different contemporary Soviet choreographers: the possibilities they tapped point again to the spectacular career in the West that he might have enjoyed.

Soloviev's work with Alexidze came amid the most artistically abundant period of his career. In 1967, he created the male lead in Leonid Jacobson's *Land of Miracles*. Jacobson, who had begun choreographing for the Kirov during the 1940s, lived in an aesthetic universe parallel to Sergeyev's. The Kirov frequently performed Jacobson's short ballets, but his long ballets were not always well-edited by him— and just as problematically they dealt with controversial subjects. During the 1960s, he created ballets based on plays and poems by Aleksandr Blok and Vladimir Mayakovsky, each of whom occupied a dubious position in the Soviet cultural pantheon. Blok died of disease and despondency in Leningrad in 1921; in Moscow a decade later, Mayakovsky was found with a bullet in the head, ostensibly a suicide.

Jacobson had wanted to stage *Land of Miracles* for more than twenty years, Janice Ross reveals in her biography of Jacobson. And he had wanted to create a ballet for Soloviev. In *Land of Miracles*, Soloviev was Russian folk

hero Yasnyi Sokol ("Brave Falcon.") It was something of a switch for Soloviev, a role in the heroic emploi, although as Valery Panov writes in his 1978
memoir, it contained "abrupt changes from a primitive hero's dynamism to
a surprisingly gentle lyricism." It was "one of the most beautiful pieces I saw
him in," Soloviev's classmate Marina Vasilieva recalled. "The reason he was
so wonderful was that the character of Yasnyi Sokol was so much what he
was like himself. So Russian."

But just like Sergeyev in *The Distant Planet*, Jacobson seems not to have
been able to resist the temptation to exploit Soloviev's virtuosity. The fact
that the steps were seasoned with a folk dance flavor made the role more
difficult rather than less. Jacobson also wanted a lot of steps performed
turned-in, an uncomfortable adjustment for a classical dancer.

After the dress rehearsal, Soloviev was "more exhausted than I'd ever
seen him," Panov recalls.

Following Soloviev's premiere opposite Makarova, Panov danced the
role opposite Evteyeva. He was "better than Yura," Legat said, "because he
was more dynamic. Yura was more Romantic." The role was also danced by
Vadim Budarin. "Each of the three was absolutely wonderful," Ostaltsov said.
"They were each different and each perfect."

Admired by many, the ballet vanished within a year—and in Panov's
telling this was to Soloviev's relief. Nevertheless, it was after this that Jacobson submitted a proposal to the Kirov that he choreograph for Soloviev a
ballet based on the life of Soviet soldier Vasily Tiorkin. The theater rejected
that, but in 1972 Soloviev made his debut as Ali-Batyr in Jacobson's *Shurale*,
created in 1950 for Askold Makarov, who was known for his heroic style.

It was around this time that Igor Tchernichov cast Soloviev as Romeo
opposite Makarova in a semiabstract treatment set to Berlioz's symphony.
It was given a studio showing attended by Dudinskaya and Sergeyev, who
were violently opposed for some reason. One year later however, Kolpakova
chose to dance it with Vadim Gulyaev at her Creative Evening.

Tchernichov then began choreographing *Bolero* as a solo for Soloviev.
Each repetition in the music became another chapter in a young man's recital
of love's serial disappointments. At the end, he could no longer tolerate the
inexorable flood of his thoughts and ran to the apron of the stage as if to

stop the orchestra on Ravel's final notes. As in *Leningrad Symphony*, Soloviev was going to be bare-chested, his curls falling over his face. In rehearsal, he "worked like a dog," said Tchernichova, who was her husband's assistant. She recalled how beautifully Soloviev performed some movements with one knee bent to his chin, his hand cupping his heel. He generated sexual electricity as well as a certain philosophical comment. "We looked at him and thought what a huge talent he head," she recalled, a talent suited above all to contemporary works. "Classical dress was too confining for him."

But Tchernichov's *Bolero* was performed at the Kirov only in a later version he made for Valentina Gannibalova.

A piece that Tchernichov made for Fedicheva and Soloviev, together with an ensemble of eight women, did make it to the stage at her 1968 benefit, the same evening at which they danced *Oresteia*. This was titled *Roman Carnival* and performed to Berlioz's overture. At the time it was radical: steps and music with no possible dramatic plot or philosophical idea that could be extrapolated. There were simply kinetic theme and motifs, relationships of movement to music, geometric progressions through space. The performance was filmed live for television. Tchernichov's choreography explored new combinations and segues between standard steps. It enabled both leads to establish a contemporary bravura—not without causing them some strain in the process. But since they never performed it again, they had no chance to polish any difficulties.

For Kolpakova's 1969 evening, Oleg Vinogradov created a one-act ballet, *The Two*, in which Kolpakova and Soloviev were lovers who survived a global conflagration. "My choreography at that time was very complicated," Vinogradov said, "especially in pas de deux, but Yuri felt dance as if he were kissed by God."

32
BARYSHNIKOV

BARYSHNIKOV AND
SOLOVIEV REHEARSE
*THE CREATION OF
THE WORLD*, 1971

"O h, oh, oh, just wait until you come to Leningrad," Soloviev told Lisa in Australia. "There's this young dancer in the company... Ah, you should see Misha! He's such a fantastic dancer. And when the girls see Misha they all go crazy."

Baryshnikov had graduated from Pushkin's class on Rossi Street in 1967, doted upon by his teacher to the same degree that Pushkin had previously lavished attention on Nureyev. Like Nureyev, Baryshnikov enjoyed the rare distinction of entering the company as a soloist. Soloviev welcomed him graciously.

"It was always very important where you would be allowed to stand in class," Baryshnikov recalled, "because in Russia you always went to the place which was assigned, and it was actually at the suggestions of the senior dancers." Soloviev and Boris Bregvadze, who had been until Nureyev the company's foremost incarnation of exotic-heroic roles, installed Baryshnikov in "a nice place, not somewhere where you couldn't see the mirror. I was honored and flattered."

In class, Baryshnikov admired Soloviev's "very beautiful sculptured face, beautiful eyes, beautiful wavy hair. An extraordinary body, like a Michelangelo: his legs, back, shoulders, hands, knees." And he admired his work ethic. "Nobody danced cleaner than he in class."

They became boon companions. "Yura was a good friend. He was one of the people I was really close to. He was a very generous man, a true gent—a mensch." Baryshnikov became close to both Yuri and his family. "Together we went fishing with Baryshnikov," Igor recalled. "In 1968, we spent the summer in the south by the Black Sea. Yura, Tatiana, Alyonka [Alyona], my mother, Misha and me."

Baryshnikov appeared very much in the stocky yet pliant physical image of Soloviev, although he was by muscular comparison cherubic. Baryshnikov was two to three inches shorter than Soloviev, but proportionately his legs were slightly longer. Temperamentally they were quite different. Baryshnikov's plastique was brighter, sharper, tauter, qualities that he exploited and heightened in the West. Technically, too, they were very different. Baryshnikov's *à terre* work—his steps on the ground—"was absolutely genius." Legat said. "Nobody could do grande pirouette like Baryshnikov."

Here the working leg is extended in second position at a ninety-degree angle. That was the very step that had partly discouraged Soloviev from trying *Don Quixote*. Retired Kirov virtuoso Nikolai Zubkovsky spent time working with Soloviev to improve his execution. "He was very good," Legat said, "and he helped him, but still Yura's working leg would drop."

But *Don Quixote* was Baryshnikov's greatest classical success in Russia. Baryshnikov, however, was found wanting in two of Soloviev's greatest roles: the Poet in *Chopiniana* and *Sleeping Beauty*'s Bluebird. He had a great jump but not Soloviev's incredible ballon.

Everything about Baryshnikov's movement on the ground or in the air was lighter. Tchernichov, who had created Mercutio in his *Romeo and Juliet* especially for Baryshnikov, began his *Bolero* solo on both Baryshnikov and Soloviev. But eventually he worked only with Soloviev: the older dancer commanded greater emotional depth, physical and temperamental weight.

But Baryshnikov had a more European face, more refined features by the standards of the Kirov aesthetic of the time. For some this would make him, hands down, more suited for prince roles. Baryshnikov, however, was not born an orthodox Kirov prince. More animated than the dreamier Soloviev, Baryshnikov's temperament and his height meant that, given the Kirov's stringent adherence to emploi, certain classical roles would have been off-limits had he stayed in Russia. And yet he turned challenges to his advantage: in the face of both support and resistance within the ranks of the Kirov, Baryshnikov provided new perspectives on these roles.

In January 1970, a few months after his debut as Basilio, Baryshnikov made his debut as Prince Désiré in *Sleeping Beauty*. Baryshnikov's *puer delicato* comeliness was perfect for this Baroque hero and his technical execution was breathtaking. Soloviev was scheduled to dance *Sleeping Beauty* two days later. The sentiments of the Kirov community went out to the burden laid on Soloviev to defend his reputation amid the afterglow of his young rival's triumph. When Soloviev began to dance that night, the audience broke out in a storm of applause. He pulled out all the stops, and that night Baryshnikov left the theater with his head down. But his talent, energy, and determination were unstoppable. His zeal "was like an explosion, like the light at the end of the tunnel," said Vinogradov. "The word 'impossible' was unknown to him. Baryshnikov had initiative and he was always offering himself, but Yura never did: Yura needed to be asked."

33
NOT JOINING
THE PARTY

Народному Артисту **CCCP**

Тов. *СОЛОВЬЕВУ*
Юрию Владимировичу

За большие достижения в развитии
советского хореографического искусства

ПРЕЗИДИУМ ВЕРХОВНОГО СОВЕТА СССР

УКАЗОМ от 30 декабря 1973 г.

ПРИСВОИЛ ВАМ ПОЧЕТНОЕ ЗВАНИЕ

НАРОДНОГО АРТИСТА СССР

С О Ю З
СОВЕТСКИХ
СОЦИАЛИ-
СТИЧЕСКИХ
РЕСПУБЛИК

Председатель Президиума Верховного Совета СССР

Секретарь Президиума Верховного Совета СССР

Москва, Кремль, 30 декабря 1973 г.

TO COMRADE YURI V. SOLOVIEV THE SUPREME SOVIET OF THE USSR
AWARDS THE TITLE PEOPLES' ARTIST OF THE USSR

Пусть ложь всё покрыла, всем владеет, но в самом малом упрёмся: пусть владеет не через меня!

Lies have trumped everything, control everything, but in the smallest of things we hold fast… they reign not through me!

—Alexander Solzhenitsyn (1974)

Soloviev steadfastly resisted joining the Communist Party. Before each tour, he and Legat were given certain papers to study and be quizzed on concerning Marxism-Leninism and the Party's interpretation of current events. "We would read them over and over again," she said, "but we didn't understand anything and we didn't want to understand anything." Regardless of talent, a dancer who could not pass the test was struck from the travel roster.

The Party's dogmas and procedures "were not organic" for Soloviev, his brother said in an elegant piece of obfuscation. Igor had joined the Party to obtain housing for his family and for career advancement. Uncle Aleksandr, who joined in the fervor of postwar patriotic sentiment, also realized it was a key to professional advancement, all tenured professors had to be party members. Igor was likely stung by his older brother's scorn at his having done so.

Nevertheless, Soloviev garnered the government titles that were coveted and often campaigned for because of the perquisites they allowed. He received Honored Artist of the Russian Federation in 1964, People's Artist of the Russian Federation three years later, and the crowning title, People's Artist of the Soviet Union, in 1973, an honor equal to being knighted by the Queen.

Soloviev was also chosen to sit on the Kirov Art Soviet committee that voted on decisions of personnel and policy within the opera house. Although unwilling to serve on it, he was chosen, Legat said, "because he was a very honest person," but the committee was largely a pro forma enterprise. "The directors were doing whatever they needed to do."

"They asked me if I liked it or not," he told Legat about a repertory question. "I said, I don't like it, and they didn't like my answer." But most of the time he just kept quiet. Seemingly he was employing a customary ruse, lending the impression that he did not consider himself sufficiently qualified to offer opinion. "For example, they would ask members of the Art Soviet, 'Did you like that opera? How did you like it? Should we release it or not?'" And he said to Legat, "I was there, I was listening to it, but is it good? Is it bad? What do I know?"

ПРИСВОЕНИЕ ПОЧЕТНЫХ ЗВАНИЙ

Указами Президиума Верховного Совета РСФСР от 9 февраля присвоены почетные звания: за заслуги в развитии советского хореографического искусства — почетное звание народного артиста РСФСР артистам Ленинградского государственного Академического театра оперы и балета имени С. М. Кирова Соловьеву Юрию Владимировичу — солисту балета, заслуженному артисту РСФСР; Федичевой Калерии Ивановне — солистке балета, заслуженной артистке РСФСР.

ВЕДУЩИЕ солисты балета театра им. С. М. Кирова, молодые, талантливые, преданные искусству и трудолюбивые, Калерия Федичева и Юрий Соловьев давно завоевали сердца зрителей. Их имена хорошо известны далеко за пределами нашего города, нашей страны. Всюду, где бы ни выступали эти выдающиеся представители ленинградского балета, их сопровождал грандиозный успех. В 1961 году во время гастролей в Лондоне, например, имел место беспрецедентный случай. Перед последним показом «Спящей красавицы» на имя дирекции театра пришло письмо, подписанное тремястами зрителями.

Просили поставить на партию Голубой птицы Ю. Соловьева.

Просьба была выполнена, и, вопреки законам академической сцены, Соловьеву после нескольких оваций пришлось бисировать. Три года спустя, во время гастролей театра в Нью-Йорке, американские газеты писали: «Ни одна труппа в мире не имеет танцовщика, который мог бы сравниться с Ю. Соловьевым... Он самый великий танцовщик... Голубая птица Ю. Соловьева стоила того, чтобы ее ждали три года».

Газета «Сан-Франциско Экзаминер» писала: «Ирина Колпакова, Калерия Федичева, Алла Сизова — три, возможно, из шести лучших балерин мира». А во время гастролей в Англии летом 1966 года газета «Вечер» отмечала: «...Наряду с большой женственностью и грацией К. Федичева равно обладает всеми необходимыми техническими качествами, которые делают ее совершенной балериной».

Большая работа в спектаклях текущего репертуара театра, частые гастрольные поездки за рубеж не мешают К. Федичевой и Ю. Соловьеву все время совершенствовать свое мастерство.

Ежедневно с утра до позднего вечера их можно видеть в репетиционных залах. В репертуаре каждого из них более 12 ответственных партий. У К. Федичевой это Одетта и Одиллия в «Лебедином озере», Китри в «Дон-Кихоте», Раймонда, Хуана в «Жемчужи-не», Лауренсия и др. У Соловьева — принц в «Лебедином озере», принц и Голубая птица в «Спящей красавице», Кийно в «Жемчужине» и др.

Последние работы К. Федичевой (Фея Сирени в «Спящей красавице», Эгина в «Спартаке») и Ю. Соловьева (Фрондосо в «Лауренсия», Принц в «Золушке») имели огромный успех у зрителей.

С большим вниманием относятся молодые артисты к расширению своего концертного репертуара. Очень интересны в этом смысле подготовленные ими хореографические новеллы на музыку Скрябина, Шуберта. Много работают они и над произведениями советских композиторов. Успеху «Ленинградской симфонии» на последних гастролях в Англии, бесспорно, способствовал яркий талант К. Федичевой и Ю. Соловьева. Сейчас у каждого из них — большая, интересная работа: Калерия Федичева готовит партию Махмене Бану в «Легенде о любви», Юрий Соловьев — партию Ясного Сокола в балете «Страна чудес».

И сегодня, поздравляя Калерию Федичеву и Юрия Соловьева с высоким званием народных артистов РСФСР, желаем им творческих успехов, интересных партий в новых спектаклях, желаем им всегда радовать зрителей своим искусством.

HONORED ARTISTS OF THE RSFSR [RUSSIAN REPUBLIC OF THE SOVIET UNION] FEDICHEVA AND SOLOVIEV NAMED PEOPLES' ARTISTS OF THE RSFSR, 1967

Nevertheless, he was not always so sanguine. After joining the Kirov in 1958, Nikita Dolgushin had distinguished himself in lyric and Romantic roles. Dolgushin was the great actor; he "immediately had wonderful acting skills," Legat recalled. His face was considered fascinating and aristocratic. But he became a nemesis to artistic director Sergeyev, whose ex-wife, former ballerina Feya Balabina, had declared backstage that young Dolgushin would be her ex-husband's successor. Dolgushin left the Kirov in 1962 and went to dance in Novosibirsk in Siberia, which together with Akademgorodok and other research centers, was an intellectual, scientific and cultural hub.

Dolgushin returned to the Kirov during White Nights 1968 for performances of *Swan Lake* and *Legend of Love*. A motion was submitted whether to readmit Dolgushin to the Kirov. Soloviev's vote was nay—seemingly a rare case of him succumbing to professional jealousy. He later told Lisa that he disliked Dolgushin and thought his mannerisms were fussy. But in any case, Sergeyev himself did not want Dolgushin back, which settled the matter. (Dolgushin later told Diane Solway that Soloviev "was an absolutely faultless dancer," but "lacked nobility and lyricism.")

If someone could share information of interest, Soloviev was always open to discussion. He spent many an hour talking to a uniquely well-rounded Party director in the Kirov. Wasn't it amazing, he said to Legat, how much this man knew! In America, they could go off together with him despite making up a unit of three, two short of the mandatory minimum of five prescribed for any type of excursion. The man even told Soloviev to be aware of another principal dancer, whom he'd bumped into in the men's room of the Big House. That dancer was a snitch. "We were so surprised," Legat said. "Him?—of all people!"

Nureyev's defection did not end the summonses. Soloviev himself received to the Big House. Over the next decade, there would be more interrogations after Makarova's defection in 1970 and Baryshnikov's four years later. More than once, Legat waited in their car for an hour or ninety minutes. When she asked what had transpired, he was evasive: "No, it's OK, they were just questioning me. Nothing happened; everything is all right."

The fact that "Cosmic Yuri" would not join the Party began to rankle in the corridors of state power. For his part, Soloviev was equally resentful about being pursued. In 1964, when he was playing with his amateur jazz combo, he had rebuffed a Party emissary by saying he'd rather play the trumpet than attend party meetings. "That was the way I sent him to the devil," he recounted to Lisa in Australia. "He understood what I meant," he added with a quick smile that said he was pleased with himself.

When the Kirov performed in Moscow, they were customarily given a gala send-off at the airport attended by top brass from the Ministry of Culture. At one going-away celebration, Culture Minister Piotr Demichev approached Soloviev. "Look, Yura, you've got such a high position. You're the embodiment of the Soviet Man, of what a Russian Communist is. You need to join the Party."

"Yes, it would be an enormous honor for me," Soloviev said with deadpan irony, "but I don't feel that I'm sufficiently mature to make a good Communist." Demichev implicitly understood how he was being treated.

As a dancer garnered more success, more government pressure could ensue. "They *made* me join the Party," Vikulov claimed. "I came back from winning the Gold Medal in Varna and they sat me down at a table. They told me: 'Now you write a letter requesting to join the Party.'"

Soloviev ridiculed his friend Aleksandr Shavrov for succumbing to pressure and joining the Party. "It's easy for you to resist, you are a People's Artist of the Soviet Union," Shavrov retorted. "I had to join. I've been divorced three times, and it's the only way I can survive." Given official puritanism, he did have no other choice. A dancer who was Party secretary in the ballet frequently buttonholed Legat: "You know, Tatiana, if you'll join then maybe Yura will join too. You've got to do it." She told Yuri and they laughed about it. But then the secretary was demoted, although he remained in the company. Nevertheless, he complained to Legat: "I lost my job because you couldn't get Yura to join the Party." He came to Soloviev and asked him to lend him some money, which was forthcoming.

Tatiana recounted that more than once it was also suggested to her that she keep her eyes open to see what was going on in the company. She received the prompts with finely tuned feigned incomprehension and ignored them.

It was Dudinskaya and Sergeyev's ability to hold on to power without joining the Party that perhaps emboldened Soloviev. Lisa imagines he reasoned that he was at least as well-known as they, so why should he join? But the power couple were consummate politicians who meticulously plotted their course, something that Soloviev had no ability or inclination to do—ever.

SOLOVIEV ON FAR LEFT STANDS APART FROM A GROUP OF LENINGRAD
WORTHIES AWARDED A STATE-SPONSORED WINTERTIME JUNKET TO SOCHI
ON THE BLACK SEA. NOTE THE THREE UNSAVORY CHARACTERS ON THE
OPPOSITE CORNER: THE HIGH-BOOTED INDIVIDUAL STILL SPORTING THE
1930'S NKVD [SECRET POLICE] GARB, THE UNRECONSTRUCTED STALINIST
DISPLAYING HIS IDOL'S ICONIC CURVED PIPE AND PYOTR RACHINSKY, KIROV
THEATER DIRECTOR, A FORMER LENINGRAD FIRE DEPARTMENT OFFICIAL

PART 3:

OUT OF

BOUNDS

A GATHERING OF STUDENTS AND FACULTY AT THE UNIVERSITY
OF MELBOURNE RUSSIAN DEPARTMENT, 1969

PHOTO TAKEN BY LISA FROM THE WINGS OF HER
MAJESTY'S THEATRE, MELBOURNE

Young like this ballet group

Mr. Michael Edgley (above), the 25-year-old entrepreneur who organised the tour of the Russian Classical Ballet, arrived in Melbourne yesterday excited about their Sydney reception.

"It's been fantastic," he said, "especially among the young people. I think the Australian Ballet Company is to be congratulated for the way it has fostered ballet here and got the young people interested."

He said that the Sydney season, of three weeks, was fully booked by the end of the first week. Extra performances were arranged for the final days.

Mr. Edgley, who has made seven visits to Russia, first saw the company in Moscow 18 months ago. He booked them on the spot.

He said the company was formed by the Russian Minister for Culture (Mrs. Ekaterina Furtseva) because of criticism that Russian ballet companies were not preparing modern works.

Fifty-fifty

She commissioned the company to give equal emphasis to classical and modern ballet and told them they could have any artists they wanted.

Galeria Fedicheva and Yuri Soloviev are prima ballerina and leading dancer of the Leningrad-Kirov Theatre of Opera and Ballet. Elena Cherkasskaya is a soloist of the Bolshoi Theatre of Moscow.

They, and 37 other dancers, have put together a programme which, according to Mr. Edgley has been an outstanding success in Russia. They are on their first overseas tour.

The company will begin their Melbourne season at Her Majesty's on Monday.

Is freedom anything else than the right to live as we wish?
Nothing else.

—Epictetus

As Russian majors at the University of Melbourne, Lisa and her classmates "jumped at any chance to meet visiting Soviets," she recalled. There were few such opportunities. First settled in 1788 as a British penal colony, Australia was an island continent in greater proximity to Antarctica than to the closest point of Western civilization. Unlike in the United States and Europe, Australia's cities had no Soviet cultural centers showing movies, distributing propaganda and providing access to the contemporary Russian language. Lisa and her classmates were taught by émigrés, either those born abroad or those who had not had even a whiff of the Motherland since the Red Army stormed the Reichstag in 1945. With the exception of Lisa and another valiant soul, Kim Bastin, a pale, blond-bearded young man who always wore the Esperantist's green star on his lapel, the Russian majors were children of largely uneducated émigrés, taken prisoner during the war, used as slave laborers for the German armament factories. At the end of the war, Stalin insisted that the Soviet laborers be repatriated, but some managed to remain in camps in Germany and eventually emigrate. Many went to the antipodes. They spoke a patois of deteriorated Russian, but they made sure that their children attended Saturday Russian classes.

Lisa and the more motivated of her fellow students devised their own ways to learn contemporary Russian. Lisa volunteered for everything. Rather than take summer jobs, she would translate for visiting delegations of every stripe. Among them were Australian Bolshevik-type trade unionists who wanted to schmooze with their fellow proletarians aboard Soviet Merchant Marine ships delivering cargo to Melbourne. She became so trusted as "politically reliable" that the Pompolit (ship political officers) would ask her to take groups of sailors on excursions to the seaside for the day. "Twenty burly blokes on a 'tram' to St. Kilda Beach," she recalled, "impeccable behavior, despite some prodigious beer consumption."

So it was that the students amassed a crazy quilt of specialized vocabularies, varying from naval to theatrical to jargon of Russian science and agriculture. They were highly competitive about who knew more current Russian slang and was thus top gun. Driving force in their adventures was Alexander—Sasha—Grishin, one year ahead of Lisa, a professor's son and president of the University's Russian Club.

During the third week of May 1969, Igor Moiseyev's "40 Stars of the Russian Ballet" arrived in Melbourne, having just opened a three-month tour in Sydney. The group was a hodgepodge of soloists from the Bolshoi, Kirov, Maly and Moiseyev companies. On the second night of the season, Grishin's gang, including Lisa, went backstage before the performance at the old and ornate Her Majesty's Theater. "Knowing all the tricks," Grishin was armed with a University of Melbourne letter of introduction he had finagled. He found out that Gennadi Vostrikov was the Komsomol chief for the performing troupe. Sasha invited some of the dancers to an impromptu party the next evening after the performance at one of the student's lodgings. Grishin was savvy enough to know to invite them directly, people more or less their age, rather than risk getting stuck with any of the old fogeys in charge who might want to tag along. Sasha asked Gennadi to choose which dancers they should invite and he agreed with alacrity.

Out of the corner of her eye, Lisa saw a man standing toward the back of the stage. In ballet tights and T-shirt, hands on hips, his head down, he shifted his weight from one foot to the other, stretching the arch of each in turn. He looked very alone, "like a small child standing at the edge of a playground, pretending to be occupied because nobody had asked him to play." She felt a pang in her heart. "Let's invite *him*," she said to Sasha, as they walked over to him. Grishin introduced himself and extended the invitation. A smile slowly appeared on his face—"as broad as the steppes of Russia and as warm as the summer sun."

"Sasha Grishin," Lisa's friend announced, extending his hand. Soloviev responded in kind: "Yura Soloviev."

"40 Stars" was presented in Melbourne by native impresario Michael Edgley in partnership, of course, with Goskontsert, the Soviet bureau for foreign appearances by performers. That spring, Soloviev was nursing an injured leg and could not dance well enough to go on the Kirov tour, but had been sent on the Australian tour, told simply to dance as well as he could. On this type of barnstorming tour, audience and critical discrimination was not expected to be razor-honed and there was good hard currency to be made for the state. Over the summer, the Kirov would be touring Japan, and once "40 Stars" finished in August, he would rejoin them for their last performances there. "Goskontsert was working Yura like a rented mule to earn hard currency," Lisa stated. "He and the other dancers were given a minuscule per diem paid directly by Edgeley International."

Edgley was the son of a British vaudevillian émigré who had become a highly successful impresario Down Under. He was still in his twenties when his father died and he took over the Melbourne-based business. Lisa knew of Edgley: Australian society was small, and they both moved in the same circles. He had already been awarded an MBE for his achievements. He was highly intelligent, tall, handsome and fashionably dressed in bell-bottomed pinstripe suits of the finest fabrics. He was proud of his "ordinary tastes" in entertainment, of the way they were in sync with the broad Australian public, thus apparently explaining his success.

As soon as the "40 Stars" arrived in Sydney, the first city on tour, Edgley had become fascinated by the seductive Fedicheva, Soloviev's partner on this tour. Brazen as always, she took no pains at all to conceal their relationship from the ubiquitous scrutiny of KGB attached to the tour.

As the days went by in Melbourne, Lisa and Grishin whittled down the dancers they could trust, and every night after the show picked them up to go out. At first Lisa conversed with Soloviev using her two Russian-English pocket dictionaries. He would hold the maroon Russian English one, she the green English-Russian. Her Russian and his English progressed to a point where they could discuss any topic freely. His English as well as his French were sufficient to allow him to read a newspaper article, or to decipher a review, or pick his way through a book. She found him "highly intuitive, in language and in most ways." He had read not only Russian classics, but such items in the English-language canon that were available in translation: Defoe's *Robinson Crusoe*, Erich Maria Remarque, Jack London, Hemingway and Dreiser. They talked about *Sister Carrie*, about Somerset

Maugham, whose writing Lisa loved. Soloviev had read Maugham's short story "Miss Sadie Thompson"—the fact that it was anticlerical made it ripe for translation.

Sergei Esenin was Soloviev's favorite poet. He knew some of his poems by heart and he recited some to her. He liked Esenin because he wrote about nature, and he liked Esenin's late poems: full of hurt, disappointment and rage. Esenin had only recently been republished after years of suppression,

LISA DANCING IN MELBOURNE UNIVERSITY RUSSIAN DEPARTMENT ENSEMBLE. PHOTO: IGOR MEZHAKOV-KORYAKIN

AT FAMILY BEACH HOUSE IN PORTSEA, NEAR MELBOURNE

his work causing a furor among the *shestisesytniki*.

Soloviev had a generosity of spirit. Lisa was about the same age as Igor, and to her he behaved very much like the older brother. He was a talented, nurturing teacher, guiding her and helping her with her Russian assignments. Particularly memorable was the way he explained the baffling Russian verbs of motion as they walked together in the park. It was accompanied by his pantomime of jumping, flapping wings and sailing motions accompanying the verb, punching them in together with the pronouns they required. "From then on, when I used the verb I could see him." She attributes to him her fluency in Russian, her success in college and graduation with 1st Class Honors (Summa cum Laude) in Russian studies.

He told her stories of his life, travels and experiences. "These and his deeply traditional Russian way of thinking were revelatory to me. So evocative of the novels I had read, yet here was someone from the twentieth century. He was the essence of what I loved about Russia: nobility and sincerity, the capacity for enormous courage and self-sacrifice at the heart of the Russian spirit. And he looked very Russian, very northern with his pale skin, platinum blond hair and blue eyes like ice on fire. Straight from the fairy tale of Ivan and the Firebird."

Soloviev, on the other hand, was intrigued by her stories of growing up around the world: in Paris, in former Maharajah of Pitapuram's palace in Madras (now Chennai), her years of convent boarding school in Kodaikanal in South India and later in England, and life in the United States. They discussed Rudyard Kipling; he had read *The Jungle Book*. He had also danced in Delhi. She missed the food, which she remembered as delicious. "Oh, no, too hot, just like the weather," he retorted. They both found the human and animal suffering and the poverty appalling.

Konstantin Sergeyev's son Nikolai was also on the tour, partnering his wife, Svetlana Efremova. Both were members of the Kirov and both were very short. Nikolai was perhaps only an inch or so taller than Lisa's own five foot two. But, unlike Efremova, Sergeyev's dancing, in Lisa's opinion, was of a quality that no one but the director's son could have gotten away with. Soloviev, in fact, told Lisa that his relationship with the senior Sergeyev had been irrevocably ruined in 1965, when he watched Nikolai's graduation performance from the wings of the Kirov. Soloviev could not suppress a snort of laughter and surprise. It was reported to Sergeyev, who never forgave him.

Soloviev certainly understood that he had learned much from Sergeyev, but he was disenchanted with his self-serving director. "You can call me any nickname you want except 'Yuronka,'" he told Lisa, Sergeyev by now having appropriated Boris Shavrov's pet diminutive. For Lisa, Soloviev performed a biting, hilarious pantomime of Sergeyev slinking about him in rehearsal, smarmy and intrusive.

Soloviev was an adroit mime, and most of his imitations were equally amusing but a good bit kinder. He might see a dog trotting down the street and mimic its gait, its manner, and then start an improvisation about the dog's reminiscence of the life it had lived and whom it had loved—"understanding, sweet and touching, albeit somewhat melancholy."

They laughed a great deal. Soloviev had a broad, generous laugh that made her laugh, too.

At the ripe old age of eight, Lisa had been packed off to boarding school. "Children like me had all learned to comfort ourselves. It produced an independence of spirit, perhaps, but in many also an aloofness, alienation or a preference for solitude." By contrast, Soloviev was very sociable, but at the same time he seemed to lack any psychological defenses at all. He "was completely incapable of consoling himself; a barb aimed at him would always hit the mark. He had no carapace. The slings and arrows of outrageous fortune cut him to the quick." Today she wonders if it was a trait from the Gamazins, his grandmother Olga and her son Vladimir, his withdrawn, invalid father.

Soloviev did not underestimate his value as a dancer: "I know what I am," he said to Lisa. Yet it was apparent that Soloviev had internalized criticism about his physique, believing his body was not the right body for ballet, perhaps responding as well to such criticisms concerning emploi.

Lisa was flabbergasted to learn that he considered his archetypal Slavic face unattractive. "Handsome, ha! As if I'm handsome!"

He hated the growth in his right eye pocket, imagining it was the first thing anybody saw looking at his face. "Why not have it removed?" she asked. "In the Soviet Union?" he replied. "You must be joking; they'd take out the whole eye!" She noticed he was also very mildly cross-eyed, which gave him a dreamy, otherworldly look. It haunted her.

She saw that his elbows were hyperextended and understood how that aided the aerial suspension he achieved, the slightly distended elbows creating their own parabolic illusion. She saw too that his feet were unique. "He not only points his feet, but seems to speak with them," Doris Hering had noted in her *Dance Magazine* review of the Kirov in New York in 1964. The pointing seemed to come naturally, or rather it was by now almost a furling reflex: his ankles wrapping past 90 degrees, then the arch and toes curling even further in what was nearly a full semicircle.

"Not very good," he said about her own arch.

"Good enough," was her retort. "But his reminded me of lily pads." Flat on the surface of the water—but supple, folding into themselves at the lightest touch.

Why, she asked, did he wear his blond curls in what looked like "a self-inflicted haircut"? Short back, sides shorn to the hairline. "Grow out your gorgeous mane, it's like a lion's and you *are* a Leo." And he might let his sideburns grow out a bit as well. Long hair on Russian men was a political statement, an identification with the West that was ridiculed and vilified by the authorities. Frequently men were upbraided by Party authorities, even stopped on the street and ordered to cut their hair by the police.

Soloviev could also be mulishly stubborn, bloody-mindedness being a very Russian trait, and had a way of pressing his point. By the time the tour had progressed to Perth, its final stop, Lisa had begun to feel more assured of her command of the Russian language. One day she mused out loud that she would like to learn German next, a language whose name could not be spoken in her father's family. "Oh, no!" Soloviev responded in mock horror. Slipping on her horn-rimmed reading glasses, he said, "Then I'll have to walk around like a German martinet!" He proceeded to give a caricature of one until he had assured himself that the point had been taken. Clearly, the Solovievs' attitude on the matter of Germany was the same as Lisa's French father.

Only rarely did they discuss politics, although Lisa recalled a heated argument about definitions of the state vs. the government. She had used the word *pravitel'stvo*—government—in a sentence about the Soviet Union. He scoffed and corrected her: *gosudarstvo*—the state—was the correct term.

Lisa argued they were one and the same. In the "Soyuz"—Soviet Union—there is a difference, he insisted; the state was the body of the people, its representatives carrying out their will. Lisa argued that the people running the government were *not* in fact carrying out the people's will. "Is there anybody in power who is not a 'representative of the people,' that is, a Communist Party member?" she spat back. Soloviev clenched his jaw. "This may be so," he replied slowly in measured tones. "But when you come to the Soviet Union, if you use the word *pravitel'stvo* rather than *gosudarstvo,* you will be making a mistake."

Lisa's heart sank; she realized she had wounded him. They were in obvious agreement about who held the power cards but she had demonstrated the gulf between their worlds. "I had grown up assured of my inalienable human rights, including the right to express my opinions. He had grown up knowing he had no such rights at all." A prolonged silence ensued.

Soloviev was a postwar patriotic Russian who espoused the collective ideals of his people without any identification with the Communist Party—similar to the nationalistic identification of *Deutschtum* among the Germans. He correctly assumed that the motivation for most to join the Party was careerism and opportunism, not ideals. He was not at all blind to the current state of affairs within the USSR, but things were getting better little by little. Sooner or later Russia would be more like the rest of Europe. Certainly he subscribed to the *shestidesiatnik* mantra that "It's not like Paris yet, but…" They spent a lot of time with young dancer Aleksandr Godunov, who partnered Tatar ballerina Ai-Gul Kasina. Godunov was twenty, and had grown up in the Baltics. He was Lisa's age, was sallow, skinny with a mouthful of metal choppers—not at all the Apollo Belvedere he later became. Always hunting for a meal, he was obsessed with saving his hard currency to buy gifts to bribe himself into the Bolshoi. He often brought up the topic with Soloviev. "Talent alone is not enough," he would explain to Lisa, typically frank about the Realpolitik of Soviet life. He had a different Weltanschauung than that of Soloviev's generation, who generally believed that Russia and the Soviet Union were synonymous. Godunov was highly verbal, very funny, quick-tempered and impulsive. Soloviev was very much a mentor as well as a friend to Godunov. He was constantly trying to stop the younger dancer from running off at the mouth in a way that could be dangerous for him. More than once Soloviev came to his rescue.

One evening, Godunov had hauled, rather than gallantly escorted, Kasina off the stage at the end of a pas de deux that had proceeded more along the lines of a tussle than a duet. Igor Moiseyev decided on the spot to send him back immediately to the Soviet Union. It could have been a career-ending incident for the talented young dancer. Soloviev intervened, talking with Moiseyev alone for hours at the hotel that same night.

He tried to calm him down but also indicated, showing no small amount of courage, that he too would leave if Godunov was forced to. Moiseyev finally relented.

On one of the dancers' rare days off, Godunov was criticizing the Soviets and Soloviev was responding tolerantly until, in exasperation, he finally said to Godunov, "Now you're not speaking as a Russian." "I *am* a Russian," Godunov insisted. They dropped the topic, partly because Soloviev knew, as the saying then went, that this was not a "subject for discussion." Ten years later, Godunov defected in New York while on tour with the Bolshoi.

35
"BELIEVE"

会うのは別かりの始まり

Au no wa wakari no hajimari.

Meeting is the beginning of parting.
—*Japanese proverb*

erformances are going well here, my legs are a little better,"
Soloviev wrote to Lisa from New Zealand, which was the
"40 Stars'" next stop after closing in Melbourne on June 24.
Next they went to Brisbane. When Lisa arrived there, she
learned that Edgley had been urging Fedicheva and Solo-
viev to defect. Both, however, were saying that it was impossible because
of family back in Russia. Besides, things at home were changing for the
better day by day.

"I am a Russian. I love my country. I do not want to leave it," Soloviev insisted. In his hotel room, he stared at a picture of five-year-old Alyona
taken right before he'd left Leningrad. In it she poked her head from behind
a doll. She had proven resistant to his attempt to snap a keepsake for his tour.
Churlish over what was going to be his long absence, she at first insisted he
photograph only the doll, not her. Then, as he said goodbye to her, he promised he would come back between the conclusion of the "40 Stars" tour in
Singapore early in August and the Kirov season in Tokyo a week later. Alyona
refused to believe him, repeating, "Goodbye 'til autumn, Papa."

"She was right," Soloviev said to Lisa with tears in his eyes. "I won't be
coming back between the two tours. And now what would happen to her
if I didn't come back at all…?"

Lisa herself never asked Soloviev to defect. She realized that emo-
tionally he could not withstand the stress of such a rupture. Soviet diplo-
mats would have been permitted to interview him and unleash a full bat-
tery of persuasion techniques: intimidation threats, emotional appeals.
Accompanying that would be a barrage of letters or even phone calls produced on instruction by the security services: wrenching pleas to return
from family, friends and colleagues. Lisa knew, too, that defection opened
the possibility that his family "would have been thrown to the wolves."

He was aware of how endangered any and all intimates would be, of how perniciously blood guilt was a cornerstone of Soviet system. Soloviev's father and brother could certainly have been harmed, but they had little status in life save as his first-degree relatives. Anna would have performed her own self-immolation. Uncle Aleksandr as well as Aunt Mira, both Party members, would have lost their status, housing and perquisites. Aleksandr, a tenured professor; Mira, an executive in the Moscow City Administration—their professional rank was conditional on absolute loyalty to the government. Nor did Tatiana have any influential patrons or family support, only a sickly younger brother, a factory worker. If the authorities had wished to set an example, Tatiana could have been terminated by the theater as punishment for his treason and reduced to doing anything, even sweeping snow in the streets, in order to keep her permit for residence in Leningrad. Alyona, as had happened to "children of traitors," might have been dispatched to a far-distant orphanage never to be seen again. After three years, if she survived, "she wouldn't even know her name," as a colleague of his later put it.

And of course the years of Stalin's most genocidal suppression were very fresh in recollection. "We all knew what our families had been through," said the Kirov's Vikulov. Born in 1938, he "grew up hearing about the Great Terror. How they would huddle together in fear in the apartment when they heard the Black Marias pull up during the night, praying together that thesecret police wouldn't come to their door. Praying they would go to somebody else's door. Doors of their friends, their neighbors. Just please not them."

"You know what happened to Pushkin?" Soloviev asked Lisa, and then abruptly went silent. Only years later did she learn what he meant. Following Nureyev's defection, Pushkin had been brought to Leningrad's Bolshoi Dom and questioned brutally about, among other things, his own alleged affair with his former student. During one workover by the KGB, Pushkin suffered his first heart attack. "He was sick with worry," said the Kirov's Arkadii Ivanenko, a former student of his. "He held all that inside of him, all that worrying. And Yura understood this perfectly." And had, of course, himself already experienced traumatic sessions with the KGB.

But, anyway, he was coming back in November. Indeed, where Soloviev was concerned, the authorities did not seem particularly alarmed. It was instead Fedicheva's behavior that became fodder for promotion-inducing denunciations to Moscow. Fedicheva proudly and flagrantly displayed an enormous ring of linked gold nuggets that Edgley gave her. She also flaunted the extensive dental work he had paid for. Like Godunov and so many Soviets, her mouth was a mass of cavity-pitted teeth and primitive dentistry. Indeed, sheer envy that she'd now been delivered from the toothaches commonly suffered might have provoked the greatest wrath. Bryzhkin, the chief KGB officer assigned to the tour, was sufficiently preoccupied with her not to spend much time vetting Soloviev.

In Brisbane, he and Lisa listened to records he had bought, including some by Russian bard Bulat Okudzhava, whose LPs were difficult to obtain in Russia. Together they translated the words and she learned the songs, as he liked her to sing to him. Lisa had brought her Russian textbooks, some records and a battery-operated portable record player. Among the records were the original cast albums of *Funny Girl* and *Hair*. Together, they liked to sing the Fifth Dimension's hit medley of "Aquarius/Let the Sunshine In," but translating the words from "Sodomy" provided a significant lexical challenge. The words themselves were certainly not in contemporary dictionaries. Soloviev shared her embarrassment as she tried to cobble together Russian translations. He ducked his head—were such things actually in the public domain? By tacit mutual consent, they moved on to the next album track. A propos, he told her he had seen only one pornographic book before he traveled to the West. He and his class buddies had read a forbidden *samizdat* translation of a Chinese book, likely the contribution of a Chinese exchange student studying in Leningrad.

Soloviev indeed, was in ways the very model of Soviet *pudeur*. Once he made mention of "the women's disease… you know, what happens to you every month."

"It's a disease if it doesn't happen," she corrected him, explaining that it was a completely normal biological process. "Oh yes, that is right," he conceded. At nineteen, the convent-and-ballet-schooled Lisa was indubitably naïve, but she had aced her science courses and knew what most adolescents in the West knew. Yet indeed, there were many occasions she would look at him in amazement and wonder: how in the world, at age 28, had his ignorance about basic human biology persisted?

Following Brisbane was a season in Adelaide and then one in Perth, the final stop. Perth was Edgley's hometown and the dancers spent time at the mansion his parents had built. He kept a dune buggy there and took Soloviev out for a ride. Edgley patronized a tailor there, and now ordered an expensive wool suit as a gift for Soloviev in the latest Mod fashion—double-breasted, widely pinstriped, with bell-bottomed trousers. Lisa went with Soloviev to that elegant establishment for a fitting. He put it on and jerked it right off again. "I'm not wearing this. I'll give it to my brother when I get back. He's shorter, they can alter the pants. I just don't have the same shape as Michael!" Edgley was six feet tall and rangy; but Yuri did keep it for himself.

Defection was indeed impossible, but the resourceful Edgley was not to be put off. He had devised a plan to bring both Fedicheva and Soloviev back to Australia: they could appear as guest artists with the Australian Ballet, which was based in Melbourne. The company was to make a tour of Australia in November; Edgley was able to secure an invitation for the two

Russians to join it as guest artists.

On one of the last evenings in Perth, Edgley gave an after-performance party at the stately family home for a dozen trusted members of "40 Stars," "*svoi*"—one of us—is one of the many expressions in the highly communal Russian worldview. Whether within the family itself or in group of friends and intimates, the world is sharply divided between "us" and "them."

As soon as he arrived, Soloviev surveyed the living room. A look of delight appeared on his face. "I want you to meet someone." He led her to a slight, dark man, clearly a Soviet, someone she had not noticed before. "Lizochka, please meet so-and-so…" Soloviev said that the pleasant-looking man was a *skripach*—a violinist. Lisa froze. She had learned from him to be wary of Soviets by then. He had once warned her when among them, "Do not to look at me with those eyes." Immediately she was concerned for his safety, having grown sensitive to his silent, reflexive cues. He thought her rigid expression meant she didn't understand. He repeated in French, *un violoniste*. The man played first violin in the orchestra. "Oh, you should hear him play!" Soloviev said, his eyes shining.

"He is the best musician in the orchestra, the most talented. We often ask him to play for us before performances. He is the most talented of all of us, the dancers, musicians, everyone." He seemed to be hearing the music as he spoke.

Three days after celebrating her twentieth birthday on July 30, Lisa returned to Melbourne, while Soloviev and his thirty-nine fellow "Stars" went on to Singapore for a week's season.

"Today was the first performance," he wrote Lisa, "but I did not dance well because it's very hot here and I cannot breathe." Nor could he sleep easily, but "it seems that we will be able to return to Australia in November. Just need to get Goskontsert to agree on this, but with the [Australian] Ballet management everything is very good."

From there he did go directly to Tokyo, as his daughter had intuited that he would. The Kirov had just performed in Osaka and he was waiting for them to arrive in Tokyo. "Today Kalya [Fedicheva] and I are sitting together and celebrating my birthday a bit," he wrote on August 10.

"On the twelfth, we dance *Sleeping Beauty*, I—Bluebird, Kalya—Lilac

Fairy. It will probably be very difficult as there will be only one rehearsal."

Edgley had also arrived in Tokyo: "Michael, Kalya and I spoke with our director about the trip to Australia and the director approved it. You cannot imagine how happy I am! Now all we have to do is get the approval of Goskontsert."

A little later he wrote her again from Tokyo: "The tour here is going well. I danced Bluebird, *Cinderella, Swan Lake.* Very good reviews. I am not dancing now; my leg is hurting again. I want to heal my leg as quickly as possible, so I can go to Australia."

Edgley then went to Moscow to attempt to negotiate with Goskontsert. But before he could speak to its representatives, he received a telegram from the director of the Australian Ballet. The invitation was withdrawn. For some reason, they were no longer interested. Lisa never knew exactly what had happened. But she was acquainted with the then-director, recalling him as "imperious and shrewd, a thoroughly nasty piece of work." An acid remark he made to her some time later convinced her that malice and sabotage had been at work on the Australian side.

Soloviev had gone to rest his legs at a spa-sanatorium in Sochi, in the southern region of Krasnodar. He had appealed for help to Dr. Natalia Karasevich, a surgeon who was an ardent fan of his and a friend to him and his family; she managed to secure a place for him there. That meant a travel permit to go through Moscow and see Edgley again. Edgley and Fedicheva later joined him in Sochi.

"There are people here, but I don't want to meet anyone," Soloviev wrote Lisa in a letter Edgley smuggled out. "In general, as soon as I left… I became a very sullen and angry person… Here it is very beautiful, many beautiful flowers… Warm sea and sun, but I cannot rest… I think day and night… All sorts of bad thoughts come into my head… The thing is, as Michael said, we cannot come to Australia in October, because the 'Australian Ballet' (director) [*sic*] sent him a letter saying they don't need us. You realize what a blow it was for me and you must be able to understand, how bad things are for me… everything has turned out so badly… especially as I do not know when… perhaps even never… Michael only got agreement on a tour in '72 but that is so long to wait… by then… It is all so horribly bad… After the tour I didn't have any discussions in Moscow (Bryzhkin) [*sic*], so all is well with that... I am all alone, it is horrible to suffer alone, pining, it would be better to be working, not resting... all my hopes have been dashed. I don't know how I am going to go on living, what to do now..."

He closed with three requests: that she study hard, that she not forget him. "Believe" was the third request.

A tempestuous outburst and then radio silence. She never heard from him again. But a year later, a manila envelope was sent to her, containing two issues of *Dance and Dancers,* with pictures and reviews from the Kirov's summer 1970 season. Lisa mourned for what might have been. But she was elated to see he had taken her advice: he'd grown out his hair and added sideburns as well. She appreciated his self-assertion. She hoped this showed she had brought him not suffering alone, but a measure of self-realization.

The envelope had no return address but the postmark was from London. She knew no one there. But she knew Soloviev had her address. Lisa assumed that a kind English friend had sent it on his behalf. "A very English thing to do," she says today. Decades later, she deduced it had been Balletomane Terence Benton.

She was relieved that his position and career had suffered no consequences for anything he had done. His dancing was unimpaired. She assumed that he had regained his footing and been able to slip back smoothly into his Leningrad life and routine, back to his theater, his world, the unattainably distant planet on which he lived.

WITH TATIANA IN TOKYO, AUGUST 1969

LENINGRAD, FALL 1969. PHOTO: COURTESY MARIINSKY THEATER

A NEW YEAR'S DINNER IN NOVOCHERKASSKAYA APART-
MENT, WITH TATIANA, FEDICHEVA AND HER NEW BEAU

WINTER 1969-70

SPRING 1970 AFTER PREMIERE OF THE NEW PRODUCTION OF SERGEYEV'S
CINDERELLA WITH FAMILY AND WELL-WISHERS, INCLUDING
DR. KARASEVICH IN BLACK HAT

PART 4:
HOPES DASHED

36
EVOLVING

BEHIND THE CURTAIN AT LONDON'S ROYAL FESTIVAL HALL,
DRESSED FOR *FLOWER FESTIVAL IN GENZANO PAS DE DEUX*,
SUMMER 1970. PHOTO: ROSEMARY WINKLEY

OPENING NIGHT GALA: OSIPENKO, SIZOVA, BARYSHNIKOV, MAKAROVA,
SOLOVIEV. PHOTO: ROSEMARY WINKLEY

eviewing the Kirov's return to London in the summer of 1970, John Percival wrote in *Dance and Dancers* that Soloviev's Albrecht was "far more dramatic than you would expect from any of his other roles (unless you remember *The Stone Flower* from their first London season); not at all an obvious performance but one of quiet and determined sincerity."

Undoubtedly he had come a long way in classical roles. During the 1960s, Mikhail Mikhailov, Rossi Street class of 1921, was still playing acting roles onstage at the Kirov as well as coaching. Soloviev was delighted when Mikhailov complimented his entrance in act 2 of *Sleeping Beauty*: how he had deployed his walking stick, taken off his cape and hat. Mikhailov said to him, "You know, you look as if you grew up in that atmosphere, that you're from that background."

As time went on, the fetters of Soloviev's own defensive mask slipped away, perhaps as well he was able to find in these roles an escape and a release. In act 2 of *Sleeping Beauty*, "Yura heard the Lilac Fairy," Legat recalled, "and went to that fantastic dream world that was so much a part of him"—her imminent entrance in the Vision scene announced in Tchaikovsky's score. In the beginning of act 2 of *Giselle,* alone on stage visiting Giselle's grave and then confronting her ghost, "There was this feeling of freedom when he could unwrap himself and do things that he was never able to do." There were no technical steps absorbing his concentration, "so he was, he told me, free to fantasize, 'to bring to life the fantasies that were inside me.'"

During the six-week season at the Royal Festival Hall, London was able to see Sizova and Soloviev dance together again for the first time since the company's debut season nine years earlier. Over the years his work had become "more thoughtful, more deep, more mature," Sizova recalled.

For Legat, their *Giselle* again confirmed her belief that Sizova was his ideal partner. "They were able to respond to each other on the same level, in the same unique way," she said. "They were in complete unison. It was the symbiosis of their two personalities that fit together so well. That was magical and was felt in the entire audience. I saw people had tears in their eyes." Sizova recalled, "When I left the stage it was covered with flowers."

In London they also performed a significant addition to their repertories: the pas de deux from August Bournonville's *Flower Festival in Genzano*, all that has survived of the 1858 full-length ballet. This was in fact the first time that the Kirov performed any of Bournonville's work. The dancers learned *Flower Festival* from a tape that Dudinskaya had gotten hold of. The duet had already been performed on concert stages in the USSR. Dudinskaya was always on the lookout for rarities to enliven the programs of dance she organized at the Philharmonic. That same year, 1970, she had been able to extend an invitation to John Taras to come to Leningrad to stage Balanchine's *Symphony in C* for one of her programs. The Khrushchev thaw was over, but cultural exchange would continue. (Four years earlier, in fact, Dutch choreographer Peter van Dijk's pas de deux The Unfinished Symphony had been taken into the Kirov repertory as a vehicle for Fedicheva and Soloviev.)

Bournonville's Danish ballet syntax is an altogether different set of stops and starts, coordination and port de bras than Russian classical. In London, Sizova was criticized by some reviewers for making her movements more expansively Russian than Bournonville demands; as she said, "It was interpreted in our own Russian style." The choreography they performed was a little more hyperbolic than the nineteenth-century text preserved in Denmark—double tours were added to Soloviev's solos. Nevertheless, Clement

FLOWER FESTIVAL. PHOTO: ROSEMARY WINKLEY

Crisp wrote in *The Dancing Times* that he had "made complete sense of the Bournonville manner."

Sizova and Soloviev were later filmed in it by famed television director Aleksandr Belinskii, who tried twice in the early 1970s to complete a documentary on Soloviev. "Both times we had to stop filming because the floor at the Leningrad TV studio was made out of stone," Belinskii recalled. "After his incredible jumps he was landing on that floor and tearing his ligaments."

In Belinskii's film, Sizova seems more centered and secure than as a young dancer. And Soloviev, too, if anything, surpasses himself. It is astounding to see rapid, multidirectional combinations performed with this kind of seamless Russian cantilena, which he sustains by just the slightest of pauses and preparations. Thus he incorporates an intelligent acknowledgment of Bournonville logic.

On this tape, his pirouettes are more impressive than earlier, at least to the modern balletic eye and sensibility. Pirouettes had never been the most exciting element in his technical arsenal. He had performed them the way he was taught, which now looks rather dowdy: a low raised leg, turning on a low relevé. For a dancer so buoyant, his pirouettes could brake jarringly into the ground, and they sometimes brake abruptly.

The 1960s saw men's style in ballet shift to higher legs in arabesque, high demi-pointe in relevé, a working leg raised higher in passé for pirouettes. Within the Kirov itself, it could be called the new style of Nureyev, who had been reviled by some for espousing it. Nureyev chose those dimensions as much because he thought it made his legs look longer. But it was just as much a part of ballet's international evolution. Alexander Pushkin, for one, added to his class after NYCB's visits what Shcherbakov described as "quick jumps à la Balanchine: we named these the 'springboard jumps.'"

When touring overseas, Kirov dancers noticed that it was much more than a question of Nureyev's own mannerisms. "We started changing, too," Legat said, although "it was actually Moscow that was the first to respond." Dudinskaya started telling Kirov dancers that they too should adjust their own styles. "We understood that the world was changing," Legat said. "Every time there was something new, of course it was interesting for Yura to see and to do and to emulate."

BLUEBIRD CURTAIN CALL. PHOTO: ROSEMARY WINKLEY

GOD, EXHAUSTED. PHOTO: COURTESY MARIINSKY THEATER

37
CREATION

WITH KOLPAKOVA AS EVE AND EVEGENI SHCHERBAKOV AS AN ARCHANGEL
PHOTO: NINA ALOVERT

s it good for me to stay?" Royal Ballet dancer Edward Arckless recalled Yuri asking him in class—he had been permitted to join the Kirov's classes in London. Out loud—just as Nureyev had asked Janine Ringuet in Paris a decade previously. "Yes," Arckless answered. However, it was Makarova who defected—much to the surprise of the KGB. The subsequent lockdown of the dancers made any further attempt all but impossible.

Baryshnikov had been as rapturously discovered by the London audience as Soloviev had been in 1961. Throughout the Kirov's six-week stay, Baryshnikov had been tailed throughout the city by KGB. Late on the night of September 3, Soloviev and Legat were sitting with Terence Benton and his Russian émigréé wife in their Rolls Royce. The Bentons were devoted to Soloviev and frequently took the couple out to dinner so he could eat steak, which was unobtainable in Leningrad. Out of the car radio came an announcement that one of the Kirov's female roster had just requested political asylum. They all tried to deduce who it could be. What they did know with certainty was that more trouble for the company would ensue. Indeed, Makarova's defection had severe ramifications. Sergeyev was replaced as artistic director and transferred to head the school. Principal dancer Vladilen Semyonov was named acting artistic director. Married to Kolpakova, he and she perhaps represented a power dyad to replicate Sergeyev/Dudinskaya.

For Soloviev, an immediate fallout from Sergeyev's dismissal was the deletion of Sergeyev's inserted variation for Albrecht in act 1 of *Giselle*. When Soloviev lodged a protest, he was informed that it "was completely out of the question," Boris Blankov writes. "The passage had been excised from the orchestral score and would not be restored."

The premiere of Sergeyev's new *Hamlet* was allowed to proceed, however. He had spent most of 1970 working on it, but no one in the theater seemed to have any enthusiasm for it. Osipenko had rehearsed the role of Gertrude but asked Sergeyev to relieve her of it. Soloviev also rehearsed the title role but also bowed out, describing the ballet with uncharacteristic acerbity as "a series of classroom exercises set to phony music" by Nikolai Chervinskii.

Panov, who saw himself as a disciple of Sergeyev's and wanted the ballet to work, nevertheless described the choreography as "massively overburdened." Following Sergeyev's dismissal, the authorities also moved to discredit and demoralize all involved with the new ballet.

In December, Baryshnikov danced two *Hamlet*s and then relinquished the part. Dolgushin was so intent on rejoining the Kirov that he agreed to appear as a guest in Sergeyev's ballet. But it was Panov who stayed with the ballet for another year, making some adjustments to the choreography along the way, until his request to emigrate in 1972 ended his Kirov career entirely.

March 1971 brought to the Kirov stage a much more lighthearted and well-liked new creation. *The Creation of the World* was a three-act ballet by husband-and-wife team Natalia Kasatkina and Vladimir Vasilyov, Moscow choreographers who were alumni of the Bolshoi. Music was by Igor Petrov, a contemporary composer who had written ballet, soundtrack and symphonic works.

Inspired by French caricaturist Jean Effel's work, *Creation* adhered to both a Russian tradition of religious satire, epitomized by Pushkin's "Gavriliad" poem, and to an integral part of Soviet ideology. The ballet took an irreverent look at turmoil in the Garden of Eden. Soloviev was God; Baryshnikov was Adam; Kolpakova, Eve; Panov, the Devil; and Fedicheva, his consort.

Kasatkina and Vasilyov collaborated with the dancers, enabling them to realize their inventiveness to the full. One day the choreographers gave Soloviev some steps to do and after watching him execute them, exclaimed: "Ah, Yura, Yura, what you did was a hundred times more interesting than what we showed!"

The Creation of the World let him project a kind of freewheeling zaniness that he had never shown before. "He was extraordinary in *Creation of the World*," Baryshnikov recalled. "Oh, he was delightful, absolutely delightful!"

Soloviev portrayed God as a selfless, prodigiously hardworking Stakhanovite *udarnik*, the prototypical Soviet "shock worker" driving himself to exceed all work norms. This was a satiric comment that the intelligentsia would have recognized in conspiratorial glee. "Because it was insulting to the communists," Legat recalled, "it was an enormous success among the intelligentsia, not just balletomanes." If anything, Soloviev's God could be said to have had enhanced reverence for deity, the very opposite of what the system wanted. Panov writes, "Spare tickets were begged at bus stops across the Neva, while speculators were busy making fortunes in the lobby."

Legat's amateur video preserves highlights of an astounding tour-de-force. Vadim Gulyaev and Natalia Bolshakova dance Baryshnikov's and Kolpakova's roles. Soloviev rages like Zeus and buzzes around with the manic energy of a silent film clown. He is as mischievous as he is magisterial. The frailties of the deity gave the satire its linchpin. When Soloviev's labors compel him to shoulder a stone à la Sisyphus, he wilts under the effort. When fatigue overtakes him, his archangels flank him and rock him in a human cradle.

In footage from Baryshnikov's personal archive, now at the Library for the Performing Arts in New York, he dances alongside Kolpakova in the roles they created. When they flee the Garden Soloviev pursues them in a staggering stag leap—no mistaking this deity's firepower!

BARYSHNIKOV'S ADAM. PHOTO: NINA ALOVERT

During rehearsals, Panov demonstrated an acrobatic cartwheel that he put into his portrayal of the Devil, and suggested that Soloviev do something similar. Soloviev demurred: "No, no, the gods cannot do such a step." Kirov dancer Vadim Strukhov recalled that it was indeed a classical purity that cloaked the deity in a balletic imprint of righteousness. His warmth toward his children and creations was overpowering.

Kolpakova also thinks that Soloviev's concept of the role stayed close to the sublime. She saw his diapason ranging from ecstasy toward "close to tragedy." In a prelude to the ballet that was later cut, Soloviev as God created the universe, floating in a zone of heavenly bliss. The world of his imagining, replete with angels and archangels, as well as Adam and Eve, all materialized before his eyes. But then later, after Adam and Eve were expelled from the Garden, he deflated, his despair crumpling him into dotage.

"He has surpassed himself," declared Russian critic Alexandra Deshicheva, describing him "the life and soul of the production."

"Of course, Soloviev had a great comic talent," Pierre Lacotte said. "He had an unlimited talent." Lacotte was visiting Leningrad at the time of the ballet's premiere. "What a marvel, all of them: Baryshnikov, Kolpakova, Soloviev." But offstage, Soloviev was now dramatically different than the young man Lacotte had known in Paris a decade earlier. "He was changed. Very sad. Everybody noticed. Kurgapkina and Kolpakova commented to me about it: 'so morose, so sad.' Osipenko especially observed it. She was highly intelligent, very observant."

Lacotte himself saw Soloviev "going about hanging his head, speaking little, walking along the corridor, always on the side, standing alone in a corner. It was awful to see. He was filled with despair. Clearly there were things troubling him."

38

FINAL YEARS

В сущности, всю мою жизнь можно рассматривать как беспрерывное старание избегать наиболее назойливых ее проявлений. Надо сказать, что по этой дороге я зашел весьма далеко, может быть, слишком далеко.
Иосиф Бродский

In fact, my entire life can be seen as a continuous effort to avoid the most intrusive of its [Soviet] manifestations. I must say that on this road I went very far, maybe too far.

—Joseph Brodsky

Soloviev's daughter Alyona had grown up in the Kirov. Her parents allowed her to watch their rehearsals provided she sat on a bench and remained silent with no fidgeting. She did so with such diligence that once Dudinskaya reported to Legat that Alyona hadn't been able to get up at the end of one of her father's rehearsals as her behind had simply gone to sleep.

Watching her parents perform from the wings of the theater, she was filled with pride, but also anxious that the performance would go well for them. She felt shy, awed by the theater, by the long shadows cast by her parents, and insignificant in contrast.

Yuri taught Alyona how to play checkers and chess, how to swim and how to fish. "He was patient, he showed well, and he made everything fun," she recalled. He and Alyona "were very close," Legat said. "They went together everywhere; they didn't take me along. They didn't include me in what they did, swimming and so forth. To tell the truth, it hurt me very much."

Yet it was Legat who enrolled Alyona in the ballet school. "Of course, I am more active," Legat said when asked about how they were different. "I also had my fears but I think I was stronger. I think that I was the center of the family; it was on my shoulders." At home "Tanya [Tatiana] ruled everything," recalled Uncle Aleksandr, which kept Soloviev in the position of junior partner as he had been when they married, an immature and shel-

tered twenty-year-old. Nor could the constant presence of his mother in their apartment have bolstered his belief in his own authority and autonomy.

On tour in Venice in 1966, he had invited colleagues Ostaltsov and Budarin to his hotel room early one evening. There on the double bed was an inflated rubber boat he had just purchased. Bottles of Italy's famous Chianti stood at the ready and were enjoyed until Legat returned from the theater and promptly showed both guests the door.

"Well, are you OK?" Ostaltsov asked Soloviev the next day. "Did anything happen? You didn't take a hit, did you?"

"Oh, I took a hit. Took a hit, and how. I always take a hit. There's nothing I know how to do, except how to dance."

In 1973, the Solovievs moved into their final apartment on Klimov Alley, which was close to the theater and secured with its help. Soloviev was entitled to a regulated amount of square meters as a People's Artist of the Soviet Union. As an Honored Artist of the Russian Federation, Legat was also allotted her regulated number of meters. When mutual meters were toted up, however, the apartment was actually three square meters larger than was legal. "Again Kolpakova went and said, 'Give them the apartment,'" Legat recalled.

It was a much more convenient location, but Klimov Alley is a narrow lane of rooming house-like nineteenth-century buildings, bleakly redolent of Dickens and Dostoevsky. The apartment was the sinister number 13. "We said hopefully, 'Maybe it will be good luck, instead.' But it was not," Tatiana recalled. "Even though we had windows on both sides, the apartment was always dark," Alyona remembered. "Why did you accept an apartment on a low floor?" the Bolshoi's Vladimir Vasiliev asked, but Moscow stars were used to privileges far beyond what the Kirov enjoyed.

In his final years, Soloviev began to be treated by the Kirov with the back of its hand. "The whole world called him the Cosmic Yuri, and then Misha came and they just kicked him out," Osipenko recounted to Joel at their very first meeting in 1998. "They completely ignored him."

"You see what happened to Soloviev?" she recalled having cautioned Baryshnikov himself. "Don't forget that the same thing can happen to you."

Indubitably, Osipenko's words were colored by her own struggles with the government and theater administrations, but it would seem that Soloviev's refusal to join the Party had finally caught up with him. He could be treated as disposable. One afternoon, another Kirov danseur cancelled his appearance at that evening's gala. Soloviev was summoned back to the Kirov from his country house to perform. He arrived at the theater in fishing gear and, after changing into his costume, muttered imprecations as he warmed up in the wings.

A long silence preceded Aleksandr's recollection of the way that his nephew would come alone to visit him in the years before his death. "He would sit down, looking bad, looking unhappy. But he wouldn't say anything about home, about how he felt. It was enough just to look at him. You could see how he felt. And I would try, but he wouldn't react, open up. He just sat there, turned in on himself. I would talk to him, try to bring him out, to get him to talk, but he would look down… How can you give advice to someone who isn't asking for any?"

"In the last years of his life, I would notice his eyes," Alla Shelest writes. "They were so sunken, and I knew that this was a bad sign. It is something that you see only in the very old, or in people who are very ill. I would think to myself, could he be sick? There was such sorrow in his eyes."

When Soloviev filmed the Black Swan pas de deux opposite Komleva in 1975, her husband, critic Arkady Sokolov-Kaminsky, found and continues to find his appearance equally disturbing. "I look with horror at the old man in the frame. And he was not even forty."

This was a time of disenchantment and disengagement from people to whom Soloviev had been close. Fedicheva's indiscretion with Michael Edgley spelled the beginning of the end of her career. Soloviev's response to the disappointment with the Australian Ballet was, characteristically, to retreat within himself. Fedicheva's was, just as characteristically, to throw caution to the winds. She not only traveled with Edgley to Moscow and to Sochi but also invited him to visit her in Leningrad later in 1969. The result was that even the apparently forgiving Rachinsky could not get her included on the Kirov's tour to London the following summer. When Moiseyev was preparing a tour to South America in 1970, he said he was not going to take her again, but that he would like to take Soloviev. Fedicheva then threatened to use such influence as she retained to block him from Moiseyev's tour if she could not go. Soloviev found out and was enraged, refusing to ever dance with her again. She pleaded with him, and theater personnel even pressed Legat to intercede with him on Fedicheva's behalf, which she did unsuccessfully. Soloviev was less than ever inclined to be forgiving.

Fedicheva's weakened position now allowed many partners to spare themselves the onus of lifting her, begging off from performances with her. She was depressed and gained still more weight. Finally, she found an American dancer, Martin Friedman, who agreed to marry her and thus allow her to emigrate to the U.S. in 1975. Unable to resume her dancing career, she opened a school on Long Island that she ran successfully until she died in 1994.

Soloviev's limited ability to analyze or observe his own psychic functioning certainly would have benefited from consultation with a psychiatrist. But like most Russians, he and his family would have known that seeking treatment could have landed him in a psychiatric hospital. Used extensively as a measure of control and repression, Soviet psychiatry was renowned for its abuses rather than its therapeutic efficacy. Institutions such as Moscow's infamous Serbsky Institute and the "Pryazhka" (Leningrad Psychiatric Hospital #2)—located uncomfortably close to Klimov Alley—were commonly regarded with horror. Psychotropic drugs and treatments forcibly administered harmed patients rather than healed them. Worst of all would have been to receive a diagnosis of aberrant personality with the fabricated catch-all disease of "sluggish schizophrenia." This was the damning diagnosis that could be applied in response to a despondent patient's unhappiness in the socialist heaven on earth that was on the way to manifesting in the Soviet Union.

And yet Soloviev's classmate Marina Vasilieva, insisted that while "of course there were those," genuine options existed as well. This was also affirmed by several St. Petersburg Bekhterev Institute psychiatrists with whom Lisa spoke in the 1990s.

"We had proper facilities," Vasilieva said, "competent psychotherapists available to treat mental illnesses. Why this was not done for him I cannot explain, since it was most certainly done for other people here."

ICARE. PHOTO: VALENTIN BARANOVSKY

39

BARYSHNIKOV'S DEFECTION

WITH BARYSHNIKOV AND IMPRESARIO MICHAEL
EDGLEY ON AUSTRALIAN TOUR, 1973

ne day during Pierre Lacotte's visit to Leningrad in 1971, Baryshnikov accidentally-on-purpose dropped his ballet slipper close to where Lacotte was sitting in a Kirov rehearsal studio. As they both leaned over to get it, Baryshnikov asked in good French, "How much do ballet slippers cost in Paris?"

"I immediately knew that he was planning to get out," Lacotte recalled. But it wasn't until three years later, on June 29, 1974, that Baryshnikov did in fact defect in Canada. He was profoundly ambivalent about this momentous decision up to and beyond the very act.

A year earlier, in the summer of 1973, the Kirov had visited Australia. Lisa had graduated from college in 1972. Four days after her final exams, she stepped on an Air France flight for Europe, severing all emotional and physical ties with Australia.

In this Australian tour, Michael Edgley booked additional work for Baryshnikov, Kolpakova and Kurgapkina apart from their Kirov performances. They danced the *Swan Lake* pas de trois in special, undoubtedly lucrative matinee performances. For all three, the pas de trois was well beneath the rank they now enjoyed in the company. Soloviev disapproved of the mercenary moonlighting. "He considered such behavior shameful for us as representatives of our country," Legat said. "We didn't earn much money, not even Kolpakova, but Yura felt we should be thankful for what we earned and maintain our dignity."

Soloviev also objected that, having been paid to perform, they didn't dance what was choreographed; instead they simplified the steps. "When I dance *Swan Lake*," he told Baryshnikov, "I dance the steps as Sergeyev choreographed them."

After one of Soloviev's performances, Baryshnikov reportedly told him that he was becoming lazy and no longer dancing up to his potential. Soloviev was offended and a rupture opened between them.

Nevertheless, Soloviev was in the Kirov audience in February 1974 for Baryshnikov's Creative Evening, where he starred in three ballets never before seen there. Legat was ballet mistress for one of them, Alexidze's *Les Petits Riens*, performed to Mozart's music. Soloviev thought that the Evening was wonderful —"We both did."

WITH TATIANA AND EDGLEY INTERNATIONAL EXECUTIVE ANDREW GUILD IN AUSTRALIA

That same year, Soloviev himself filmed a new addition to his repertory, the Russian-born French choreographer Victor Gsovsky's 1949 *Grand Pas Classique,* dancing opposite Komleva. This was another bridge or series of bridges across the cultural divide. "Eva Evdokimova showed it to me," Komleva recalled. "She had prepared it with Yvette Chauviré," who created the pas de deux opposite Vladimir Skouratoff in 1949.

Soloviev retained the ability to learn new material fast. Unlike Komleva, he had never danced it before, and they had only one rehearsal together. Dancing it "practically from scratch," as she recalled. Nevertheless, they performed it "on the level of dance mastery that Yura possessed." In *Grand Pas* he is thinner as well as more Western in manner than ever before, as befitting the material itself and reflecting too his by now long exposure to Western trends. His beats and brisés are breathtaking as always: so nimble, so sparkling, and look so effortless that they almost seem like optical illusions. He dances with extraordinary speed while maintaining clarity and detail. His vivacity, charm and nonchalance bring out the best in his ballerina; Komleva dances with meticulous strength and delicacy.

At this particular time, different options for private enterprise were being allowed certain figures in the ballet world. Baryshnikov was in Canada as part of a tour organized by Aleksandr Lapauri of the Bolshoi. At the moment that Baryshnikov defected, Legat was on a similar tour of North Africa organized by the Kirov's Askold Makarov.

At the Kirov, Baryshnikov had fast been becoming Kolpakova's preferred partner, which Soloviev experienced as a rebuff. One report is that Soloviev had been originally scheduled to partner her in Canada but had been deleted once she had managed to convince the wary authorities that Baryshnikov was not a security risk.

For Soloviev, Baryshnikov's defection was somehow the beginning of the end, perhaps awakening resentments and regrets that festered. An occasional impulsive comment on Soloviev's part later revealed some glee that Baryshnikov's defection had given the regime a black eye.

To longtime Kirov wardrobe mistress Natalia Semyonova, he said something different. Semyonova adored Soloviev. She recalls in Mshanskaya's documentary that after Baryshnikov's defection, he was more despondent than she had ever seen him. Had it been he who had gone to Canada, "I would not have stayed there."

In his words we hear a forlorn jeremiad. He had been good, loyal, often selfless in his service to his company, his ballerinas. He brought the Soviet Union prestige, honors, millions in hard currency and international acclaim. He had turned down one offer after another that could have brought him riches and freedom. And where had it led him?

Baryshnikov's defection meant that Kolpakova was left in Canada without a partner. Soloviev was apprised that he would be flying to Canada immediately to replace Baryshnikov for the remainder of the tour. But he refused. Legat heard about it when she arrived home from North Africa. "It was a scandal," she recalled. "Everyone was saying, 'Are you a fool? Why don't you want to go?' He said, 'They didn't take me from the beginning and I won't go.'"

When Kolpakova returned to the USSR and the new season began, Soloviev might have treated her as he had Fedicheva. But his wife urged him not to precipitate a breach. In class, "I would make him go over and greet her." Soon he was again Kolpakova's regular partner and, whatever he was feeling inside, he continued to support her flawlessly.

In 1972, Igor Belsky had become the Kirov's director, replacing Semyonov. He had begun the ballet *Icare* [Icarus] on Soloviev as well as Baryshnikov, who ultimately refused it. Now it became Soloviev's ballet, but he wasn't particularly keen either. "There was a lot of virtuoso allegro and Yura wasn't so young or so strong," Ostalstov said. Of course virtuoso allegro was

CUBA, 1975. KOLPAKOVA LEFT

still a hallmark of many of his roles, but Ostaltsov describes this as "Belsky allegro—very dry. Yura didn't like it." Belsky made some changes Soloviev requested, but it was not a project to rank with his *Leningrad Symphony* thirteen years earlier. Nevertheless, Soloviev danced it—the tale from Greek mythology now tragically pertinent to his particular situation. In excerpts from the ballet preserved in Legat's collection of amateur footage, he performs with almost frightening intensity.

By 1974 Lisa was working in Germany. For her, Baryshnikov's defection, extensively documented in the media, was a painful reminder of what could have been. "I blocked everything out, I couldn't stand to hear or read anything about it. It was absolutely gut-wrenching."

40
COACHING

leksandr Pushkin had died of a final heart attack in March 1970. The Kirov's Shcherbakov thought that Soloviev could have been chosen to inherit Pushkin's men's company class. "It would have been good for the Kirov and good for Soloviev." Soloviev had an extraordinary ability "to grasp movements instinctively," he recalled. Once on tour in Egypt, the Kirov was taken to a souk to watch belly-dancing. Afterward, Shcherbakov confessed himself amazed. How in the world could the women do that? "It's obvious how," Soloviev replied, then lifted up his shirt, pushed down his slacks to below the hip bone and provided a seemingly perfect recreation. In 1964, Shcherbakov asked Soloviev for help when he began dancing Soloviev's role in *The Distant Planet*. Soloviev's words and his demonstration were "so clear and so beautiful. He was brilliant." But Soloviev was never political enough to fight for such an important position as Pushkin's. Which current or retired dancers were allowed to teach or coach could be a highly contested, highly political process, subject to internal theatrical as well as larger state considerations. Communist Party membership was increasingly a sine qua non. "He would never have come to the chief and asked, 'Let me become a coach,'" Ostaltsov said. "He couldn't plead for something."

Soloviev was also at a disadvantage because of his own doubts. "When I stop dancing, what do I do?" he asked Legat. "What else? You will become a ballet master." Legat herself was coaching while she was still on stage. It is a transition that is often not at all difficult for dancers far less talented, but Soloviev was daunted. "No, I don't know anything about how to do it," he told his wife and his friend Shavrov. "No, it is very difficult," he insisted.

On one occasion, Soloviev's old teacher Boris Shavrov was going to be away for ten days and asked Soloviev to replace him in class on Rossi Street. Soloviev walked unannounced into the studio, and the boys were of course beside themselves with surprise and excitement. During the center adagio, one was trying so hard that he hyperventilated and fainted to the ground. Soloviev was afraid that it might have been his fault. Afterward, he asked some of the other teachers if they thought the problem was that he had given combinations that were too difficult. Everybody laughed it off; it was just that the boy had been overwhelmed at being taught by his idol.

Earlier in the 1970s, Soloviev had rehearsed his own role in *The Stone Flower* with a young dancer who was being tried out in some principal roles. "He was big, but he had no talent," Legat said, "but he was the boyfriend of a ballerina."

"My God, I've been stuck with this guy," Soloviev complained to his wife. "He did everything to pull whatever there was out of this person," she recalled, but he finally told her that he was ready to concede defeat: "There was nothing I could do with him." Soloviev now saw some type of sabotage at work. "And look what's going to happen: because what they're going to say is, 'Ha, you see, Soloviev is no teacher. Soloviev is not able to do it, because we gave him this boy and he wasn't able to do anything with him.' And it's going to look like it's me. And it's not."

Kolpakova sat next to Soloviev in the director's box during the performance and remembered how nervous he was as he watched. "The guy was not really good," she said, but the performance "wasn't bad. It was professional, you could see the style, you could see everything, but I don't think Yura was satisfied."

For whatever reason, Soloviev did not see possibilities for himself here. A couple of months before he died, he ran into his former classmate Elena Shatrova, who was then married to Vinogradov and working as a ballet mistress staging his ballets. "You have a future," he told her.

41
THE LOOK IN HIS EYES

… И с отвращением читая жизнь мою,
Я трепещу и проклинаю,
И горько жалуюсь, и горько слёзы лью,
Но строк печальных не смываю

… And loathing it, I read the record of the years,
I curse and tremble like one baited;
For all my bitter groans, for all my bitter tears,
The lines are not obliterated.

—Alexander Pushkin
(Babette Deutsch, tr.)

"In the last period of his life," Gabriela Komleva recalled, "he was somehow intense… and grim. Something was weighing heavily on him. He was very intense… and very morose."

Soloviev's workload prompted his father to compare it to the routine of a factory worker. Given his seniority, the Kirov should have treated him with extra consideration. Instead, it worked him relentlessly. The fact that he apparently didn't protest or refuse was likely due to his pronounced awareness of artistic, professional and patriotic obligation, but also to paralyzing depression and inertia as well as a streak of masochism as woefully archetypal as Russian expansiveness and self-abnegation. Lisa had witnessed in Australia the way that Soloviev "brought out the venom in malicious individuals. I saw the viciousness in their eyes, a pack of hyenas gripped by the thrill of the kill, having finally managed to encircle and pull down a magnificent lion."

In Soloviev, a seething, sullen rancor persisted. Vikulov recalled sitting in the common dressing room where they used to change before class. One day Soloviev turned to Vikulov: "You are a premier danseur. I am premier danseur. And so what? We are both sitting here in this shit." After hearing his patriotic affirmations in Australia in 1969, Lisa was startled when Vikulov told her bluntly in 2016 that by this point Soloviev "hated this country."

Wardrobe mistress Tatiana Semyonova recalled that in 1976, while the company was on tour in Poland, she asked if she could take a photo of him. He agreed, but she was appalled when he stepped on a tree stump and assumed a cruciform position. His head hung down to the right and his eyes were closed, like the depiction of Christ in old Russian icons. "Oh, please, not like that," she pleaded, "smile for me…" But he insisted.

IN POLAND, 1976. PHOTO: NATALIA SEMYONOVA,
COURTESY MARIINSKY THEATER

Soloviev appeared to have retreated gradually into an internal exile, a reverie, his psychic isolation exacerbated by his own nature and that of the silence of his art form.

Kirov artistic director Igor Belsky was formidable and equivocal. He was personable enough that Osipenko, for one, adored him despite knowing that he was as close to enemies of hers as he was to her. Director of the Maly ballet in the 1960s, he slipped an anti-Soviet message into his own choreography and enjoyed presenting fare that was more adventurous than what would be allowed at the Kirov. At the same time, he knew how to propitiate authority sufficiently to take over the Kirov from Semyonov in 1972.

Belsky would not give Legat a full-time position as a Kirov coach, and she was not working steadily at this time. Ostaltsov and his wife, Kirov dancer Natalia Spitsina, urged Soloviev to lobby for her with Belsky. But he was not going to do for her what he could or would not do on his own behalf, no more now than when Nureyev had instructed him to do the same years earlier. "If they need her, they will come and offer it to her." However, Legat was asked to go to Yugoslavia to teach for several months. She turned down the offer because of her anxiety that out of sight, she would be very much out of the running in her own theater. Later, she came to the regretful conclusion that Soloviev might have lived had he been in another environment altogether, one more clement in every way.

During this final year, Soloviev, usually sitting alone in their third bedroom, what they called his "music room," played the soundtrack from Ken Russell's *Lisztomania* at high volume obsessively on his lavish stereo system. One evening, he and Ostaltsov listened to it for more than an hour without speaking, interrupted only by Tatiana bringing in some dinner for them. Ostaltsov understood his need for companionship as well as his inability to verbalize his problems.

He had told Lisa in Australia that as much as he loved Leningrad and the Kirov, where he wanted above all to be was in the country, "in freedom, in nature." Years earlier, Uncle Aleksandr had suffered a grave disappointment at work. "He made a number of discoveries in the field of radio communications," his cousin Mira recalled. "But these did not meet with success; somebody blocked them." Distraught, he left and went to Lake Ladoga to rest, to restore his equilibrium before returning anew to his profession.

Now, as Igor recalled, Soloviev himself dreamed of retiring to the woods, even becoming, so he had told Shatrova, a forest ranger. Yet, as Igor said, "I can't believe that he wouldn't have become a teacher. He couldn't live without ballet. It was his life."

Ballet, however, was even more Legat's life. Concerns about the end of her own dancing career and concern with Alyona's progress at the Academy likely increased her already laser-sharp focus. "The sad thing was that Tatiana would push him very hard to fulfill obligations that he felt no longer able to accomplish," one of his classmates recalled. Perhaps she did not want to entertain the idea that his fabled career could be coming to a close a bit prematurely. "She would say, 'You've GOT to do this, you've GOT to do that… You can't refuse to do this; you've got to perform. You've got to rehearse that; you've got to go to rehearsal. It doesn't matter, you've got to do it all.'" In pain physically and mentally, however, he simply no longer could. Nor did he want to.

Part of him remained alert to the satisfaction of artistic expression. In 1976, Igor Tchernichov was creating a duet for him and Valentina Gannibalova to be performed at a gala she had organized in Moscow. But for some reason the piece didn't come off as planned. However, Soloviev was excited about dancing Leonid Lebedev's *The Infanta* as a guest artist at the Maly opposite Kolpakova. "We saw something that Lebedev had done and thought, Ah!" Legat recalled. The score was by S. A. Kosholkin, a dancer in the company and had a Spanish flavor. Soloviev was a page in love with his mistress, whose indifference drives him to suicide. The ballet "was difficult for us, because it wasn't classical," Kolpakova recalled. "We both worked really hard." But the work was pleasant: Lebedev was "calm and quiet and polite," recalled Elena Kunikova, then a young dancer in the company. The little piece was around fifteen minutes. Both dancers were on stage throughout, dancing alone, then together. The result "was extraordinary," Legat recalled, so much so that Lebedev declared that no one else would ever dance the duet again. The two dancers were "warm and regal," Kunikova recalled, the performance "incredibly beautiful. You would never have known it was difficult for them."

WITH KOLPAKOVA IN *THE INFANTA*

During the spring of 1976, Soloviev was in Moscow with the Kirov, where it performed in honor of the 200th anniversary of the Bolshoi. The troupe was about to begin a two-month tour of Japan, its first major tour since Baryshnikov's defection two years earlier. It had become disconcerting to dance with Soloviev, Sizova recalled. Their old emotional rapport onstage was not there. In their final performances of *Giselle* and *Leningrad Symphony*, "I felt his empty eyes on the stage. I couldn't reach a connection with him." Some of this disaffection is visible in the *Sleeping Beauty* that was transmitted from Moscow over Japanese television prior to the company's visit. Soloviev's body is thin, but a spiritual heaviness intrudes. At times his face wears not the beatific look of the 1963 film, but rather an inscrutable stoniness. He doesn't bother to take a bow after his Act 3 variation. At the same time, it is a greatly expanded interpretation. His artistry has grown: he has an enhanced feeling for pose, beauty of line. He conveys a complete Baroque characterization apparent in the way he extends his foot delicately and walks on the front of the foot to simulate an appropriately dainty gait in the mime passages. His arms, his gestures open with a confident entitlement. No longer the princeling he was in the 1963 film; he is now a prince of the world.

However low his morale, Soloviev once again brought out the best in his partner. Not customarily known for eroticism, Kolpakova's épaulement here suggests the hint of an erotic languor in the sleeping Aurora. In the act 3 grand pas de deux, her classic precision is sparked with an air of spontaneity and ecstatic impulsiveness. Also in Moscow, he was filmed partnering her in the *Chopiniana* waltz at a gala: another flawless performance by both—and by both together.

In Japan, Soloviev again shouldered an onerous workload, dancing the full-length classical ballets as well as *The Stone Flower* and *Leningrad Symphony*. For Emi Yamauchi writing in *Dance News*, Soloviev's Prince Désiré made clear that he could "still defeat a wicked old Carabosse any old time he feels like it. Soaring leaps, clean batterie and brilliant tours en l'air (in which he invariably lands facing front in perfect fifth position) are his technical trademarks." But just as much appreciated was "the human vulnerability he gives his characterization as Désiré; after courageously conquering Carabosse and his fiendish demons, and kissing the sleeping Aurora, he bashfully retires to the side, waiting for the Princess to introduce him to her newly awakened parents."

They returned to Leningrad in September just before the new season opened. Kolpakova left for a vacation, but according to Legat, the theater made the shocking demand that Soloviev not take any time off but return immediately to work. "They are exploiting me," he complained to Aunt Mira, using the Russian *ekspluatiruiut*, a loaded word used to indict capitalistic abuse of workers.

Belsky had invited Romanian choreographer Vadim Elizarov to create *Tyl Eulenspiegel* at the Kirov for Soloviev and Kolpakova. Elizarov was Belsky's student at the Leningrad Conservatory. A trickster figure from medieval German folklore, Tyl might have been the perfect vehicle for Solo-viev a few years earlier—a follow-up to his comedic triumph in *The Creation of the World*. But circumstances were far different this time.

"The rehearsals were awful," Legat said. "He gave Yura all kinds of extremely difficult things to do," steps in line with Tyl's scalawag identity, but punishing to his interpreter. At one point he had to spin on his head, with the result that in rehearsal a splinter pierced his skull. To retrieve it, the top of his head had to be shaved. At home he raged about the ballet, but "he would go back and push himself to the limit in the rehearsals, no matter what."

Now plagued by insomnia, Soloviev went for acupuncture treatments, but found more efficacious the traditional Russian soporific. Alcohol con-sumption had soared to epidemic levels in the despair of the Brezhnev era. Osipenko shuddered as she recalled a friend of hers who lived near the Solovievs, who described walking home past their apartment at night. The façade was dark except for their kitchen window, through which she could see him sitting alone, drinking.

Kirov colleague Anatole Gridin said that he "didn't like the crowd that surrounded Soloviev at the end, they made him drink too much. He was a gentleman, he always behaved well before an elder like me, but there was a bad influence on him. It was hard for Tanya [Tatiana], I'm sure she suffered."

Finally, Soloviev found a way "to kind of slip out of" *Tyl Eulenspiegel*, Legat recalled. Its lifespan on the Kirov stage was very brief.

It was during these months that he seemed to be flirting with the pos-sibility of suicide. Soloviev was ordinarily a superb driver, but driving to the country with Aleksandr Shavrov, he suddenly sped up as they approached a dangerous bridge near his house. "Now we go slip quietly into the water," he announced to his friend. "Maybe you want to die, but I don't!" Shavrov shrieked. Another time driving with Shavrov, Soloviev slalomed his Volga from snow bank to snow bank. "He would do things like that all the time," Shavrov recalled. "More and more."

At the end of 1976 Osipenko saw Soloviev in the studios of the Maly. Why did he look so sad, she asked. "I am so tired of everything," he told her. "Tired or not tired, but maybe you have to try to change your life. Try some-thing else." Perhaps he should join the Maly full-time. There he could build on the success of *The Infanta*—continue to create interesting new work made especially for him. "I'm too tired to start anything again," he told her. The emptiness in his eyes was more disturbing to her than if he had been sobbing.

Sometimes Legat would walk into his music room and, if he noticed her, he might slip a book he was holding into a position that made it seem as though he had actually been reading. But he hadn't been reading at all, for she saw that the book was upside down. She realized that he was far away, entirely lost in his thoughts.

Aunt Mira had been planning to visit Leningrad for the New Year, but canceled her trip. "At that time I had my own family problems," she recalled. "Thus I think about it: I always accuse myself. If I had come up, I would have helped him to solve his problems. He was overwhelmed by them. He pleaded, 'Auntie, come, Auntie, Auntie, come...'"

OVERLEAF: MME OHTA WAS A JAPANESE TEXTILE MAGNATE, A FERVENT FAN OF THE KIROV AND OF SOLOVIEV, WHO REGULARLY COMPLIED WITH HER ON-STAGE, POST-PERFORMANCE REQUEST THAT HE SWEEP HER UP INTO A BALLETIC LIFT. SHE IS SHOWN HERE BACKSTAGE AFTER A 1976 *SLEEPING BEAUTY*, FLANKED LEFT TO RIGHT BY, AMONG OTHERS, DUDINSKAYA, KURGAPKINA, VIKULOV, TATIANA UDALENKOVA, VLADILEN SEMYONOV, LEGAT, SOLOVIEV

42

"YOU CAN IMAGINE WHAT I SAW THERE"

До свиданья, друг мой, до свиданья.
Милый мой, ты у меня в груди...
В этой жизни умирать не ново,
Но и жить, конечно, не новей.

Farewell, good friend, farewell.
You are always in my heart...
In this life, to die is not new...
Nor is staying alive.

—Sergei Esenin
Untitled final poem

I n the final week of Soloviev's life, he talked to Marina Vasilieva at the Ostaltsovs' apartment. "I—just—cannot—go—on—anymore. I can't do it. I don't know what to do. You're intelligent, you have a future. I have no future. I have nothing. What am I, a fisherman?"

Several friends debated whether it was easier to choose death than to endure life's vicissitudes. "It's easier to die," Soloviev insisted over the objections of another guest.

He appeared to be putting his affairs in order. Boris Blankov was startled to see him early in the new year washing his car on the street outside his apartment. This was not something Leningraders usually did in minus-twenty-degree weather.

On January 6, he was scheduled to dance Lavrovsky's *Romeo and Juliet* opposite Kolpakova. He was experiencing some difficulty with his legs and tried to persuade her to let someone else dance with her. "Kolpakova said, 'No,' categorically 'No,'" Ostalstov recalled. Although not difficult technically, Juliet was an arduous role for Kolpakova. Since *The Stone Flower* in 1957, she had frequently been coached by former Kirov ballerina Tatiana Vecheslova, a great dance actress. "She was lucky that she had Vecheslova, who pushed and pulled and pounded," said Legat. "If she hadn't had her, she would never have been able to do *Romeo and Juliet*." Perhaps Romeo was a difficult role for Soloviev, too—it was certainly a late addition to his repertory. He had first danced it in 1975. Pyrotechnics were the least important part of it.

However, at this point that was what worried him. Romeo's one solo, in the balcony scene, was short but still he feared that it was going to be too much for him. Kolpakova urged him to simply cut his variation. Better not to dance the performance at all, he told her. Legat advised him simply to improvise some poses to fill up the music. He found that kind of subterfuge repellent. He was Yuri Soloviev, a People's Artist of the Soviet Union. "How can people come to the theater and say, 'But he didn't dance?'" She told him it didn't matter. "Any pose that you do, you will do it right and beautifully and everybody will love it."

On the morning of the performance, Soloviev went for treatment to the local medical clinic that served the Kirov. He decided to go ahead with that night's ballet. Before the first act, however, Ostaltsov went to Soloviev's dressing room and saw him in a black mood, not at all the radiant young lover he was about to portray. "Yura, why are you so sad?" he asked. "Motherfucker! They don't work!" he said, implicating his legs. (Before the final years of his life, Soloviev was almost never heard to use profanity.)

He told Kolpakova that "he didn't feel well, his leg and back," but nevertheless, "It was a wonderful performance," she recalled. "How he was Romeo: unbelievable!"

BALCONY SCENE, FINAL *ROMEO* WITH KOLPAKOVA

There is dispute about whether or not he did include the variation that night. Bothersome enough was the running he had to do. "He was in such pain," Legat said. "He couldn't run. He still ran, because he felt he had to."

Future Kirov ballerina Lubov Kunakova, who had recently joined the company after training in Perm, watched from the first row of the orchestra section. "It was extraordinary, heart-wrenching," she recalled. "So sincere, so beautiful, so tragic, it was hard to watch."

Kunakova and a group of balletomane friends went backstage to congratulate him. He clearly did not want to hear them. One member of the group asked him to autograph a photo. "Hah, what kind of Romeo am I?" he said more to himself than his admirer. He turned and walked away.

At home, he was just happy that he hadn't disappointed anybody—Kolpakova, the public: "Thank God I got through everything."

On Sunday, January 9, Soloviev and Legat went to New Year's dinner at Igor's apartment. Russians celebrate twice, once on the first of the year and again two weeks later in observance of the Julian calendar that the Russian Orthodox Church continues to use to this day. "My brother looked very tired and old," Igor told Russian journalist Fiodor Razzakov. "Something incomprehensible was going on inside him." A New Year's dinner like this was an important family occasion to which attendance was obligatory. But Soloviev and Legat did not stay long.

Soon after, Soloviev called Igor and asked him to go with him to the country. Igor told Razzakov: "I refused, because on the following Monday I had to go back to work. My brother kept insisting, but was unable to persuade me. Clearly, it was not just on a whim that my brother asked me to go with him. Something clearly was tormenting him. He needed someone to speak to, to pour out his soul."

"I had to work," was all that Igor said to Lobenthal. But to Razzakov he explained that he was expected back at work only on January 17. That was days after Yuri was planning to return, and thus hardly the likeliest explanation for Igor's decision not to go to Koloskovo.

Undoubtedly, Soloviev and Legat's hasty departure from the family party was a breach of etiquette. Was this why Igor, in turn, refused Yuri's request to go with him to the dacha? It very well might have been that Igor lived the rest of his life with a burden of guilt.

Yuri's request to Igor seems like a final attempt to allow fate to forestall his intentions. Soloviev didn't drive, but instead took the train to Koloskovo—the first time and the last that he traveled there by train. It was reported he had been seen drinking as he walked from the station to his house. At the dacha was a weapon, an *otrubka*—a sawed-off rifle—a war trophy given him by a retired officer, a dacha neighbor and admirer. This was the weapon of choice of organized crime and possession was a criminal offence. Legat had banned it from their apartment, but he had refused all her efforts to persuade him to get rid of it altogether.

Soloviev hadn't told Legat when he was coming back, but when he failed to show up for rehearsal with Kolpakova, the ballerina dispatched a posse of his friends. They went to check his garage and found his car, and decided that he was still in the city. But Tatiana and Anna saw that the chewed-up old fur hat he wore to the country was missing. They discovered the newer fur hat he wore in the city, as well as the contents of his pockets, his wallet, keys, jewelry. They were convinced that something was very wrong. Finally, on January 15, Shavrov drove to the dacha. "You can imagine what I saw there," he later told Lisa.

43

DISCOVERY

t six o'clock in the morning, Ostaltsov was wakened by a call from Shavrov. "Yura is no more." Ostaltsov was baffled. "Where on earth are you calling from?" Shavrov was already back in Leningrad. "I went there, Yura is lying there, holding a weapon, and not breathing." That was all he could or would say over the phone.

That same day Ostaltsov, accompanied by some executives from the Kirov administration as well as several police officers, was bussed out to the dacha. "They were all in the hot seat for it," Ostaltsov said. Soloviev was not only a star but a Peoples' Artist of the USSR, one of the Soviet Union's highest awards, and any scandal involving such a public figure was sure to bring down much collateral damage.

Police swarmed around the dacha. They wrapped Soloviev's frozen body in a sheet. With Ostaltsov they drove to the main Priozersk-Leningrad road, hailed a truck, and told the driver he was to drive the corpse to the morgue. The driver's documents were confiscated as insurance that he did as he was told. Ostaltsov was seated next to the truck driver. More police and other officials, both in and out of uniform, were awaiting them at the morgue. Soloviev's body was undressed, his clothes now part of a police investigation. Ostaltsov insisted on being shown the body to verify that it was indeed Soloviev. He knew that there would be questions. Could the unthinkable really have happened? He did everything he could not to look at the head. Shavrov had already given him a description.

Sergei Vikulov was then touring the Soviet Union. "But when I got back, all my family were waiting for me at the airport. I never allowed anyone to see me off or to meet me, so I knew something terrible had happened. I was not surprised. Everybody said, 'What a shock, what a shock.' What shock? It was not a shock for me. It was horrible. A tragedy. But not a shock."

"My head is breaking open," Aleksandr Godunov wrote Legat from Moscow. "I cannot comprehend it. A person with the rarest soul has left us, and a great dancer. My beloved nightingale." Osipenko would later tell Lisa that Soloviev's suicide remained for her "a weeping wound." Certainly it continued to haunt other colleagues as well. Ninel Kurgapkina staged *La Bayadère* for Nureyev at the Paris Opéra in the months before his death in

1993. In 1998 she recalled, "I know from his words" that among Kirov danseurs Nureyev "valued Soloviev most of all, and he was always very interested in him and his career and he always asked about his end."

As is traditional for Kirov stars, the funeral service was held in the
Grand Foyer behind what is traditionally called the Tsar's Box (although the
Imperial family preferred to sit in the less visible stage right box). The crowd
overflowed into the street. Each of the female dancers in the Kirov placed a
rose on the closed coffin. Ostaltsov considered that appropriate: "He always
gave roses, he and Tanya [Tatiana] received flowers for their performances.
He loved flowers, having flowers, roses at home. The coffin was covered in
roses; you couldn't even see it anymore.

"We were all weeping. Even all the men were weeping, because it was
unbearable, because it was totally unexpected, totally incomprehensible.
And for a person who was more often in the air than on the ground."

44

AFTERMATH

Und wenn du lange in einen Abrund bickt,
Blickt der Abgrund auch in dich hinen.

And if you gaze long enough into an abyss,
The abyss will gaze back into you.

—*Friedrich Nietzsche*
  Beyond Good and Evil

As a dancer, Soloviev had reached the pinnacle of his art. As a man, he was at thirty-six incompletely evolved, psychologically the product of a repressive society as well as an individual family that did not encourage self-reflection. His uncle Aleksandr complained that following Soloviev's death, "Nobody would talk about it," Aleksandr's own brother included. "I wanted to talk, but Anna Vasilievna and Volodia [Vladimir]… nobody would talk. That was how they handled it." Vladimir's blood pressure began to spike, and he died of a stroke four years later.

"I still can't understand it or believe it," said Igor. "He had no reason. There was one possible explanation: that he was killed. Maybe. The police did not investigate it." An autopsy had not been conducted. The initial reaction of the Kirov ensemble also was that he had been murdered. But there was only one set of footprints in the snow, Shavrov asserted to Lisa.

As he had almost certainly intended, Soloviev's death was a terrible embarrassment to the state. By the time, place and manner of his death he had committed the gravest crime possible for a Soviet citizen: breaking away from the collective. He ended his days not as a cog in the "we," but as an "I." He was guilty, too, of the felonious destruction of state property, namely himself. He still had considerable amortizable value to the Ministry of Culture.

Frantically engaged in damage control, Moscow and Leningrad officials each tried to keep the other as peripheral to the case as possible. A car had been dispatched to pick up Alyona from the winter camp where the Rossi Street students were spending their vacation. Legat recalled that she and Anna "went through everything, everything" in the apartment, "hoping to find a note that he might have left for Alyona. At least that, for her. But we found nothing. He left nothing. Not even for her."

And yet Soloviev "adored his daughter," as Baryshnikov said and many others had also observed. Progressing at warp speed as the Leningrad winter approached, his agony had obliterated his sense of self and connection to reality, including his ability to comprehend that he was loved or would be missed by Alyona or anyone else.

Soloviev's mother "suffered so terribly," Tatiana recalled. "She grieved so horribly." Yet in her grief she also tried to save her granddaughter. Thirteen-year-old Alyona shut down after Yuri's death, which was followed soon after by the additional trauma of coming home from school one day to find out that their apartment had been robbed.

At home, she closeted herself in her room. Both Tatiana and Anna's entreaties were futile. "Anna and I were at our wits' end."

In desperation, Legat took her to a pediatrician. "Something has happened to this child!" he said, correctly diagnosing psychological trauma. Tatiana told him what that was.

Legat began a regimen: picking Alyona up at school and taking her on long walks around Leningrad. "I recounted all I knew about the buildings, the architecture, the history. And little by little she came out of that condition and we became so close."

Legat wanted Soloviev buried in Serafimovskoe cemetery, where she believed her mother reposed in a mass grave of siege victims. The theater commissioned a sculpture carved out of red boulder standing on its end that no one in his family liked. It disturbed Lisa when she first saw it in the late 1980s, "standing out like a sore, swollen thumb, an eyesore in the surrounding somber beauty. It was a massive, naturally red blob of Soviet kitsch, a bludgeoned-out bas-relief," patterned after a photo of Soloviev as the Underwater God in *The Little Humpbacked Horse*. He was "given a bulbous nose," Lisa complains, "a face squashed as flat as a Mongol warrior and his right arm hung behind his head at an angle indicative of a dislocated shoulder." "That arm!" Legat later protested to Lisa. Igor also made a point of saying to Lobenthal that he didn't like it either. However, Legat was told that she was to pay for the monument, and she did.

For Lisa, its one redeeming quality is a shallow carving of a phoenix rising out of the ashes on the obverse. To her it suggests a first sketch that had been rejected by Party hacks for suggesting the whiff of a belief in an afterlife.

That fall, Vinogradov replaced Belsky as the Kirov's artistic director. Belsky's watch had seen repeated scandals: the emigrations of Fedicheva, Panov and Ragozina, Baryshnikov's defection, and now Soloviev's death.

In January 1978, Igor's wife Anna, off for a vacation with her children, gave her mother-in-law a goodbye kiss on the forehead. "Why do you kiss me on the forehead, as people do saying farewell to a corpse?"—a Russian Orthodox custom at funerals. "Oh, Mama, what nonsense!"

When she returned to the city, however, she discovered that Anna's remark had been self-fulfilling: on the first anniversary of Soloviev's death, his mother hanged herself in her own apartment. She had already been buried by the time Igor's wife and their daughter returned to the city. As with Yuri's death, "nobody spoke," Anna said. But "I can understand her," Legat said. "For her, Yura was her everything, what she lived for. What she had fought to keep alive and to keep alive for during the war."

PATH TO GRAVESTONE AT SERAFIMSKOE CEMETERY. PHOTO: S. KUZNETSOV

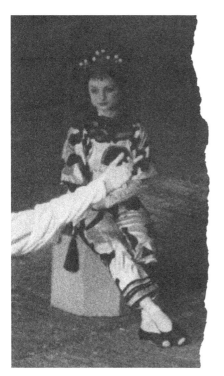

ALYONA'S NUTCRACKER CHINESE
DANCE. ROSSI SCHOOL PERFORMANCE

TATIANA AND ALYONA

PART 5:
ODYSSEY

LISA ON AMMO, HER ARABIAN HORSE. PHOTO: CORAL REISS

45

THE SCARLET LETTER

It can't last longer than two weeks.
But even ten days of happiness in a woman's life
Is a wonderful and rare thing.

—Jolie Gabor, Countess de Szigethy

O stracism had followed Lisa's return to Melbourne in August 1969. Much to her mother's shame and fury, her daughter had plummeted from princess to pariah. A veritable Australian Hester Prynne. Her mother returned from social functions to give chapter and verse of remarks overheard: "What a disgrace to her family, that girl! Can you imagine, running off with a Russian, a dancer, a-a-a… *communist!*" Never again would Lisa be invited to Government House, never admitted back to the Ladies Circle in the Members' Box on Opening Day of the racing season. Lisa's diplomat father permitted himself a single, laconic told-you-so: "Ça finit toujours mal avec les Russes"—"Things always end badly with the Russians."

Every cloud has a silver lining, of course. She had now been provided plenty of time for her studies, the opportunity to learn much at Melbourne University. In that winter of 1969–70, emotions were her greatest enemies, the intellect her greatest friend. The traveler from a distant planet had come to earth briefly, and then was gone. Every new Russian word learned was a word he might have used, every literary work one he had read or was reading at the moment, perhaps one of the banned books he'd told her he had dared to explore. Ballet class develops both muscle memory and a good ear. She could hear turns of phrases Soloviev had used and modeled, contemporary phraseology he had spoken and wrote. After final exams that year, a professor remarked, "When I read what Lisa writes, I hear her voice." "Not my voice," she reflected silently.

Translating for the Soviet Merchant Marine took on a greater significance. As most of the cargo ships were from Leningrad, she could ask the crew members to tell her about life there. How did they live, did they happen to go to the museums and the theater? Mostly, they didn't. Whenever it was possible, she would be there when the ships weighed anchor, watching them slip away slowly over the horizon, taking with them her own stowaway prayers.

She also continued her work for Edgley's company, translating and performing with visiting Russian troupes, as well as performing the English readings onstage with Russian *Shestidesiatnik* poet Andrei Voznesensky on his tour of Australia. Even more memorable was performing with U.S. poets Lawrence Ferlinghetti, Allen Ginsberg, together with Voznesensky; it was hard to say which of the latter two was more wildly uninhibited than the other.

Working in West Germany after she'd graduated from college in Australia, she married an Army officer, became a U.S. citizen, and lived and worked in Heidelberg at USAREUR HQ until 1975.

46

CAMBRIDGE, MASS.

Я кончился, а ты жива.
И ветер, жалуясь и плача,
Раскачивает лес и дачу.
Не каждую сосну отдельно,
А полностью все деревá
Со всею далью безпредельной...
А чтоб в тоске найти слова
Тебе...

I am gone, but you live.
And the wind, complaining and wailing,
Rocks the forest and the dacha.
Not each pine tree alone,
But all the trees in the endless distance...
To find words for you in your grief...

—*Boris Pasternak, Doctor Zhivago*

Early in the winter of 1976–77 Lisa, now working at Harvard University's Widener Library, began thinking about Soloviev incessantly, obsessively. A pall had fallen on her that she could not shake; at work her focus was markedly impaired. She tried to banish the thoughts by sheer will. Finally, she realized that she had to tell someone. She had not mentioned Soloviev's name since early 1970, when Edgley returned from visiting Fedicheva in Leningrad. He had seen Soloviev there. "He's fine," Edgley told Lisa. She understood that she would not be hearing from him again.

But now whom could she tell? Whom could she trust? Who would keep her mouth shut? She decided upon Oksana Procyk, the curator of the Widener's Ukrainian collection. An attractive, intelligent woman, she reminded Lisa vaguely of her own lawyer mother. Oksana kept largely to herself, distancing herself from coworkers. But she had volunteered to Lisa that her father, a Ukrainian who grew up in what had been Poland, had been at Auschwitz. As this was the sort of topic not readily shared with others in the Slavic Department, Lisa felt that she could tell her about Soloviev without compromising him.

One morning she met Oksana by chance in the marble corridor behind the main staircase of Widener. She told Oksana that she had once known a Soviet Russian. Oksana's eyes opened wide—how could this possibly have happened, she asked. Soviet citizens were followed everywhere in the West and she knew that Lisa had never had been to the USSR. Lisa clarified: he was a dancer; she had spent two and a half months with him while he was on tour in Australia. "Who is it? Where is he from? What company? What's his name?" Lisa stood there dumb. Wavering. Could she mention his name without compromising him? Oksana kept hammering, "Who is it? Who is it? Well, who IS it?"

"Yuri Soloviev, with the Kirov."

"You mean the one who just killed himself? I read about it last night in *Time* magazine."

Lisa said no more to Oksana. She spoke no more of him to anyone until 1988.

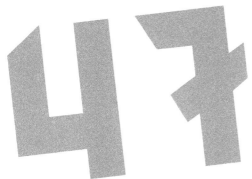

47

SINGAPORE, 1988

Lisa and her family had recently moved to the lovely island nation on the South China Sea. In those pre-Internet days, access to information there was limited. Bookstores had very little to choose from due to government censorship. Lisa reread all the books she had brought with her, some dating from college years. One of them was *Enemy at the Gates* by William Craig, about the Battle of Stalingrad. Interviewed by the author, a West German woman recalled the fiancé she had lost in the battle. She astounded the author by asking him, "Perhaps I should go there and look for him?"

An expat Englishman owned the local video lending library. He stocked it well, clearing all imported material through the censors at Customs and picking up a new video cargo on Monday mornings. Lisa took her two sons, Max and Alexander, there every Thursday afternoon. One Thursday, as she walked in, he bellowed, "I've been waiting for you!" and disappeared into the backroom. She came up to the counter and waited. He approached, hands behind his back. "You're a cultured person, I've been saving this all week for you." He shoved a videocassette up to her face.

She was stunned to see Soloviev's photo on the cover. She had not looked at a picture of him since his death. It was the only ballet video the proprietor had ever ordered. He couldn't tell why he had done so; he usually stuck to current films and children's videos, which were the moneymakers.

The Glory of the Kirov featured footage from *The Sleeping Beauty* performed by Kolpakova and Soloviev in 1976, just months before his death. Lisa played it over and over again. Watching act 2's Vision pas de deux and act 3's grand pas de deux was an existential experience for her.

It had been filmed at the Bolshoi in Moscow during a visit by the Kirov, transmitted live over Japanese TV to promote their upcoming tour.

Lisa knew that Soloviev had often danced in Japan; indeed, this was his fifth and final Japanese tour with the Kirov. Clearly, his artistry struck a chord in the Japanese soul, and they adored him.

Both Lisa and her father had lived in Japan, he before World War II, she in the early 1980s. She had learned Japanese and recognized that *Beauty* had been filmed by a cinematographer steeped in its traditions, with the Zen-like minimalism of haiku, a silent scream of the deepest of human emotions.

A highlight was the masterfully filmed close-up of his expert one-handed slow turns of the sleeping Aurora in deep arabesque. What must have been evident, she thought, to anyone who had known him was the cri de coeur of his performance. Masterful, impeccable in his mature command of technique, the resigned absence in his presence was haunting. A part of him had already gone away. A part remained in a distilled, haunting beauty. Spare and dignified, he seemed to silently speak W. H. Auden's words: "Life is a process whereby one is gradually divested of everything that makes it worth living, except the gallantry to go on."

Every defense that Lisa had created over the years was shattered. Carefully laid protective layers, bulwarks, and reinforcements crumbled.

She had to go to Russia. The pull was as irresistible as if 1969 had been yesterday. Despite the video proprietor's repeated request that she return the cassette, she informed him that nothing, including arrest, caning, and deportation, would persuade her. He allowed her to buy it. "It's against policy, I'll have you know," he told her almost sternly. But when she nodded, he smiled back.

A Russian-born neighbor, Natalya, and she had become dear friends. Natalya was married to American lawyer John Sheedy and had children the same age as Lisa's. Lisa and Natalya had hired on that year to translate for the Soviet delegation to the Singapore Film Festival. Attending were Soviet film directors Eldar Ryazanov, Gennadii Ogorodnikov, and functionaries from Gosfilm, the film distribution unit of the Ministry of Culture.

One morning Lisa was translating for an interview of Ogorodnikov conducted by Singapore's *Straits Times*. The director was from Leningrad—bullish, brash, in his mid-thirties, one of the Young Turks who was beginning to film the kind of social commentaries that Perestroika had begun to make possible. He was accompanied by an English-speaking "Third Secretary" from the Soviet Embassy—that is, KGB. The interview was progressing in the usual measured fashion. The reporter asked about things that were of little interest to the director; the director in turn discussed things the reporter had never heard of.

All of a sudden, Ogorodnikov launched into the most vituperative, damning diatribe against the Soviet Union that Lisa had ever heard out of a Russian, much less a Soviet citizen holding a ticket back home with an agent of the secret police sitting at his elbow. Lisa was stunned. The Third Secretary blinked. "Protect this guy," was Lisa's first thought. He was headed for oblivion. Without looking directly at Ogorodnikov, she asked him, in Russian "You want me to translate THAT?"

"Translate it."

"Word for word?" she asked.

"Word for word."

Out of the corner of her eye she watched the Secretary, waiting for his response. But he didn't move a muscle, didn't say anything at all. And so Lisa translated, word for word. That was the blinding, stunning, thrilling moment that she knew: The Party was over! Soviet power, once seemingly monolithic, was finally crumbling. She could find out what had happened to Soloviev without causing harm to anyone there. She could find his family.

"Find the medallion, you will find your answer," she told herself, feeling sure she would be guided in her way, would enable her to vector in toward her goal. She had given Soloviev the gold St. Christopher's medallion her parents had given her at birth. On one side was engraved St. Christopher carrying the Infant Jesus across the waters; on the obverse was her name and birthdate in French. She had worn it with the cross on her neck all her life. As she had to explain the meaning of the medallion to him, Soloviev was sure nobody else in Leningrad would know what it was when he wore it.

48

WHITE NIGHTS

В Петербурге мы сойдёмся снова,
Словно солнце мы похоронили в нём.
Осип Мандельштам

Четверть века прошло за границей,
И надеяться стало смешным.
Лучезарное небо над Ниццей
Навсегда стало небом родным...
Тишина благодатного юга,
Шорох волн, золотое вино...
Но поёт петербургская вьюга
В занесённое снегом окно,
Что пророчество мёртвого друга
Обязательно сбыться должно.

—Георгий Иванов

In Petersburg we will meet again,
As though we had buried the sun there.
Osip Mandelstam

A quarter of a century has passed abroad,
And hoping has become ridiculous.
The radiant sky over Nice
Has become my own forever...
But in St. Petersburg a blizzard sings
In a snow-covered window,
That the prophecy of a dead friend
Surely will come true.

—Émigré poet Georgii Ivanov

espite Gorbachev's Perestroika, travel advisories for Americans to the Soviet Union remained in effect, particularly for proactive anti-Soviets like the Whitakers. Lisa encountered stiff resistance and stern warnings. Finally, a Pilate-like washing of the hands ensued when she enlisted Natalya as travelling companion. So it was not until May 1989 that she was able to leave for Leningrad, released by her husband with a terse, "You won't look good in the Gulag."

Natalya had studied at the Herzen Institute in Leningrad and had a friend, an alumnus who was one of the "New Russian" entrepreneurs. He was Sergei V. Kuznetsov, son of the prominent folklorist Vladimir S. Bakhtin, grandson of the Countess Bakhtin nicknamed "Kuzya." A delightful bon vivant with a degree in French and German, he seemed to step out of a nineteenth-century novel. Having received an exclusive contract with Fujifilm to develop film for Leningrad tourists, he had a small photo shop near the city's principal thoroughfare, majestic Nevsky Prospect. Using the new travel possibilities available to Soviet citizens, he had asked Natalya to send him an invitation so he could go abroad for the first time in early 1988. Going to Singapore seemed as good a place as any, since he would have a place to stay. Hard currency purchase for travel was far too limited to afford a hotel.

Natalya asked him to find out where Soloviev was buried. Kuzya arrived in Singapore with more information than she expected. A photographer friend had gone out and taken pictures of his grave, in Serafimovskoe Cemetery. How appropriate, it seemed to Lisa, that winged Soloviev was in a place named after the biblical six-winged Seraphim.

The June light in Leningrad ("Белые Ночи—Belyye Nochi") the White Nights when the sun barely sets, was for Lisa a surreal experience, contributing to the dreamlike atmosphere induced by the emotion of finally being there. The Neva River was a strange steel color, stately, its waters heaving and flowing in slow motion, evoking in her memory, Soloviev's ballon, his slow takeoffs and landings in deep pliés. She watched the river for hours, standing alone on the many red granite embankments, from the Petrogradskaya Storona where Kuzya lived, or across the river standing in front of the Winter Palace, or the appallingly named Robespierre Embankment. She was too tense to sleep much, physically strained by wandering all over the city. Her day began with long jogs along the Neva when awakened by the sun at three a.m. and continued until midnight when darkness finally arrived. Kuzya and other kind friends of his often volunteered to guide her. They had a lot of free time, having quit their ill- or non-paying government jobs to venture out on their own, becoming the New Russians. They were intelligent and entrepreneurial, refusing to languish and die in poverty.

49

PRIMARY SOURCES

ellist Oleg Bedran, another friend of Natalya's from her student days and a member of the Maly Theater Orchestra, had asked around and told her that a friend of Soloviev's was willing to meet a foreigner to speak about him. One afternoon in the Maly artists' cafeteria, the cellist sat her at one of the tables and went to the counter. A man who met him there was brought over to her, introduced, and then Oleg walked off.

This was Yuri Vasilkov, a former principal danseur at the Maly. Although slight, he had a redoubtable look. Most remarkable were his ice-blue eyes and a manner that indicated this was not a man to be crossed. Sitting directly opposite her, nose-to-nose across the small table, he leaned in on one elbow, locked his eyes on her, and without any attempt at small talk or preamble—including the question of who the hell she was—came at her and "let it rip." Clearly, this was a man who had waited a long time to have his say.

He always remembered the encouragement Soloviev had given him as a young dancer—above all, the words of support Soloviev offered at his graduation-night performance at the Kirov. Subsequently, they became friends.

Vasilkov and his wife Irina Gorokhova, a retired Kirov dancer, helped her over and over again in her quest. Irina loaned her photo album to Kuzya to copy, as Lisa had no photographs of Soloviev. Vasilkov made pleas and phone calls to people who had known him, but all refused to meet with her. Lisa spent hours at their apartment on Vasilievsky Island, while they taught her all about the past: their past, Soloviev's past. They gave her what she describes as one of the greatest courses on the Soviet Union she had received. Gradually she was beginning to understand things. Vasilkov was the first, and, for a long time, the only person who would talk about Soloviev's death. "Lizochka, he died of old wounds, of many old wounds."

Kuzya was on friendly terms with Andrei Kuznetsov-Vecheslov, son of Kirov principal dancers Tatiana Vecheslova and Sviatoslav Kuznetsov. Lisa was invited to meet him. Kuznetsov was willing to speak about the Kirov in general terms, but refused to discuss Soloviev save for the recollection of the last time he saw him. "I should have done something to help him." These words were repeated to Lisa by many others over subsequent years.

It was known that Alyona and Tatiana had left Leningrad years ago, but where might they be? Neither Vasilkov nor Kuznetsov knew, and her additional inquiries were met with a unanimous stone wall.

50

TRINITY SUNDAY— KOLOSKOVO

uri Vasilkov had given her the address of Soloviev's dacha; he and his wife had visited there in the old days. Lisa would have preferred to see it alone, but was unable to find a way to go by herself in those still-secretive post-Soviet times. Foreigners were forbidden to travel outside a twenty-five-kilometer radius from Soviet cities. She couldn't simply go out into the country and make her way around, and she certainly couldn't ask directions. Even in the city center, people recoiled in horror when they understood that it was a dreaded foreigner addressing them in Russian.

But one day, after she revisited Soloviev's grave, Kuzya and his friend Andrei Telkov, one of the few who had a car in those days, told her that they would drive her to the dacha. She was very grateful for their courage. "When we leave Leningrad, don't speak a word to anyone," Kuzya warned her.

As they were about to leave, Natalya called. "Today is Holy Trinity Sunday." Russian Orthodox Church calendar is still per the Julian Calendar—all their Feast Days were, and remain, two weeks after our Gregorian Calendar. This hadn't occurred to Lisa, who had already celebrated Trinity Sunday in Singapore. "You have to go back to Serafimovskoe cemetery today," Natalya insisted. "On Trinity Sundays everyone always goes to pay respect to their loved ones." "I *am* going to pay respect to a loved one," Lisa answered.

It was an extraordinarily sunny day. They arrived at Koloskovo by the Priozerskii Road; Andrei and Kuzya stayed by the car while she went up to the low fence. No longer owned by the Solovievs, their former dacha was a ramshackle wooden cabin that had expanded via small increments, including a *banya*—a sauna. Soloviev had added it since the heat relieved his back pain, she was later told. In true Russian style, after roasting himself, Soloviev would run from the sauna and jump into the Maloe Sushchie Lake, some 100 yards away.

Just as Lisa reached the gate, it swung open. Startled, she saw a large dog trot out, deep dark eyes in a brindle head observing her. She lowered her eyes and slowly nodded to it. Just as slowly, he lowered his head, responded with his own slight nod and walked off, leaving the gate wide open. She stepped inside. A tiny cloud appeared overhead, sprinkling a few drops of rain on her as she prayed. It felt to her like a blessing. She seemed to hear

Soloviev say matter-of-factly, "Не молись тут только за меня: Ne molis' tut tol'ko za menya—Don't pray here for me alone." Only afterward, when they were leaving Koloskovo, did she see a plaque not far off from where the car was parked:

"Our village is named in honor of Sergeant Aleksandr Petrovich Koloskov, heroically fallen here on 28 June 1944 during the liberation of the Karelian Isthmus from German-Fascist invaders."

So she had prayed for them all, Russians like Soloviev, Finns, Germans, whoever they were, whose remains were left long after the battle had passed on from that lovely little lake.

51

"MIGHT YOU BE COMING TO MOSCOW?"

isa and her husband found themselves decidedly unsuited to each other, but she remains grateful to him for her sons. A brilliant man, largely absent, he graduated from West Point before women were admitted; his disapproval of all things Russian was axiomatic.

Still, she managed to get back to Leningrad. On her second trip, she met again with the Vasilkovs and Andrei Kuznetsov, but was stymied in her search, unable to make further Kirov contacts. She did, however, meet Sergei Albert, a colleague of Kuzya's at the Fuji concession, and his wife, Natalia Bespalova, an associate professor of English at the prestigious Bonch-Brue-vich Institute of Telecommunications. Unbeknown to each other, Soloviev's uncle Aleksandr taught there as well. It was Natalia who later made the contact with Soloviev's best friend, the late Aleksandr Shavrov, when all other efforts had failed.

Sergei, a tall man whose appearance, British-accented English, and timbre of voice reminded her of one of Hollywood's most elegant baddies, the St. Petersburg–born British actor George Sanders, became a true friend and great help to Lisa in the years to come. A linguist by training, he possessed a sharp wit and knowledge of his native language, which provided great joy and a significant boost to her armamentarium.

Now having resettled in Connecticut with her family, she asked her mother to stay with her sons while she made her third trip in the fall of 1990.

She reminded herself of the Russian proverb "God loves the Trinity." "This time it will work," she told herself.

In Leningrad she stayed once again with Kuzya and his family in their spacious Art Nouveau apartment building on the Petrogradskaia Storona, near the Peter and Paul Fortress. Vasilkov gave her the telephone number of Natalia Krasovskaya, the doyenne of Soviet ballet critics. There was a slight chance she might help find Tatiana and Alyona. Lisa called that same evening and gave Krasovskaya her mantra: she was a foreigner, she had traveled to Russia several times to learn of Yuri Soloviev and his fate.

She cringed, feeling like a travelling salesman trying to jam his foot in the door before it gets slammed in his face.

"Why are you calling me?" returned Krasovskaya's harsh, high-pitched voice. "Call Tatiana Legat!"

"I cannot find her. She doesn't live in town."

"She's in Moscow. Here's the phone number."

Lisa repeated the number to be sure. Krasovskaya hung up before Lisa could say thank you.

Lisa picked up the phone again and dialed the number. Legat answered. Lisa identified herself once more and repeated her mantra, adding, "I wasn't able to find you until Vera Krasovskaya gave me your number."

Legat retorted that it was not possible: she was the only Legat listed in the Moscow telephone exchange, the only Legat in the city!

"I am a foreigner, Tatiana Nikolaevna," Lisa entreated, "I didn't even know what city you lived in."

A long silence ensued, Lisa's heart dropped, but she hung on and waited. Finally, a small, very different voice inquired, "Might you be coming to Moscow?"

"I will buy a ticket for tomorrow's Red Arrow. I will be in Moscow day after tomorrow."

Kuzya took the phone and asked Tatiana for the address. He had kindly agreed to accompany Lisa to Moscow. He would meet with Fujifilm representatives there and bring back things that were impossible to buy in Leningrad. "Laundry detergent, for one," his wife Lena shouted from the kitchen.

The Red Arrows were the only passenger train foreigners were allowed to take between Leningrad and Moscow. It was an exclusively overnight train that ran nonstop: foreigners intending evil wouldn't be able to alight and go snooping.

The train arrived at Moscow's Leningradskii Vokzal—Leningrad Station. Lisa went to Legat's apartment nearby and rang the bell. Legat opened the door, tears in her eyes. Behind her was a lovely slight person with Soloviev's face. His Alyonushka.

Legat and Alyona led Lisa directly to the kitchen, bypassing the formality of the living room. They were determined that she have something to eat after her journey. Then Tatiana began to speak. Her words tumbled over each other, waves and waves in rapid succession. Of Yuri and the family and what had happened to them after he died, about Alyona, about life in Moscow.

She had left Leningrad when Alyona graduated from the Rossi Street academy in 1982 because the Kirov had declined to accept her. Legat was informed that Alyona, shorter than her mother, did not suit them. It was an unthinkable affront: the heir to the Legat-Soloviev dynasty rejected. Other less talented legacy graduates had been given places at the theater. Legat resigned from the Kirov and immediately received an offer from Maya Plisetskaya to join the ballet staff of the Stanislavsky-and-Nemirovich-Danchenko company in Moscow. Alyona had joined the state ballet company in Vilnius, Lithuania, then an outpost of anti-Russian sentiment, clamoring for independence from the Soviet's 1944 occupation of the Baltics. Legat bought a large apartment in Moscow from the proceeds of the sale of the car and the dacha.

Legat spoke for thirty minutes without pause, her eyes and Lisa's never leaving each other. "And you?" she finally asked, with a slight tilt of her head.

A letter from Legat arrived a few weeks later, postmarked New York. A trusted friend who was travelling to the U.S. had mailed it for her. Legat wrote to "Dear Lizonka" that she had been deeply moved by their visit, meeting someone "who so loves and remembers my beloved Yurin." She signed the letter, "Loving you, Tatiana."

52

1992

n January 1992, the Soviet Union was dissolved. Widespread economic disruption and infrastructure collapse were particularly felt in the health-care system, causing great hardship, particularly for the most vulnerable populations. Nonprofits in the United States became active in providing assistance.

In the spring of that year, Lisa joined Americares, a medical humanitarian relief organization located in New Canaan, Connecticut. It had recently begun providing assistance to the ex–Warsaw Pact countries. She became its project manager for Eastern Europe and the former Soviet Union.

For her first solo airlift, 115 tons of medical supplies transported by a massive U.S. Air Force C-5A Galaxy, Lisa chose Vladimirskaia Oblast, a district east of Moscow. One of the trucks picking up the donated medical supplies was from an outlying hospital in the district, delightfully named Iurievo Pole—Yuri's Field. The Chief Nurse, a formidable-looking Russian woman of the old school, briskly signed the manifest and departed, only to return some time later, jumping off the truck and running toward her. Panting as she climbed the steps of the warehouse, she said to Lisa, tears in her eyes, "I'm not from this district, I'm from Leningrad, a *blokadnitsa*—a siege survivor—and I have high blood pressure. We have had no beta blockers to control it for many months until this donation. You have saved my life. This is for you," she said as she removed the lacquered brooch pinned to her heaving, massive breasts and gave it to Lisa. Looking at it as she held it in her hands—she saw it was Danila in *The Stone Flower*.

Travelling back through Moscow after another airlift, Lisa went to see Tatiana and Alyona. While Tatiana was working, Alyona and her friend Alexei took her sightseeing. She stayed with them overnight rather than go back to the hotel. The next day as she was leaving, she was surprised and concerned that only Alyona accompanied her to the door. Tatiana had remained in the kitchen, quite contrary to the Russian custom of *provozhat*, that everybody sees the guest to the door. Had she offended, Lisa wondered? As she turned to walk out the door, Alyona called out to her. Lisa turned around. Alyona had pulled out the gold chain she wore beneath her sweater. "Lisa, is this yours?" she asked, holding the medallion up to her— inscribed "Lisa Jacqueline 30 Juillet 1949."

"Yes, mine," Lisa said.

"Papa wore it all his life. When he died, I took it and wear it."

PART 6:
EPILOGUE

LISA AND TATIANA IN ST. PETERSBURG, NOVEMBER 2016
PHOTO: VALENTIN BARANOVSKY

53
COMING TO AMERICA

ALYONA AND TATIANA IN NEW YORK CITY, AUGUST 1992

Legat had remained under a travel ban since Soloviev's suicide. It was only through Plisetskaya's efforts that it was temporarily lifted. She wanted Tatiana to rehearse a group of dancers Plisetskaya had assembled for a month's tour of Italy. Now after Perestroika, travel restrictions were lifted. A summer teaching position in England, then a position at the Boston Ballet had become available. Tatiana asked Lisa to expedite and to bring out his film archive. On August 22, 1990, Lisa met Tatiana and Alyona at LaGuardia Airport in New York. They stayed with her in New Canaan until the contract with the Boston Ballet began. Tatiana was quite overwhelmed by having left Russia. She and Lisa spent many hours talking after the others had gone to bed.

Tatiana and Alyona did well at the Boston Ballet and elsewhere. Tatiana's student Sarah Lamb subsequently became a ballerina in London's Royal Ballet. Intelligent and capable, Alyona danced and staged—and also bought houses, renovating them and turning them around. It became possible for them both to obtain permanent resident status. On May 20, 1997, Alyona gave birth to a son she named Yuri Legat. She asked Lisa to be his godmother. Alyona later married Andrey Shevaldin, a former Bolshoi Ballet dancer, and bore a second son, Nikolai, in 2003.

ALYONA DANCING THE SUGAR PLUM FAIRY IN *THE NUTCRACKER*

OFFLOADING AN ILYUSHIN-76 TRANSPORT PLANE WITH AMERICARES
PHOTOGRAPHER PHIL FARNSWORTH IN RUSSIA

54

SWORDS INTO PLOWSHARES

or five years in the mid-1990s, Lisa, often accompanied by now-colleague Sergei Albert, crisscrossed Russia and the former Soviet Republics, off-loading airplanes loaded with tons of vaccines and medical supplies from Siberia to Samarkand, Chelyabinsk to Chechnya, above the Arctic Circle, to the deserts of Central Asia in temperatures ranging from +130 to -45 degrees Fahrenheit. While sending medical humanitarian aid to St. Petersburg, she also founded the Americares-Yale Medical School Cardiology and Cardiac Surgery Program with Dr. Robert Jarrett, then medical director of Americares. Together they brought teams of doctors to the St. Petersburg Institute of Cardiology to teach U.S. best practices in adult and pediatric heart surgery to their Russian colleagues.

While in St. Petersburg, Lisa was invited to the Vaganova Ballet Academy Museum on Rossi Street. It was run by former dancer Marina Vivien, daughter of the great Leonid Vivien—actor, director, and then artistic director of the Leningrad Pushkin Academic Theater. Of French extraction, Vivien spoke French at home with her husband, the son of idealistic French communists who had come to the Soviet Union during the Great Depression and remained stranded there.

As Vivien showed Lisa around, there were all manner of portraits of contemporary dancers, but not one of Soloviev. There were in a cardboard box a few pictures of him, but nothing more. "There's no money for it. Look at the ones we have," Vivien said as she turned a picture around to show the frame had once been around a portrait of Felix Dzerzhinsky, founder of the Cheka, the Soviet secret police. "But if you can help, we can make this side wall for Soloviev, next to Vinogradov."

Lisa arranged for enlargements of the photos she had collected through Kuzya's Fujifilm subsidiary. Frames were made for them and when she returned to St. Petersburg, the Soloviev wall was extant.

In 1997, the Russian government declared there was no further need for humanitarian aid. Lisa left Americares soon after and, much like Davey Crockett who had said "You can go to hell—I'm going to Texas," moved to Houston with her family.

She continued her close connection to St. Petersburg, spearheading a program that created a telemedicine link between the University of Texas Medical School and the three medical schools in St. Petersburg. Students and faculty were now allowed real-time online access to Grand Rounds lectures and the UT medical library.

Now CEO of The Living Bank, the Texas nonprofit organ donor registry, Lisa returned to St. Petersburg in summer 2005 to review a Rotary Medical Service Grant she had obtained for the city. By now, it had become much easier to find and talk with Soloviev's former friends and colleagues. When she told his ex-Kirov colleague Evgenii Shcherbakov how much she would have liked to have seen Soloviev in *Giselle*, the kind, gentlemanly former dancer escorted Lisa to see it at the Mariinsky. At least to see where he danced it, he insisted, overriding her reluctance. Watching it was a bittersweet moment for her.

In 2008, while Lisa was again abroad, Legat received an invitation to coach at the newly renamed (back to Imperial) Mikhailovsky Theater (the Maly in the Soviet era). Tatiana jumped at the chance to return to her beloved St. Petersburg and her family followed. Alyona has devoted herself to bringing up her sons, frequently declining opportunities in Russia and abroad that would interfere, but from time to time she still returns to America as guest teacher.

Andrey requalified as a massage therapist. Although Russian now predominates at home and in school, Soloviev's two grandsons speak English between themselves.

RESTING UNDER A MOTHBALLED USAF COLD WAR BOMBER BEFORE AIRLIFT
PHOTO: PAUL MCGUIRK

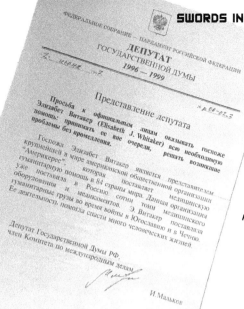

ФЕДЕРАЛЬНОЕ СОБРАНИЕ — ПАРЛАМЕНТ РОССИЙСКОЙ ФЕДЕРАЦИИ

ДЕПУТАТ
ГОСУДАРСТВЕННОЙ ДУМЫ
1996 — 1999

Представление депутата

Просьба к официальным лицам оказывать госпоже Элизабет Витакер (Elisabeth J. Whitaker) всю необходимую помощь: принимать ее вне очереди, решать возникшие проблемы без промедления.

Госпожа Элизабет Витакер является представителем крупнейшей в мире американской общественной организации "Америкерес", которая поставляет медицинскую гуманитарную помощь в 84 страны мира. Данная организация уже поставила в Россию сотни тонн медицинского оборудования и медикаментов. Э. Витакер поставляла гуманитарные грузы во время войны в Югославию и в Чечню. Ее деятельность помогла спасти много человеческих жизней.

Депутат Государственной Думы РФ,
член Комитета по международным делам

И.Мальков

LAISSEZ-PASSER
FROM THE DUMA
[PARLIAMENT OF
THE RUSSIAN
FEDERATION]

AT A RUSSIAN ORPHANAGE AFTER A DISTRIBUTION
PHOTO: MELANIE BAROCAS

55

THE
SUMMING UP

Die Vergangenheit hört nicht auf.
Sie korrigiert sich in der Gegenwart.

The past does not end.
It corrects itself in the present.

—*Siegfried Lenz*

n September 2016 Lisa interviewed Pierre Lacotte by phone from Paris. His outrage at Soloviev's fate intensified her own sense of mission. "Il vous a demandé de ne pas lui oublier!" he thundered at her. "Faites ce qu'il vous a dit! J'exige, Madame, que vous écriviez le livre!"

"He asked you not to forget him! Do as he told you! I demand of you, Madame, write the book!"

Perhaps in English, the words would not have struck so primordial a nerve. But delivered in her father's language, they fell upon Lisa like a command thundering from the heavens.

She returned to St. Petersburg in November 2016. Faithful friend Kuzya met her at the airport. "It's snowing!" he roared with delight. "It hasn't snowed in St. Petersburg so early for years. It is to welcome you back to the Motherland." Picking their way to Kuzya's gleaming imported SUV, they exited the parking lot, packed with every manner of late-model foreign makes. An elevated highway fed into the city, which gleamed and glowed as they drove through the winter wonderland. Kuzya delivered her to the Soloviev's apartment on the elegant Fontanka Embankment near the Mariinsky. Tatiana had invited Lisa to stay with them. "You can stay in Yurka's room as he's in Moscow and it will be easier to do your work. We are very busy, so we won't disturb you."

Tatiana, sparkling and unchanged by the years, met Lisa at the door with pretty Alyona and tall, elegant Andrey. Their son, Nikolai, who had just won a Junior Pre-Olympic Team 220-meter race that day despite a sore heel, limped in after them to greet Lisa. The apartment had been skillfully remodeled by Alyona. It brimmed with memorabilia of the legacies of both Legat and Soloviev families. On Tatiana's bedroom dresser, a small framed

LISA WITH TATIANA. PHOTO: VALENTIN BARANOVSKY

picture, dark with age, showed her and her brother as teens with their beloved Babushka. A picture-postcard of a very young Soloviev striking a matinee idol pose, his jacket thrown over his shoulder, hangs on the wall at the foot of the bed.

"That is the first thing I see when I wake up in the morning. I like to remember him like that."

"Oh, if Yura had lived…" is an oft-repeated preamble when Tatiana speaks of life today.

Tatiana had arranged to go to the Vaganova Academy Museum the next day. She was donating the pages of handwritten notes to the ballet *Spectre de la Rose* given to Soloviev in New York by Andre Eglevsky. As they came in, they both looked to the right, both women remembering the spot. The Soloviev wall was gone. Not the actual wall, but the framed portraits of Soloviev and the casement with the photo albums. Marina Vivien was also gone, repatriated by the French government to the city of Lyon. Her replacements were Tatiana Gorina and Alyona's classmate Elena Adamenko. No, they had no knowledge of the fate of the Soloviev wall or the albums. But they did have some photos of Soloviev they could look through. With that, they produced a cardboard box, making Lisa feel as if she had come full circle—all the way back to the cardboard box of photos produced for her twenty years earlier. Gorina and Adamenko plan to expand the museum's collection significantly, which will include many Soloviev artifacts, including his Bluebird costume, donated by Tatiana and the family.

German, Tatiana's brother, also came by to see Lisa again. Tall and gaunt, he was still possessed of an indomitably sunny disposition that had served him well throughout a life that had included blockade, starvation, orphanages, the Gulag, several marriages, and now, a posse of grandchildren. Tatiana sat next to him as Lisa interviewed him. She would comment, "I didn't know that" or "Ooh, you never told me that before," the three often sighing, often laughing together. No, he said, he didn't remember their mother, only a woman in a red beret.

Later, sitting at the dining room table that she had taken over as her desk, Lisa scanned all the Soloviev-related materials, including his final report cards, newspaper clippings from all over the world, photographs

SOLOVIEV'S GRAVE WITH GRANITE EFFIGY
IN BACKGROUND. PHOTO: LISA WHITAKER

and documents from Anna Solovieva, Igor's widow. Igor had died in 2009 of a brain tumor.

Lisa came across Clive Barnes' obituary of Soloviev in *The New York Times*. Barnes had written of Soloviev's "dark and desperate passion" in his portrayal of Albrecht. As Lisa read, Tatiana came by and sat down. The women read and re-read the obituary together. They spent much time at the kitchen table or the desk/dining room table. Tatiana's eyes glowed or grieved, remembering.

From the moment in 1992 when Tatiana had asked in a soft, hesitating voice, "Might you be planning to come to Moscow?" Lisa had felt at ease in her company. Their backgrounds and attitudes were often strikingly different, even jarringly so, but the feeling was not. She had never felt like a stranger.

Tatiana was rehearsing the Mikhailovsky corps in *Giselle*. "There is only one performance at the Mikhailovsky before you leave St. Petersburg. You will sit in my Repetiteur's seat in the Parterre."

"Oh, *Giselle*," Legat said with a sigh, going on to recount how Soloviev had danced it. "In the second act, Albrecht dances brisés in a diagonal heading downstage and then turns and continues his brisés as he returns upstage. He is pleading with Myrtha, perhaps for his life, perhaps to be with Giselle. Soloviev performed the brisés downstage, then returned upstage instead in a series of pas de poisson leaps. His arms and eyes were pleading with Myrtha downstage; his eyes never left her. Nobody else could do that," Legat proudly declared. "It was electrifying. You must put it in the book."

"How did he play Albrecht?" Lisa asked. "Like a spoiled man doing as he pleased, amusing himself with a peasant girl?"

"Oh, no, no! His Albrecht was honorable, like his own nature. He truly loved Giselle. He was foolish, thinking he could… and then he broke her heart and killed her. It tormented him."

Why was this Soloviev's favorite role, Lisa mused as Tatiana spoke. Did he feel that it was an allegory of his life? Was that why he began to dance it with such intensity? Like the aristocrat Albrecht, Soloviev had status and honors as a premier danseur, a member of a privileged, if powerless, Soviet elite. She wondered if the appeal in dancing *Giselle* was that it was a mute

ALBRECHT. PHOTO: JENNIE WALTON

soliloquy on the regrets Soloviev may have had. Did he see in Albrecht a character who was similarly constrained by society, circumstance, and his own only too human failings? And, as well, the siren's song that the resolution is in death.

Inexplicable, enigmatic Russia. Every Westerner who has ever claimed to understand it has been proven wrong. Often dead wrong. "The only way to figure the Russians," Clark Gable, playing a Moscow correspondent, quips in the 1953 film *Never Let Me Go*, "is to put two and two together, make nine, add seven, divide by four, and give up."

A land where a total stranger will go to extraordinary lengths to help you just because, and a land where someone whose day job is to help you will leave you hanging by your neck, slowly swinging in the wind. The land of the most pernicious of all breeds of civil servant, the infamous, widely loathed *chinovnik*.

The former imperial capital now restored, gleaming with gold and marble majesty, land of endless, ferocious natural beauty and indescribably horrible history. St. Petersburg is once again what Peter the Great intended, a thoroughly European city, with French restaurants, American bars, English pubs, and English-language translation everywhere. A friend of Lisa's fumed about his daughter's insisting that she needed a new iPhone: "The young people don't realize what it was like!" But thank God they don't, he and Lisa agreed.

What had also disappeared was the boundless public drunkenness that had astounded Lisa when she first traveled to the Soviet Union. As a friend remarked, "This is today's Russia. Before, everybody drank and there was nowhere to go and drink. Sit freezing in the park or sit at home looking at your relatives, and drink. Both horrible. Now there are these establishments on every corner and nobody drinks anymore. Look at me! Did you ever see me before with a glass of water?"

Nonetheless, the Russians are not like you and me, to paraphrase F. Scott Fitzgerald. But to Lisa, behind even the blandest-faced everyman there lay something riveting and endlessly compelling.

In St. Petersburg, Lisa was enormously helped by Mariinsky photographer Valentin Baranovsky, a former TASS News Agency photojournalist.

When Lisa mentioned she had only driven by 64 Fontanka, where Soloviev had grown up, Baranovsky drove her there in the snow. Splashed by mud from passing cars, the two examined the plaque on the façade commemorating him. Inexplicably, the massive entrance door stood open. They made their way up to the fifth floor where the Solovievs communal apartment had been, Baranovsky snapping photos all the way.

The hour was approaching, always the saddest hour, when the time for departure had come. Now Baranovsky arranged for Lisa's interview with retired Kirov character dancer Anatoli Gridin. Gridin had said he no longer wanted to submit to interviews, but Baranovsky persuaded him. Lisa was eager. In 1957, Gridin had created the role of the evil bailiff Severyan in Grigorovich's *The Stone Flower*. Lisa had seen the video of act 1, filmed in London in 1961 with Gridin, Soloviev, Osipenko, and Sizova.

"Meet me at the synagogue nearby, not my building," Gridin instructed her. The next day, cutting and blustery, she met a slim man with bright pale eyes peering from under a ski cap, a white Fu Manchu mustache and long straight hair, looking like a benevolent version of Severyan. He peered deeply into her eyes, tearing now from the wind.

"You are not a *korrespondent*"—a journalist—"'Lisa, Lizaveta,'" quoting lines from an old ditty.

"No, I am not."

"This synagogue"—he gestured—"was open all through Soviet times, providing meals to the hungry. Shall we go in and see what they'll give us to eat?"

"No, let them provide for the needy, I would like to take you to lunch"

"I am not accustomed to having ladies take me out."

"You could get used to it."

"Hmm, I could," he replied with a grin. "Why did you want to interview me?"

Lisa said she had seen him in 1964 on stage and recently on DVD as Severyan. She was intrigued watching his performance. She felt sure that he would have something interesting to say.

"And I do?"

"Yes you do," she said, continuing the rapid verbal handball game that marked the interview. Gridin must be a formidable chess player, Lisa mused.

He spoke about how kind Tatiana's grandmother was to him while he and Legat lived as boarders on Rossi Street. Babushka had given him an apple one winter. "Could you believe it, a piece of fruit in Leningrad in those times?" The grandmother had asked him, a well-behaved older boy, to look out for Tatiana.

He and Lisa linked arms to resist the blasts of arctic wind blowing down Dekabristov Prospect. Kuzya was due to pick her up. Lisa suggested that Gridin leave her there and go home: "That is such a light jacket, you must be cold."

"I am a Siberian," was his reply, and then, continuing as much to himself as to her, Gridin reflected: "So, Soloviev, Soloviev, hmm… He was a great artist. *Sviatoi*"—saintly, sainted. "Do you understand the meaning of the word *sviatoi*, Lisa-Lizaveta?"

"Yes, I do."

"And, indeed, how is it that you speak Russian so well?"

"That was from him, too."

"That was a great gift Yura gave you."

Amen, she thought.

FOYER OF FONTANKA 64. PHOTO: VALENTIN BARANOVSKY

… И пусть фиксированные и бронзовые веки
Как слезы, тающий снег тает,
И голубь тюрьмы позволил ему пройти вдалеке,
И корабли тихо идут вдоль Невы.

—Анна Ахматова
   Реквием

… And may the melting snow flow like tears

From the motionless bronze eyelids,

May the prison dove release him into the distance,

As the ships on the Neva, to slip softly away.

—Anna Akhmatova
"Requiem"

NOTES

All remarks from firsthand sources are taken from author interviews unless otherwise stated. Interview citations are given only the first time they occur in the text. We do not give review titles, most of which are generic.

Quotes from Tatiana Legat are taken from numerous conversations with Whitaker beginning in 1992, interviews by Lobenthal in September 2000, and August 2004.

Quotes from Aleksandr Soloviev taken from interviews by Lobenthal, April 2005, and Whitaker, July 2005.

Quotes from Nikolai Ostaltsov taken from interviews with Lobenthal, February and August 2001, and with Whitaker, November 2016.

PART 1: BEGINNINGS
CH 1: INTRODUCTION
"hanging in the air," Lobenthal interview with Ib Andersen, February 2012.

"you would get goose bumps," Whitaker telephone interview with Emma Minchonok, February 2017.

"made to stand in line," Whitaker interview with Evgenii Shcherbakov, July 2005.

"the most terrific accusation," Iulia Iakovleva,
https://www.afisha.ru/performance/65571/review/342722/

"dropping out of international consciousness," Clive Barnes, "Dance View: A Pall Is Cast Over Leningrad's Kirov Ballet," *The New York Times*, January 23, 1977.

"a Stradivarius," Natalia Makarova, *A Dance Autobiography*, New York: Alfred A. Knopf, 1979, 72.

CH 3: RECLAMATION
"a rare chance to discover," Anna Kisselgoff, "A Magic Trio Revisited: Seeing What the Ballet Legends Were All About," *The New York Times*, January 21, 2000.

CH 4: HIS PARENTS
"someone from the intelligentsia," Whitaker telephone interview with Mira Baklanova, March 2017.

CH 5: CHILDHOOD

"There were no toys," Lobenthal interview with Igor Soloviev, February 2001.

"very supportive letters," Lobenthal interview with Alla Osipenko, May 1998.

CH 7: ON ROSSI STREET

"a pint-sized prince," Lobenthal, "Yuri Soloviev," *Ballet Review*, Fall 2003.

"always recognizable," Whitaker interview with Aleksandr Chavrov, July 2005.

"with such admiration," Arkady Ivanenko interview with Marina Tcherednichenko, March 2017.

"not just how to dance," Whitaker telephone interview with Gabriela Komleva, December 2016.

"headed for fame," N. I. Gorbachev, included in *Yuri Soloviev: His Life and Work*, edited by Boris Blankov, St. Petersburg, Russian Federation: Dean Publishers, 2005, 137–141.

"didn't wear a comic makeup," Elena Tchernichova, *Dancing on Water: A Life in Ballet, from the Kirov to the ABT*, Boston: Northeastern University Press, 2013, 78.

"Not aggressive, not sad," Lobenthal interview with Evgenii Shcherbakov, May 2002.

"open-minded," Lobenthal interview with Elena Shatrova, February 2002.

"some kind of sadness," Lobenthal interview with Oleg Vinogradov, August 2001.

PART 2: THE KIROV
CH 8: NUREYEV, PISAREV, PUSHKIN

"found stabbed to death," Lobenthal interview with Elena Tchernichova, December 1990.

"everything for Yuri Soloviev," Diane Solway, *Nureyev: His Life*, New York: William Morrow, 1998, 87.

"You think I'm good?" Julie Kavanagh, *Nureyev: The Life*, New York: Pantheon, 2007, 52.

"threatened to punch," *Rudolf Nureyev: Dance to Freedom,* directed by Richard Curson Smith (BBC Two, 2015).

"do everything perfectly," Whitaker interview with Sergei Vikulov, November 2016.

CH 9: TATIANA
"Stalin liked ballet," Whitaker interview with Andrei Kutznetsov-Vecheslov, 1989.

CH 12: ALLA SIZOVA
"always closer to me," Lobenthal interview with Alla Sizova, February 2002.

"a wonderful pair on stage," Alla Shelest, "God-Given Gifts," included in Blankov, *Yuri Soloviev: His Life and Work,* 133–134.

"a great artist," Belsky, remarks at memorial evening honoring the fifty-fifth anniversary of Soloviev's birth, 1995. Included in Blankov, *Yuri Soloviev: His Life and Work,* 98–99.

"uniquely spiritual," Doris Hering, *Dance Magazine,* November 1961.

CH:13-16
In addition to specific citations listed below, we consulted accounts in Kavanagh, *Nureyev: The Life*; Solway, *Nureyev: His Life*; Peter Watson, *Nureyev: A Biography*, London: Hodder & Stoughton, 1994; and Otis Sturat, *Perpetual Motion: The Public and Private Lives of Rudolf Nureyev*, New York: Simon & Schuster, 1995.

Electronic sources include:
www.aktualnizpravy.cz
www.cairn.info/revue-les-cahiers-sirice
www.chtoby-pomnili.net
www.kino-teatr.ru
www.kinozal.tv/persons
www.kommersant.ru
www.kp.ru
www.kulturologia.ru
www.liveinternet.ru
www.nureyev.org
www.psj.ru
www.telegraph.co.uk

www.terpsyhora.ru/interviu
www.theaustralian.com.au
www.theguardian.com
www.thesundaytimes.co.uk
www.tracker.nova-lan.ru
www.ufppc.org
www.vault.fbi.gov
www.versia.ru

Source documents include:
KGB (Committee of State Security) of the USSR:
Chairman Aleksandr N. Shelepin, to Politburo:
 1.   Note of 3. VI.1961,
 2.   Note of 19. VI.1961: Treason to Motherland of ballet Artist R. Kh. Nuriev.

Prosecutor General of the Russian Federation
   Case Materials, Archive Number 50888: April 2, 1962, Criminal Offenses Chamber, Leningrad City Court. Sentenced Rudolf Kh. Nureyev (in absentia) to seven years in custody in a strict regime colony with sequestration of property, under Article 64a of the RSFSR Penal Code on the charge of refusal to return to the Soviet Union from abroad while touring France with the ballet troupe of the Kirov Opera and Ballet Theater.

RSFSR Penal Code Article 64a has a capital offense provision. The state-appointed defense lawyer Otmegova successfully argued for a mitigation of the sentence, "considering Nureyev's personality and the circumstances under which the offense was committed."

Documentaries:
Rudolf Nureyev: Dance to Freedom, directed by Richard Curson Smith
(BBC Two, 2015).
Контракт со смертью. Рудольф Нуриев (РОССИЯ 1—*Russia Channel 1*, 2005)
Kontrakt so smert'yu. Rudol'f Nuriyev (Rossiya 1—*Russia Channel 1*, 2005),
Точка невозврата: Нуреев, Барышников, Годунов (НТВ—*NTV-TV*, 2011)
Tochka nevozvrata: Nureyev, Baryshnikov, Godunov (NTV—*NTV-TV*, 2011)

CH 13: PARIS
"old-fashioned clothes," Whitaker telephone interview with Pierre Lacotte,
September 2016.

"the sensation in Paris," Whitaker telephone interview with Claude Bessy, October 2016.

CH 15: LONDON

"a huge ovation," A. H. Franks, *The Dancing Times,* July 1961.

"justifiably and inevitably," John Martin, *The New York Times*, June 28, 1961.

"conquering London," Andrew Porter, *The Financial Times*, June 26, 1961.

"no one like him," Andrew Porter, *The Financial Times*, July 17, 1961.

"overwhelming role," Oliver Merlin, *Le Monde*, May 25, 1961.

"breathtaking," John Martin, *The New York Times*, June 24, 1961.

"not a showcase," *Ballet Today*, October 1961.

"at times inept," Fernau Hall, *Ballet Today*, August-September 1961.

CH 17: AND NOW AMERICA

"grave misgivings," John Martin, *The New York Times*, October 15, 1961.

"the two foreign dancers," Anatole Chujoy, *Dance News*, November 1961.

"a rising ballerina," Lobenthal interview with Mimi Paul, January 2009.

"a fantastic dancer," Lobenthal telephone interview with Allegra Kent, October 2017.

"as graceful on his feet," Louis Biancolli, *The New York World Telegram and Sun*, September 23, 1961.

More Melnikova photos of the Kirov can be seen at http://melnikova-ballet.ru

CH 18: DUDINSKAYA AND SERGEYEV

"hated Soviets so much," Kavanagh, *Nureyev: The Life*, 130.

"creative and physical strength," Shelest, "God-Given Gifts," 133–134.

"In his whirlwind rotations," N.I. Gorbachev, "Strolls Around Town With Yuria," 137-141.

CH 19: DANSEUR NOBLE
"wanted most to dance," Anatole Chujoy, *Dance News*, November 1961.

"lacked the noble manners," Boris Blankov, "Soloviev's Albrecht," *Ballet Review*, Fall 2005.

"I thought, my God," Lobenthal interview with Irina Kolpakova, May 2002.

"The audience gasped," Arkady Sokolov-Kaminsky email to Whitaker, July 2017.

"a finicky painting," Tchernichova, *Dancing on Water*, 129.

"always so beautiful," Oliver Merlin, *Le Monde*, December 1, 1965.

"slightly girlish cast," Mike Davis and Fernau Hall, *The World of Ballet and Dance*, London: Hamlyn, 1970, 74.

"more like a weight lifter," A. H. Franks, *The Dancing Times*, July 1961.

"a great deal of weight," Clive Barnes, *Dance and Dancers*, September 1967.

"he will never look slight," John Percival, *Dance and Dancers*, October 1970.

CH 20: THE SLEEPING BEAUTY, 1963
"taut, inspired," Shelest, "God-Given Gifts," 133–134.

"much more style," Alexander Bland, *The Dancing Times*, November 1965.

CH 23: INTERESTS AND HOBBIES
"very kind," Whitaker interview with Yuri Vasilkov, 1989.

"a connoisseur of theatrical scripts," N.I. Gorbachev, "Strolls Around Town With Yura" 137-141.

CH 24: "WHEN YOU DANCE WITH YOUR BALLERINA…"
"grown as an actor," Doris Hering, *Dance Magazine*, November 1964.

"considerably huskier," Arthur Todd, *Dance and Dancers,* November 1964.

"high-heeled shoes," Nicholas Dromgoole, London *Daily Telegraph*, September 6, 1966.

"new warmth and confidence," Mary Clarke, *The Dancing Times*, October 1966.

CH 25: PERSONAL STYLE
"power in reserve," Mary Clarke, *The Dancing Times*, October 1966.

"jumped even higher," Lobenthal, "Yuri Soloviev," *Ballet Review*, Fall 2003.

"made everything look easy," John Percival, *Dance and Dancers*, October 1966.

"a harmony in him," Lobenthal telephone interview with Jean-Pierre Bonnefoux, April 2017.

CH 26: NIJINSKY REPERTORY
"much more beautiful," Lobenthal interview with Mikhail Baryshnikov, May 2010.

"new dimension of male dancing," Tamara Karsavina, "My Partners at the Maryinsky," *The Dancing Times*, December 1966.

"any other in my experience," James Monahan, *The Dancing Times,* October 1966.

"still in the air," Lobenthal interview with Irina Baronova, January 1982.

"persuade him to defect," Whitaker interview with Anatole Gridin, November 2016.

CH 27: WORLD TRAVELER
"the greatest male dancer," Richard Buckle, London *Times*, September 18, 1966.

CH 28: A *GISELLE* DEBUT
"phenomenally well," Blankov, "Soloviev's Albrecht," *Ballet Review*, Fall 2005.

CH 29: DEFECTION?
"We couldn't do anything," Whitaker telephone interview with Arkady Ivanenko, January 2017.

CH 30: GEORGI ALEXIDZE

"master of classical style," Georgi Alexize, "I Am Happy," included in Blankov, *Yuri Soloviev: His Life and Work*, 135–136.

"Yura breathed together," Evgenii Shcherbakov interview with Georgi Alexidze, May 2002.

"inner qualities of a dancer," Whitaker telephone interview with Marina Alexidze, February 2018.

CH 31: CREATIVE EVENINGS

"worked like a dog," Lobenthal, "Yuri Soloviev," *Ballet Review*, Fall 2003.

"had wanted to stage," Janice Ross, *Like a Bomb Going Off: Leonid Jacobson and Ballet as Resistance in Soviet Russia,* New Haven, CT: Yale University Press, 2015, 323.

"a surprisingly gentle lyricism," Valery Panov, with George Feifer, *To Dance*, New York: Alfred A. Knopf, 1978, 225.

"one of the most beautiful pieces," Whitaker interview with Marina Vasilieva, November 2016.

"more exhausted," Panov, *To Dance*, 226.

CH 33: NOT JOINING THE PARTY

"lacked nobility and lyricism," Solway, *Nureyev: His Life*, 124.

PART 4: HOPES DASHED

CH 36: EVOLVING

"far more dramatic," John Percival, *Dance and Dancers*, October 1970.

"made complete sense," Clement Crisp, *The Dancing Times*, September 1970.

"we had to stop filming," Aleksandr Belinskii letter to Lobenthal, 2001.

CH 37: CREATION

"had been excised," Blankov, "Soloviev's Albrecht," *Ballet Review*, Fall 2005.

"massively overburdened," Panov, *To Dance*, 268.

"tickets were begged," Panov, 275.

"a classical purity," Lobenthal interview with Vadim Stukhov, June 2012.

"surpassed himself," Alexandra Deshicheva, *Sovietskaya Kultura*, April 17, 1971, reprinted in *Dance News*, October 1971.

CH 38: FINAL YEARS
"made everything fun," Lobenthal/Whitaker interview with Alyona Solovieva, July 2016.

"I would notice his eyes," Shelest, "God-Given Gifts," 133–134.

"the old man in the frame," Whitaker telephone interview with Arkady Sokolov-Kaminsky, July 2017.

CH 41: THE LOOK IN HIS EYES
"calm and quiet and polite," Lobenthal telephone interview with Elena Kunikova, September 2017.

"any old time," Emi Yamauchi, *Dance News*, October 1976.

"so sincere," Whitaker interview with Lubov Kunakova, November 2016.

"looked very tired and old," Fedor I. Razzakov. *How Our Idols Departed: The Glow of Unexpended Stars*. St. Petersburg, Russian Federation: Eksmo, 2010, 164.

"always asked about his end," Ninel Kurgapkina, "The Dancer's Legacy: A Tribute to Rudolf Nureyev," seminar at the New York Public Library for the Performing Arts, New York City, March 8, 1997.

CH 44: AFTERMATH
"kiss me on the forehead," Whitaker interview with Anna Kakabadze Solovieva, November 2016.

CH 55: THE SUMMING UP
"dark and desperate passion," Clive Barnes, A Pall Is Cast Over Leningrad's Kirov Ballet," The New York Times, January 23, 1977.

Page references in *italics* indicate an illustration.